THE
IMPROVEMENT
OF THE
ESTATE

THE IMPROVEMENT OF THE ESTATE

A Study of
Jane Austen's Novels
by Alistair M. Duckworth

The Johns Hopkins Press · Baltimore & London

Chapter 1, somewhat altered and expanded, is reprinted from *Nineteenth-Century Fiction*, 26 (June 1971), 25–48, by permission of the Regents of the University of California.

Quotations from D. H. Lawrence, *A Propos of "Lady Chatterley's Lover,"* are reprinted by permission of Laurence Pollinger Ltd. and the Estate of the Late Mrs. Frieda Lawrence; William Heinemann Ltd.; and Random House, Inc.

Copyright © 1971 by The Johns Hopkins Press
All rights reserved
Manufactured in the United States of America

The Johns Hopkins Press, Baltimore, Maryland 21218
The Johns Hopkins Press, Ltd., London

Library of Congress Catalog Card Number 75-161839
ISBN 0-8018-1269-0

TO MY MOTHER AND FATHER

CONTENTS

Page references inserted in the text are to:

The Novels of Jane Austen, ed. R. W. Chapman. 5 vols. Third Edition. London: Oxford University Press, 1933.

The Works of Jane Austen, ed. R. W. Chapman. Vol. VI: *Minor Works*. London: Oxford University Press, 1954.

Jane Austen's Letters to Her Sister Cassandra and Others, ed. R. W. Chapman. Second Edition. London: Oxford University Press, 1952.

All page references in parentheses to the letters will be preceded by *L*. Only where needed for the sake of clarity will the individual novels be indicated by their initial letters. *MW* stands for *Minor Works*.

PREFACE

GIVEN THE NUMBER of Jane Austen studies that have appeared in the last decade, some justification for this book is called for. It offers perhaps two original proposals: first, it makes the unusual assumption that *Mansfield Park* is fundamental to Jane Austen's thought—not the counter-truth it has traditionally been considered—and second, working from a detailed and positive reading of this controversial work, it proposes a thematic unity to her fiction. As my title implies, such a unity resides in Jane Austen's conception of the "estate" and in her idea of "improvement." For Jane Austen, in *Mansfield Park*, the estate as an ordered physical structure is a metonym for other inherited structures—society as a whole, a code of morality, a body of manners, a system of language—and "improvements," or the manner in which individuals relate to their cultural inheritance, are a means of distinguishing responsible from irresponsible action and of defining a proper attitude toward social change.

After considering *Mansfield Park* in chapter one, I have sought to identify in her other mature novels an authentic commitment to a social morality and a continuous awareness and exposure of attitudes destructive of social continuity. Though her early and relatively immature novels—*Northanger Abbey* and *Sense and Sensibility*—are evidently different in tone and texture from her later writings, they are not different in their social and moral assumptions. Working within the traditions of eighteenth century fiction, these works do not support the theme of this study in the convincing way that the four great novels and the last fragment do, but neither do they contradict it and, as I argue in chapter two, when their ironical modes are properly understood, they are consistent with the outlook of her later and greater novels.

Pride and Prejudice, discussed in chapter three, is the culmination of her early mode and the greatest example of the novel of antitheses; here Jane Austen puts forward a positive vision of society as she artistically enacts in the marriage of Elizabeth and Darcy her notion of proper social "improvement." Elizabeth's final entry into the estate of Pemberley is not, as some critics would have it, a conventional escape (for Elizabeth) from a life of penury and mediocrity, or (for Jane Austen) from troubling insights into the nature of society; rather it is the responsible commitment of an individual to a heritage which, though basically sound, is in danger of becoming static and moribund without "improvement."

The two novels which follow *Mansfield Park* continue the estate theme, though in different ways. The central thematic opposition in *Emma,* discussed in chapter four, is between the traditional culture which Knightley represents and the "games" world inhabited by Churchill. This is another form of the opposition in *Mansfield Park* between "house" and "theatre," or between responsible and "Reptonian" modes of estate improvement. When Emma chooses to cleave to Knightley's world rather than to Churchill's, she repeats Edmund's mature preference for Fanny Price over Mary Crawford. Nor, in view of the threats to the "estate" that Churchill and the Crawfords are shown to represent, are we to lament the rejection of their vitality, which is of quite another order from that of Elizabeth Bennet. Artistically more satisfactory than Edmund's marriage to Fanny, Emma's acceptance of Knightley serves, like the former union, to guarantee the continuity of a traditional society, grounded in religious principle, guided by historical example, and "improved" by individual energy.

In *Persuasion* a change in the direction of Jane Austen's emphasis is evident, one greater than that usually considered to occur between *Pride and Prejudice* and *Mansfield Park.* Kellynch Hall is rented by its egregiously vain owner, and with this voluntary abandonment of an inherited estate Jane Austen brings into central focus a question always present but formerly resolved in her fiction. On what "grounds" should the socially deprived individual base his moral actions? As I argue in chapter five, Jane Austen's answer, suggested principally through the conduct of the heroine, Anne Elliot, is not radically different from that implied by the actions and characters of previous heroines: to retain one's personal integrity while remaining faithful to inherited principles of behavior, to act "usefully" whenever possible, to exhibit "resources" in the face of adversity—these remain the positive and estimable virtues of Jane Austen's individualism. While these qualities result in a happy ending for the heroine, however, *Persuasion* uniquely fails to suggest through the marriage of its protagonists a wider stability in society at large. Wentworth's naval virtues of frankness and energy are not, finally, brought to the improvement of Kellynch or, indeed, of any estate, and his marriage to Anne provides private happiness without the corresponding sense of public good suggested by the marriages in earlier novels.

The loss of a morality "grounded" in religion and tradition, and manifested ideally in the structure of an estate, is clearly intimated again in *Sanditon*, where Mr. Parker follows in the line of all the other false stewards in Jane Austen's fiction, from General Tilney and John Dashwood to Rushworth and Sir Walter Elliot. His estate at Sanditon is no longer his in trust, to be passed on, properly improved, to his heirs; instead, it has become an object of "speculation," a seaside resort to be used for the making of a fortune. With Jane Austen's last fragment the tendency of *Persuasion* is confirmed, as a brief comparison with Jane Austen's earlier fragment, *The Watsons*, shows, and it seems fitting, therefore, to close with a postscript pointing to the Victorian novel in which society, considered as a valid sanction for individual morality, is seldom encountered. But a secondary concern throughout the study has been to establish what is meant when Jane Austen is termed a "transitional" novelist. Thus, to mention my introduction last, I here attempt not only to counteract various "subversive" readings of her work but also to place her in the tradition of English fiction between what may be briefly termed the "providential" fiction of Fielding, Richardson, and other eighteenth century novelists, and the "contingent" fiction of the Victorians. The argument here is necessarily tentative and conducted at a level of generality which some may find unsatisfactory, but it will serve its purpose if it suggests the seriousness of Jane Austen's intellectual position and the sincerity of her artistic response.

To Earl Wasserman and Hillis Miller of The Johns Hopkins University I am deeply indebted not only for reading this study in an earlier form but for their inspiring teaching and brilliant scholarship. Professor Miller's work on Dickens, on the Victorian novel generally, and now on Hardy, is deservedly well known. Professor Wasserman's major work has been concerned with poetry, and perhaps only those who have had the privilege of hearing him lecture on the eighteenth century novel can know how original and illuminating he is on this genre too. To my colleagues at the University of Virginia, Francis Hart, Martin Battestin, and Anthony Winner, who have read and commented upon my manuscript, I am most grateful, as I am to Frederick Dennehy and David Robnett for help with research. To the research committee of the University of Virginia I would like to express my thanks for generous funds to cover typing and photography costs. My greatest debt is not, however, academic. To my parents, who have not yet read this study, but who may after reading it—and for all its faults—consider it some compensation for the uncertainty of my setting forth, I dedicate this book.

Photograph courtesy of the Library of Congress.

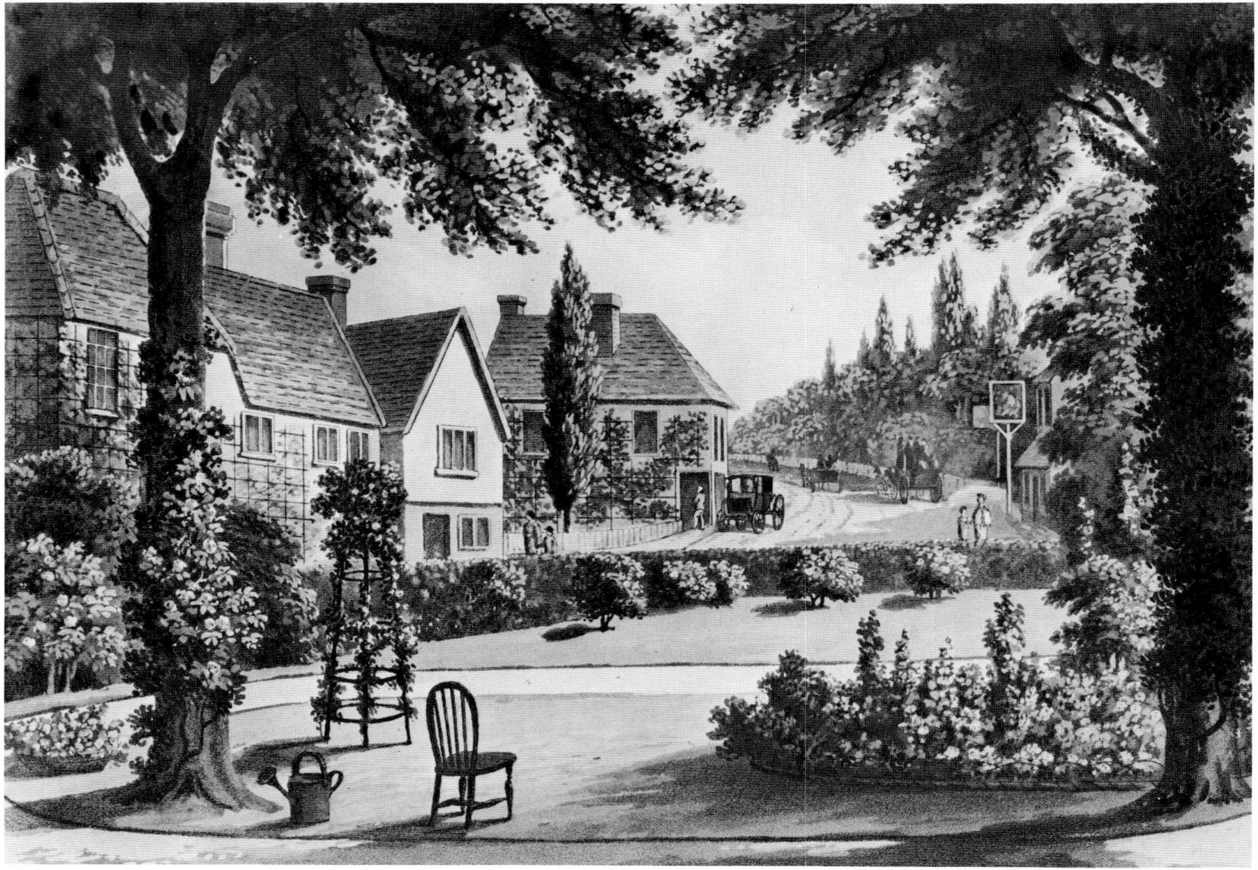

View from my own cottage, in Essex. From Fragments on the Theory and Practice of Landscape Gardening,
by Humphry Repton (London, 1816).

THE
IMPROVEMENT
OF THE
ESTATE

INTRODUCTION:
SOME CRITICAL
AND LITERARY CONTEXTS

The family of Dashwood had been long settled in Sussex. Their estate was large, and their residence was at Norland Park, in the centre of their property, where, for many generations, they had lived in so respectable a manner, as to engage the general good opinion of their surrounding acquaintance.

THE SITUATION of the Dashwood family at the beginning of *Sense and Sensibility* reflects the sense of inherited security that is the birthright of the self in Jane Austen's world. Initially, existence is enclosed and the estate into which an individual is born provides him with a little world of harmony and peace. As he lives at the center of his property, so he belongs to a family which is surrounded by other families and has been "for many generations" settled in its place. He comes to consciousness in a community that is corporate and structured in all areas. In the possession of a public language and of common modes of behavior, in the very disposition of buildings and landscape, such a community manifests an organization that has evolved over a long period of time. Though it is a human organization, it is complete, inherited intact, and it has about it an air of consecration. It seems to be "truth . . . come to dwell anonymously upon the earth."[1] Preceding human consciousness and serving as a framework of order external to the mind, society, at the beginning, both protects and supports the individual self.

Soon, however, the self in Jane Austen's world loses its birthright, the initial security is withdrawn and in its place a very different world appears. It is a world which receives its most extreme expression in the description of Mrs. Smith in *Persuasion*:

She was a widow, and poor. Her husband had been extravagant; and at his death, about two years before, had left his affairs dreadfully involved. She had had difficulties of every sort to contend with, and in addition to

[1] I borrow the phrase from José Ortega y Gasset's chapter, "The Concept of the Generation," in his *The Modern Theme*, trans. James Cleugh (1931; rpt. New York: Harper Torchbooks, 1961), p. 17.

these distresses, had been afflicted with a severe rheumatic fever, which finally settling in her legs, had made her for the present a cripple. She had come to Bath on that account, and was now in lodgings near the hot-baths, living in a very humble way, unable even to afford herself the comfort of a servant, and of course almost excluded from society. (152–53)

Mrs. Smith, a minor character in Jane Austen's last novel, is important as the final embodiment of a fate that haunts all her novels. Here at the last is the entirely unsupported woman, reduced to bare existence without husband, society or friends. Though she appears at the end of Jane Austen's writing life, Mrs. Smith has always existed as a latent possibility in the novelist's thought, an unvoiced threat, the other possible pole of existence. Meeting her old friend after twelve years, Anne Elliot comes face to face with her own possible fate; but Mrs. Smith is also a more unfortunate Miss Bates, or an older and socially unrescued Jane Fairfax. Further, she is the possible outcome of a Marianne Dashwood, an Elizabeth Bennet, or a Fanny Price. For this is the danger facing many of Jane Austen's heroines, that present security may become total isolation, that residence "in the centre of their property" in the enjoyment of "the general good opinion of their surrounding acquaintance" may be exchanged for life "in lodgings" without the money even "to afford . . . the comfort of a servant."

At one level, the danger that presents itself is that of "degradation." The Dashwoods, "long settled . . . for many generations" at their large estate in Sussex, are required to leave the protective confines of Norland Park and to travel into Devonshire, "so far from hence" (25), where they exist, somewhat in the manner of dependents, in a cottage at some distance from the great house. In *Pride and Prejudice*, it is true, the Bennets are not evicted from Longbourn, but they live in some danger of social dislocation. Their estate, in default of a male heir, is entailed upon the egregious Mr. Collins, and should their improvident father die, the income of the five sisters will be quite insufficient to keep them in the comfort to which they are accustomed.[2] In *Persuasion*, finally, "degradation"

---

[2] £5,000 is settled on Mrs. Bennet and the children. Mr. Bennet's estate brings him a considerable £2,000 a year, but he has saved nothing of this. Should he die, Mrs. Bennet and her five daughters will be in an uncomfortable, if not impecunious, position. Though Mrs. Bennet had a fortune of £4,000 on marriage, it is unlikely that any of the Bennet girls could command much more than

becomes a central theme as the Kellynch estate is rented by its self-centered owner, and Anne Elliot is forced to leave the cherished space of her home.[3]

At a deeper level, however, the degradation that threatens Jane Austen's heroines has implications beyond the social, implications that are metaphysical or theological in nature. Isolated from a stable and inherited "estate," an individual suffers more than loss of station; he is, more importantly, excluded from his "grounds" of being and action. Without the customary reference points of a structured inheritance, he may feel at a loss how to act. First and last in Jane Austen's novels, in *Northanger Abbey* and *Persuasion*, exclusion from home is literal as Catherine and Anne travel into worlds where few received principles are found exemplified in social behavior. Anne Elliot's is much the more troubling journey. Forced to leave Kellynch when it is rented to the Crofts, she travels to Uppercross, Lyme and Bath, and finds it difficult to discover in any of these localities a pattern of order or continuity. Mrs. Smith in the same novel is "almost excluded from society," and the immediate meaning is clear: she is unable on account of her sickness to visit the Assemblies in Bath. But the phrase may also be read to mean that society, considered as a support and protection for the self, as a body of public manners and conventions in accordance with which the self may act, is denied Mrs. Smith. In such a con-

---

their share of the settlement, that is £1,000, or £50 per annum. Mr. Bennet suspects that his brother-in-law must have added to Lydia's portion in order to effect her marriage to Wickham, for "no man in his senses would marry . . . on so slight a temptation as one hundred a-year during my life, and fifty after I am gone" (*PP*, 304). This in mind, there are clear economic reasons for the "gulf impassable" (311) between Elizabeth and the very rich Darcy, who commands £10,000 a year. I deal at more length with the thematic significance of incomes in Jane Austen's fiction in chapter two.

[3] For a more psychologically oriented consideration of degradation in Jane Austen's life as well as in her art, see Brigid Brophy's "Jane Austen and the Stuarts," in *Critical Essays on Jane Austen*, ed. B. C. Southam (London: Routledge & Kegan Paul, 1968), pp. 21–38. I am less willing than she to read Jane Austen's fiction in terms of Jane's own psychological, and her family's social, predicament, and I cannot wholeheartedly accept her commitment to a Freudian explanation of Jane Austen's artistic development. Nevertheless, Miss Brophy provides persuasive biographical reasons for the fear of degradation that seems to underlie much of Jane Austen's fiction. She had, Miss Brophy suggests, "a strong sense that her whole family had been dispossessed of something they had a right to," and her fiction reflects this sense, as, for example, in Fanny Price's experience (of "present exigency in contrast to previous grandeur") at Portsmouth.

tingency, the reduced self may resort to subversive stratagems to ensure survival.[4]

Persuasion, particularly, apprehends a world in which traditional grounds of selfhood no longer obtain; but the apprehension in lesser degree attaches to all the novels. And it is perhaps a recognition of the failure or weakness of the self's social inheritance that has led a number of readers to sense in Jane Austen's fiction a dislike of society and of traditional forms, and to discover in her work a tendency toward ethical subjectivism. Such a reading receives support from the discovery that the deprivation that comes or threatens to come to many of Jane Austen's heroines can be attributed to parental failure. Like Mrs. Smith's husband, who had been "extravagant" and "left his affairs dreadfully involved," the heads of families in the novels—Henry Dashwood, Mr. Bennet, Sir Walter Elliot—are irresponsible or deficient in the performance of their duties as husband, father, landlord, and trustee. When to these failures are added the too complacent common sense of Catherine Morland's parents, the hypochondria and old-maidishness of Mr. Woodhouse and the errors of Sir Thomas Bertram in respect to his children's education, a hypothesis that has long been favored by a persistent tradition of Austen criticism seems inescapable. Through the failure of parents properly to provide for their children the typical Austen heroine is deprived of a secure inheritance and called upon early in life to act as a "centre of self-responsible moral judgement."[5]

Taken so far, the hypothesis is unexceptionable; it is the argument that sometimes develops from this point which I find unacceptable. No longer supported by the social structure, the argument runs, Jane Austen understandably responds in a subjective and ironical manner to the debased world she encounters, discovering value and order only in herself or in a closed friendship with a sister or brother (as Elizabeth Bennet confides in Jane, or as Fanny Price shows affection for William). Her subjective response and social withdrawal, however, cannot be made openly in her art but

---

4 I discuss Mrs. Smith at greater length in chapter five.

5 D. W. Harding, "The Character of Literature from Blake to Byron," in *From Blake to Byron*, Vol. V of the *Pelican Guide to English Literature*, ed. Boris Ford (1957; rpt. with revisions, Harmondsworth, Middlesex: Penguin Books, 1962), p. 59.

must be suppressed and disguised in the interests of family harmony, or under the pressure of a conventional society, which is, after all, the only arena of her existence and self-fulfillment. As Reginald Farrer, one of her first critics in this mode, put it on the centenary of her death:

[Jane Austen] was obviously ill-served by her circumstances. Behind the official biographies, and the pleasant little empty letters, and the accounts of how good she was to her mother and wouldn't use the sofa, we feel always that she really lived remote in a great reserve. She praised and valued domesticity indeed, sincerely loved her own family, and made domestic instincts a cardinal virtue in all her heroes. But the praise and value are rather official than personal; her only real intimate at home was her sister Cassandra, and it is significant that only upstairs, behind her shut door, did she read her own work aloud, for the benefit of her chosen circle in the younger generation. Yet more significant, though, is the fact that nowhere does she give any picture of united family happiness.... This ... speaks volumes, in its characteristically quiet way, for her position towards her own family. She was in it; but she was not really of it.[6]

Extend Farrer's view of the relation of Jane Austen to her family to the relation of Jane Austen to society as a whole, and we have here in embryo an entire modern attitude—an attitude that has received its most extreme and articulate expression in the works of D. W. Harding and Marvin Mudrick, the deans of what has come to be called the "subversive" school of Austen criticism.[7]

[6] "Jane Austen," *Quarterly Review*, 228 (July 1917), 2–3.

[7] The first critic to read Jane Austen as an ironic judge of her own society was Richard Simpson in an unsigned review in *North British Review*, 52 (April 1870), 129–52, of James Edward Austen-Leigh's *Memoir of Jane Austen* (now available in D. W. Harding's edition of *Persuasion* [Baltimore: Penguin Books, 1965]). Simpson's review is conveniently collected in *Jane Austen: The Critical Heritage*, ed. B. C. Southam (London: Routledge & Kegan Paul, 1968). Harding took up the suggestions of Simpson and Farrer in his "Regulated Hatred: An Aspect of the Work of Jane Austen," *Scrutiny*, 8 (March 1940), 346–62. This is perhaps the most articulate and succinct interpretation of Jane Austen as a subversive. Harding argues that "her books are ... enjoyed by precisely the sort of people whom she disliked; she is a literary classic of the society which attitudes like hers, held widely enough, would undermine." After Harding in this approach comes Marvin Mudrick's *Jane Austen: Irony as Defense and Discovery* (Princeton: Princeton University Press, 1952), and I would also include articles by Mark Schorer, David Daiches, Geoffrey Gorer, and Kingsley Amis—later to be mentioned and documented—in this tradition. For an excellent brief history of critical attitudes to Jane Austen up to 1963, see Ian Watt's "Introduction" to *Jane Austen: A Collection of Critical Essays*, ed. Ian Watt (Englewood Cliffs, N.J.: Prentice-Hall, 1963).

The extreme opinions of the "subversive" critics—that Jane Austen undermines the social values she seems to affirm, that she can discover personal equilibrium in a society she detests only through the secret ironies of her art—are implicitly opposed throughout this study. Here the emphasis which this criticism places on Jane Austen's moral individualism, on "the detachment and autonomy of the individual as a centre of self-responsible moral judgment," in D. W. Harding's words, may be briefly questioned. There are occasions, indubitably, where such individualism is admirable (one need only recall the splendid response of Elizabeth Bennet to Lady Catherine), and a recurring requirement of Jane Austen's moral vision is that the formal and static façade of authority be enlivened and regenerated by individual energy. But this is a long way from saying that individual action of a subversive or antisocial nature is sanctioned, even unconsciously, in Jane Austen's novels. True, her heroines often find themselves in an insecure world through no fault of their own, but what is remarkable is how positively they respond, either consistently or finally, to the endangered world they encounter. Indeed, in one instance, that of Fanny Price in *Mansfield Park*, it is precisely the resistance of the heroine to those forces endangering her world which permits the continuity of an integral society. Given the irresponsibility of others, we might say, it is the more incumbent upon the Austen heroine to support and maintain an inherited structure of values and behavior.

Furthermore, Jane Austen has a continuous awareness of the dangers as well as the values of individualism. This is surely the point of *Emma*. As a heroine, Emma Woodhouse is unusual in having no apprehension as to her social place and social future. Socially and financially she is at the opposite pole from Mrs. Smith, and unlike Fanny Price or Elinor Dashwood she has no cause to exhibit fortitude in the face of adversity or isolation. In one sense only has she been deprived: she has lacked firm adult supervision since her mother's death, and has consequently "a disposition to think a little too well of herself" (5). But even if the lack of parental direction is considered partly responsible for Emma's individualism, it is by no means a wholly adequate explanation. As is true of Marianne Dashwood and Elizabeth Bennet before her, Emma's self-assertion is a characteristic inherent in her nature which has been given license rather than brought into being by her father's incompetence. Emma glories in her freedom to define her world outward from a center of self, yet we are to be aware of how closely she comes to fragmenting the little world of Highbury with her "schemes" and of how heinously she fails in her social responsibility when she insults Miss Bates on Box Hill.

Against the regulated hatred, the detached irony, and the subversive morality that much recent criticism has stressed, it is necessary to take more seriously a Jane Austen "thoroughly religious and devout," who has the additional "merit . . . of being evidently a Christian writer."[8] In this connection it is appropriate to mention one important response to deprivation that is dramatized in Jane Austen's novels which seldom finds its way into critical commentary. At times of greatest distress the "reduced" self in Jane Austen's fiction is apt to fall back on its "resources," an idea which suggests a Christian stoicism, an inner resilience in the face of adversity. Elinor Dashwood, Fanny Price, and Anne Elliot all at times approach a kind of Christian heroism which recognizes that, whatever the distresses of the moment, this world is not after all the place of ultimate reward.

Such a tone, genuine enough when it is sounded, is never of course dominant in Jane Austen's fiction; her religion, as Archbishop Whately first noted, is not obtrusive. Moreover, the isolation and, often, real despair that her heroines experience is followed by a reinstatement into society. After dispossession comes possession, as each heroine in the novels (with the significant exception of Anne Elliot) is finally located in a properly organized space for her socially responsible activity, in a "suitable, becoming, characteristic situation" (*E,* 358) such as Donwell Abbey, Delaford, Pemberley, or the Mansfield parsonage. The typical Austen plot may move in the direction of isolation and subjectivism, but in the end there is a rapprochement between self and society.

This formal relocation of the individual protagonist in society is perhaps what the "subversive" critics find hardest to reconcile with

---

8 The first quotation is from Henry Austen's admittedly panegyrical "Biographical Notice of the Author," included in the posthumous edition of *Persuasion* (1818); the second is from Archbishop Whately's unsigned review of *Northanger Abbey* and *Persuasion,* in *Quarterly Review,* 24 (Jan. 1821), 352–76. Both pieces are collected in *Critical Heritage.* Among modern critics, C. S. Lewis, in "A Note on Jane Austen," *Essays in Criticism,* 4 (Oct. 1954), 359–71, most clearly recognizes "the religious background of the author's ethical position."

their view of Jane Austen as an author who commits a covert assault on society's values. Often, it appears, her plot resolutions are considered as acts of "bad faith," as refusals to accept the responsibility of her intuitions or the implications of her "original choice." She is a heretic to her own early recognition of the inadequacy of society, and in affirming finally that society is the proper context of individual behavior she evades the burden of achieving personal equilibrium outside of crumbling—but comforting—conventions.[9] Discovering meanings beneath or beyond her explicit formulations, "subversive" criticism has presented us with an author who in different circumstances would have permitted her dislike of social values to surface in her fiction and proclaimed the unfettered freedom of the intelligent self to define its own morality and order.

As I am well aware, such views have not gone unchallenged in recent criticism.[10] Nevertheless they remain prevalent, and for understandable reasons. Brilliantly destructive of the cult of "gentle

[9] No critic to my knowledge actually accuses Jane Austen of the Sartrean "*mauvaise foi*," but a Sartrean vocabulary seems natural to describe a common discovery of incipient but suppressed individualism in her novels.

[10] Howard S. Babb's *Jane Austen's Novels: The Fabric of Dialogue* (Columbus: Ohio State University Press, 1962), a close study of Jane Austen's language, is a good corrective to "subversive" criticism. Babb notices the "public" meanings of Jane Austen's conceptual nouns and the careful balance of her syntax, features which provide a linguistic backdrop of order against which the solecisms and lexical vulgarities of her immoral characters may be judged. Following Trilling's "Manners, Morals, and the Novel" (in *The Liberal Imagination* [New York: Viking Press, 1950]), Babb argues that manners, considered as "indexes to major cultural and personal values," may define a comprehensive and substantial reality" (p. 5). A. Walton Litz, in *Jane Austen: A Study of Her Artistic Development* (London: Chatto & Windus, 1965), also opposes the assumption of the "subversive" critics that Jane Austen's "characteristic (and only valid) artistic vision was marked by an aloof and defiant irony" (p. 85), by showing how grounded her work is in eighteenth century ideas. Inheriting eighteenth century dualisms—art and nature, sense and sensibility—her persistent attempt is that of "accommodating reason and feeling, of regulating sympathy without destroying it" (p. 68). *Contra* Mudrick, Litz argues that Jane Austen's work is to be seen as a series of attempts to capture a complex vision in novel form and that her failures are artistic and not ideological, not the submission of insight to social pressure. Frank Bradbrook's *Jane Austen and Her Predecessors* (Cambridge: Cambridge University Press, 1966) and Kenneth L. Moler's *Jane Austen's Art of Allusion* (Lincoln: University of Nebraska Press, 1968) take up F. R. Leavis' suggestion in *The Great Tradition* (London: Chatto & Windus, 1948), p. 5, that Jane Austen, in her indebtedness to others, provides an illuminating study of the nature of originality. By relating her individual talent to tradition, moreover, these scholars shift the critical emphasis from a consideration of Jane Austen's peculiar psychological situation to an assessment of a shared concern with more general and social questions.

Janeism" as they are, armed with the weapons of Freudian insight,
secretly enamored, perhaps, of an existentialist morality, they present a more "interesting" Jane Austen—just as Lytton Strachey
presented a more interesting Florence Nightingale when he proposed that her faith and efficiency (her confusion of the deity with
drains) were suspiciously motivated. Yet, if one believes that Jane
Austen genuinely affirms the prior, objective existence of moral and
social principles in her fiction, such views are unacceptable—unacceptable because they misread the nature and quality of her moral
commitment.

One way to support my argument is to consider the typical
pattern of Jane Austen's plots, not as an expression of her submission to social pressures or as a fictional response to her own biographical predicament, but as an indication of her attitude to
society and to the individual's place in society. If her fiction looks
forward to modern themes and responses (as in *Persuasion* and
Sanditon I believe it does), it also grows out of an eighteenth century novelistic concern with the predicament of the dislocated individual. It is in the eighteenth century novel that the recurring
pattern of Jane Austen's plots—the movement from a condition of
initial security to a period of isolation and then to a final reinstatement in society—finds its origins. It is there, too, that individualism,
often viewed in religious contexts, has interesting implications for a
consideration of Jane Austen's fiction. By setting her novels in the
context of what might be termed the "providential" fiction of the
eighteenth century, we may qualify the subversive readings of her
moral vision. Then, by briefly looking ahead to the "contingent"
fiction of the nineteenth century, we may suggest ways in which her
novels do indeed anticipate later nineteenth century novelistic preoccupations.

EIGHTEENTH CENTURY fiction, at least until the emergence of
the Gothic and of Godwin, tends not to question the constitution, however much it may deplore the conditions of society.
"Things as they are" are given, cannot be essentially otherwise, and
the eighteenth century novelist, generally speaking, defines the individualism of his protagonists within these assumptions. A glance

at the structure of representative works will reveal what is meant by "things as they are."

Wherever we look, the protagonist begins life experiencing harmony and peace. Robinson Crusoe is brought up in "the upper station of low life," a situation considered to be the "best state in the world" by his father; Tom Jones grows up at Paradise Hall, the pleasant country seat of Squire Allworthy; Rasselas lives initially in the Happy Valley; the Vicar of Wakefield inhabits "an elegant house, situated in a fine country and a good neighbourhood." In all cases, however, a separation from initial security occurs. Robinson Crusoe disobeys "the will, nay, the commands of [his] father," leaves his "father's house," and the eventual consequence of his "original sin" is his complete isolation on the island. Tom Jones is expelled against his wishes from Paradise Hall. Rasselas is impelled by "original curiosity" to escape from the the "security and delight" of the Happy Valley, and to seek with Imlac a "choice of life." Parson Primrose is suddenly relieved of his fortune and parish; his eldest son is forced to go out into the world to seek his fortune; his house is burned and his cattle driven off; one daughter is thought to have died, another is abducted; and the vicar is reduced to a condition of life that makes a mockery of his early deuteronomic belief that the righteous in this life are always rewarded.

All these heroes (and many others) find themselves, like many of Jane Austen's heroines, excluded from "a state of happiness," either through voluntary choice or through factors over which they have little or no control. But in every case their dislocation is a temporary, if sometimes desperate, state. Always the hero returns after his experiences to a more or less stable existence; usually he is reintegrated into society, having undergone a growth of awareness en route. Crusoe is rescued from his island and, after "Farther Adventures," returns home an old man, conscious of the "value of retirement and the blessing of ending our days in peace" and fully prepared to take "a longer journey." Tom Jones, after narrowly escaping hanging, marries Sophia and, having learned enough in the way of prudence to survive in a postlapsarian world, returns to Somersetshire. Rasselas, less happily it is true, finds neither marriage nor lasting peace; nor, though he returns to Abyssinia, may he ever re-enter the Happy Valley. But if his project to rule a little kingdom seems doomed to continual frustration and his experiences seem to have taught him only that "human life is everywhere a state in which much is to be endured and little to be enjoyed," there still remains for him, as for his sister, the Princess, the "choice of eternity." Parson Primrose, after all his tribulations, is restored to his former prosperity through the help of Sir William Thornhill, and at the end has "nothing now on this side of the grave to wish for."

Beyond all the manifold differences—of morality, tone, genre—that undoubtedly exist among these works, one similarity is striking and significant: the circularity of the plot structure. Evidently based to a quite explicit degree on the myth of the fall, such a structure may be used in different ways and for different effects by different authors. But one general effect of their common use of the *felix culpa topos* is surely this: individual isolation in their novels is rendered explicable in terms of universal Christian experience. Expulsion from paradise is the common lot of all men since Adam, but the fall, like Adam's, is not entirely unfortunate and the possibility exists for a return, not of course to the untrammeled bliss of Eden, but to the modified happiness that is proper to the mortal condition, or, if this too seems unattainable (as in *Rasselas*), then to the eternal happiness of the afterlife. By secularizing the structure of the fortunate fall (as Fielding does), or by writing in the tradition of spiritual autobiography (as Defoe does), or by cutting his fictional cloth to a scriptural pattern (as Goldsmith uses the story of Job in the *Vicar of Wakefield*), these authors reveal a belief in a world directed according to God's providential plan.

Of course, qualifications need to be made. Clearly these novels are not merely prosaic versions of *Paradise Lost*. Even in *Tom Jones*, where we are asked to see Tom's journey in Adamic terms, the use of the fortunate fall is not entirely serious, and Fielding is obviously aware of the comic (as opposed to cosmic) lengths to which the analogy of Tom to Adam and of his work of God's creation can be taken.[11] Then again, readers of *Rasselas* may doubt the consolatory effect in this somewhat lugubrious work of Johnson's use

---

[11] In his prefatory essays, Fielding (or his dramatized narrator) plays with the idea of author as God: first, he is a master cook preparing an appetizing meal, next a king ruling his subject-readers, then the author of a work which "may, indeed, be considered as a great creation of our own," and finally the creator of a prelapsarian land about to be endangered by "reptile" critics.

of the myth of the fall. If the apologue has a religious meaning, one might argue, it is closer to Ecclesiastes than to the New Testament. And even in *The Vicar of Wakefield*, a novel which explicitly attempts to "explain" existence in orthodox terms, problems arise. Like Job, *The Vicar* brings into question the doctrine of rewards and punishments; the righteous man is not necessarily to rest secure in the belief that he need never go begging for his bread. But (again as in Job) *The Vicar*, after plunging its protagonist into terrible hardship, returns him to a condition of even greater prosperity than before. Parson Primrose's renewed prosperity is brought about by the watchful benevolence of Sir William Thornhill, and it may be that Goldsmith intends us to read the knight as a secular Christ. Despite this, one is left somewhat uneasy by the ending of the novel. Having raised the specter of unrelieved misery in this life, can Goldsmith so easily effect a happy conclusion? Sir William seems more like a *deus ex machina* than a redeemer.

Such demurrers made, however, it is nevertheless possible to argue that the eighteenth century novel generally reflects faith in a society whose grounds are divinely validated. Though no generalization can adequately cover a genre whose representative forms include the psychological structure of *Tristram Shandy* as well as the ontological structure of *Tom Jones*, there are sufficient family resemblances among major eighteenth century novelists (Sterne excepted) for us to say that, while individualism is coextensive with the "rise" of the novel, it is an individualism for the most part contained within traditional, religious terms.[12] However comically

---

[12] Ian Watt's excellent *The Rise of the Novel* (1957; rpt. Berkeley and Los Angeles: University of California Press, 1962) argues that the "rise" of the novel is closely related to the "rise" of social, philosophic, and, especially, economic individualism. Thus, for example, Robinson Crusoe's "original sin" is not to be read literally as Crusoe's repetition of Adam's sin; really it is the "dynamic tendency of capitalism itself, whose aim is never merely to maintain the *status quo*, but to transform it incessantly" (p. 65). And Crusoe's island is not a place of spiritual banishment where he may be led to repentance and an awareness of God's providence, but a territory to be exploited for capitalistic purposes: "Profit is Crusoe's only vocation" (p. 67), his frequent religious reflections mere "Sunday religion" (p. 81). In emphasizing the sociological at the expense of what is genuinely religious in Defoe's novel, however, Watt has failed to allow for the continued existence, in the thought and literature of the eighteenth century, of a controlling theological view of life. See G. A. Starr, *Defoe and Spiritual Autobiography* (Princeton: Princeton University Press, 1965), and J. Paul Hunter, *The Reluctant Pilgrim* (Baltimore: Johns Hopkins Press, 1966), for important

Fielding uses the fall story in *Tom Jones,* for example, his fiction is in other than simple allegorical ways a convincing expression of Christian optimism. Eden may not be recreated in the world—the impossible hope and mistaken strategy of Mr. Wilson in *Joseph Andrews*—but human life can be structured satisfactorily in this world, for beyond the viciousness, hypocrisy, and vanity that mark society as a fallen structure there is a natural moral order, just as behind the corruption of such words as "honour" and "prudence" there are fixed, normative meanings. It is the duty of the individual to discover this moral order, to ascertain the true meaning of moral concepts, and, having done so, to live within these valid structures.[13]

A brief examination of perhaps the greatest eighteenth century novel will suggest the importance of an understanding of eighteenth century attitudes to society for a reading of Jane Austen's fiction. Richardson's *Clarissa* may seem far from the mood of Jane Austen's novels, but many of the issues Richardson treats are less absolute concerns in Jane Austen, and in some interesting ways the dilemma and response of Richardson's heroine looks forward to, and comments upon, the dilemmas and responses of Jane Austen's heroines. The basic conflict of *Clarissa,* moreover, that between the individual and authority, recurs in most of Jane Austen's novels, and since it is precisely in the matter of how this conflict is resolved that critics are in disagreement, an examination of Richardson's masterpiece is in order.[14]

---

qualifications of Watt's hypothesis. From these works it is evident that Crusoe is as much a spiritual pilgrim as an economic capitalist and that Defoe's novel, while it undoubtedly celebrates man's self-sufficiency, also reveals his deep need of divine support. One need not insist that the theological context, any more than the sociological, is a complete interpretation. Both reveal existing aspects of *Robinson Crusoe* and together define, perhaps, a significant tension at the heart of the work between a residual providentialism and an emerging individualism.

[13] For an excellent discussion of the kind of lesson to be learned in *Tom Jones* and of the various meanings that "prudence" carried at the time, see Martin Battestin, "Fielding's Definition of Wisdom: Some Functions of Ambiguity and Emblem in *Tom Jones," ELH,* 35 (June 1968), 188–217.

[14] In suggesting *Clarissa* as a gloss for Jane Austen's fiction—indeed in briefly examining Defoe, Fielding, Johnson, and Goldsmith—I am not arguing for direct influence. Much of what Jane Austen learned from the eighteenth century novel was filtered through later novels and particularly through Fanny Burney, though she had a good knowledge of Fielding and Richardson too. For a good general study of the later eighteenth century novel, see J. M. S. Tompkins, *The Popular Novel in England: 1770–1800* (1932; rpt. Lincoln: University of Nebraska Press, 1961). The influence of the Richardsonian tradition on particular Austen novels

Required by the "family plan" of the ambitious, social-climbing Harlowes to marry a man she hates, Clarissa is at the same time tempted by the aristocratic Lovelace to leave her home. Both abhorrent possibilities are for a time successfully resisted: she will not marry the rich but toadlike Solmes, nor will she accede to Lovelace's scheme. But Clarissa's situation cannot long remain in such precarious balance. The coercion of her father and brother reaches the point that she is convinced that a forced marriage to Solmes is imminent; at the same time Lovelace's overtures become more persuasive and impelling to a degree which Clarissa does not consciously realize. The crucial scene in which Clarissa is separated (or separates herself) from her family takes place at the garden door of Harlowe Place.[15] Clarissa is aware that in leaving her father's house she will be "taking a step which nothing but the last necessity could justify" (I, 461), but against her conscious will she is tricked by Lovelace into fleeing.

In leaving her "father's house" by way of the garden, Clarissa is clearly, in some sense, repeating the expulsion of man from Eden. In a later conversation between Clarissa and Lovelace the parallel is explicitly made when Clarissa says: "here, sir, like the first pair (I, at least, driven out of my paradise), are we recriminating" (I, 502). But in broad historical rather than mythic terms, Clarissa's journey from the garden is the journey from the corporate life of a traditional society, in which the individual (in Jacob Burckhardt's famous formula) knew himself "only as a member of a race, people, party, family, or corporation,"[16] into a modern capitalistic world in which competitiveness and individualism have separated man from a society of enclosure and support. There is, of course, no implication here that *Clarissa* is the first literary work to suggest this historical transition or that its date (1747–48) indicates the inception of a crucial change in the structure of human consciousness. My

---

is assessed in Henrietta Ten Harmsel, *Jane Austen: A Study in Fictional Conventions* (The Hague: Mouton, 1964). Frank Bradbrook's *Predecessors* investigates certain literary, ethical, and aesthetic traditions of the eighteenth century in which Jane Austen's thought had its roots, while Kenneth L. Moler's *Art of Allusion* pays close attention to more immediate literary and ethical contexts.

[15] *Clarissa*, intro. John Butt (London: J. M. Dent, 1965), I, 473–74. All subsequent references will be to this, the Everyman's Library edition, and will be made in parentheses in the text.

[16] *The Civilization of the Renaissance in Italy*, trans. from 15th ed. by S. G. C. Middlemore (1929; rpt. New York: Harper Torchbooks, 1958), I, 143.

point is merely this: a great many novels, including Jane Austen's, treat the dilemma of an individual in a society in which traditional and corporate values are giving way, or are felt to be giving way, to new economic and individualistic ones. Whatever precise date is assigned to the transition, the radical change in values and in an entire social orientation that has accompanied the emergence of the modern world has been a central theme of prose fiction from *Lazarillo de Tormes* to Lawrence's *The Rainbow*.

A more important consideration than the presence of such a theme in a given novel, however, is the nature of the response elicited from a novelist in face of the transvaluation of morality he experiences. Here it is necessary to distinguish Richardson's response (as it is also necessary to distinguish Jane Austen's) from other responses that are commonly discovered in fiction. There is, for example, the individualistic response of the picaresque hero in which moral action is identified with the available means of survival. Smollett's Roderick Random may serve as typical of the picaresque response in English fiction. His whole life a series of hardships, Roderick has arrived at a philosophy of adaptive individualism:

> If one scheme of life should not succeed, I could have recourse to another, and so to a third, veering about to a thousand different shifts, according to the emergencies of my fate, without forfeiting the dignity of my character beyond a power of retrieving it, or subjecting myself wholly to the caprice and barbarity of the world. (*Roderick Random*, chapter 23)

Life is assumed to lack order and the world to be inimical to individual security. Society must be resisted and circumvented. Yet society is nevertheless the necessary backdrop for individual adaptability and it usually becomes, as in Roderick's case, the final domicile of the hero. Moreover, the thought that society may be a historically determined structure capable of change would never enter the head of a picaresque hero or author.

Just such a thought, of course, is at the heart of Scott's historical fiction, where a choice between cultural attitudes existing in time, rather than between moral attitudes existing in an atemporal realm, transforms the novel from a genre treating ethical antitheses to a genre offering dialectical possibilities. Before Scott's novels, however, such a choice between cultures is rarely, if ever, found in

English fiction. What we face in *Clarissa*, as in modified form in Jane Austen's fiction, is a choice between "things as they are" and individual resistance. Precisely here caution is necessary. What is the nature and quality of Clarissa's resistance? For the Marxist critic, Clarissa appears as a historical "type," the nexus of forces in flow in mid-eighteenth century England, and her resistance to her family carries revolutionary overtones for the capitalist society in which she lives. Such Marxist individualism is not, however, descriptive of *Clarissa*. It is true, as Alan McKillop has said, that Clarissa comes into "conflict with the whole system,"[17] but she becomes neither a Roderick Random adaptively changing to the coloration of a temporary background, nor a revolutionary protagonist in dynamic opposition to a corrupt system. Expelled from "all other protection and mediation," she reaches a state of extreme subjective isolation; she must become "father, mother, uncle" to herself (II, 294). Her reduced state, however, leads her neither to the pragmatic expediency advised by her friend Anna Howe—to marry Lovelace as soon as possible—nor to a disaffection with the true values of her culture. In the end, she sets out "with all diligence for [her] father's house" (IV, 157), expecting in heaven the happiness denied her on earth, and even asserting with her dying breath that it was good that she was "afflicted" (IV, 346). Her resistance to the economic corruption of her home is not revolutionary but reactionary. Though she sets herself in heroic opposition to those forces that would compromise her principles, her opposition is not subversive, for she is affirming the religious principles which ideally underlie society. The quality of her resistance looks forward to the individualism of Jane Austen's own Christian heroines, Fanny Price and Anne Elliot, both of whom are likewise under pressure to accede to proposals which violate their social and personal beliefs. The price Clarissa has to pay is of course great. No reintegration into society is possible and only in heaven is Clarissa's virtue to be rewarded.

Clarissa's absolute allegiance to a theological interpretation of conduct underscores the suspicion of excessive individualism that is a feature of eighteenth century fiction and (a point that is also im-

---

[17] *Samuel Richardson: Printer and Novelist* (Chapel Hill: University of North Carolina Press, 1936), p. 127.

portant in a reading of Jane Austen's fiction) reveals that isolation from society need not lead to a "survival morality" or to disaffection and subversive attitudes. Nevertheless, the conflict in which Clarissa is engaged, while it affirms the necessity of acting always in accordance with religious principles, also reveals the "pull" of individual freedom. Something of the tension between providentialism and individualism that is discovered by modern readers in *Robinson Crusoe* reappears in *Clarissa*. Richardson, however, is conscious of the incipient individualism that his novel contains and is genuinely successful in exposing its theological insufficiency.

Free individual action in *Clarissa* finds its advocate, of course, in Lovelace, but it is important to recognize that Clarissa, too, "falls." Like Eve, she is seduced by a diabolical figure to go against her father's command, and like Eve she is culpable. Although it seems harsh to blame her for leaving her father's house—since he has through his greed and cruelty forfeited all claim to stand in god-given authority over her, and she has even so refused voluntarily to disobey him—Clarissa is herself guiltily aware that she has permitted an unsanctioned secret correspondence with Lovelace, and she need not, after all, have gone to meet him at the garden gate. In this act, particularly, we are aware of a slight, if unconscious, movement on Clarissa's part toward the freedom which Lovelace offers her. Richardson's description of the actual interview at the garden door, replete with the imagery of keys and locks and of swords and sheaths, not only gives an appropriately sexual tone to Clarissa's fall but suggests that she is genuinely tempted by his words and actions. Indeed it might be argued that it is precisely at this point that Clarissa symbolically loses her virginity (the later rape, done while she is drugged, leaves her blameless and only permits Lovelace to discover, in Yeats's phrase, "the perpetual virginity of the soul"). Certain it is that Clarissa sees her action in leaving the garden as irrevocable and one by which she has "laid up for [herself] *remorse for [her] whole life*" (I, 509).

Clarissa, expelled from (partly choosing to leave) the garden, is forced (partly forces herself) to be free. But her freedom is something she fears and ultimately rejects in her submission to God. She takes the traditional view of the fall, that it is a sin of ultimate consequence by which she has forfeited the security and peace of her enclosed home. But need the fall, which leads to her freedom, be considered such an irrevocable step? Need it even be considered a sin? Such questions enter *Clarissa* almost in spite of Richardson. From another point of view, the journey out of the garden is the first real, human act—that act whereby an individual first defines himself in specifically human terms. This point of view is held in the novel by Lovelace. Recognizing that Clarissa's "sudden transition" has caused her to treat him with coldness, Lovelace is at first confident that she will soon have the gratitude to "distinguish between the *confinement* she has escaped from and the *liberty* she has reason to rejoice in" (I, 494; my italics); and his belief is sincere (if ultimately mistaken, in Richardson's view). A relativist and an individualist, Lovelace rejects all systems except that which he confidently places in his own breast. From his faith in his own sufficiency he is able to tell Clarissa that he will be "a father, uncle, brother, and . . . a *husband* to [her], all in one" (I, 480). All the security she has lost in leaving her father's house, she will rediscover in the intense and passionate relationship he offers her. Nor in her new state is it simply that he will be "all" to her; she, for her part, will be "all" to him. At several points in the novel, Lovelace sees Clarissa as his "salvation," or as a person with ultimate power over his life. He cries, "Include me in your terms; prescribe to me; promise for me as you please; put a halter about my neck and lead me by it . . ." (II, 80). In the intensity of such pleas his outlook is revealed as not only extreme and self-contradictory but heretical. Promising to "provide" for Clarissa, Lovelace desperately needs Clarissa to "provide" for him. If he has said that he will replace the whole family structure in Clarissa's life (and beyond this, by implication, God's authority), then she, the "divine" Clarissa, will act as God to him, will be the "ground" of his being. As novel after novel in the nineteenth century will insist, no person can act as the "providence" and "substance" of another.

Clarissa's heroic refusal to submit to Lovelace's impassioned appeal is to be understood, therefore, in the context of theological orthodoxy. Driven from a family enclosure that has been economically corrupted, unable to accept the expedient morality of Anna Howe, Clarissa cannot "sanction" or "sanctify" (the words are again and again repeated) the passionate union Lovelace offers her, for this would not only defy her father's authority but go against God's law. Lovelace may have led her to forfeit all her "temporal" hopes, but she is determined he will not destroy her eternal happiness. Her "soul disdains communion with him" (III, 521); she has more pleasure in thinking of death than of such a husband. Something of this conflict between religious obedience and passionate love recurs in the character of Marianne Dashwood in *Sense and Sensibility*, and while Jane Austen, like Richardson, gives a good deal of sympathy to passion, no less than Richardson does she reject the possibility of a passionate relationship becoming a substitute for the relation between an individual and God. Like Richardson too, as we shall see especially in *Emma*, Jane Austen is fully aware of the "evils" of complete subjective freedom, of the problems attendant on the departure from the "father's house."

Clarissa testifies to its author's sincere faith that the world is structured according to divine plan. As long as such a faith persists, one might conjecture, it is unlikely that we will find many novels granting ultimate sanction to the individual to define his own order. But with the loss of a deeply experienced faith in God's providence, will not such a sanction be claimed and exercised? Looking ahead to later English works that take the conflict between father and child as a central theme, one discovers very different resolutions. The individual protagonists of such works as *The Ordeal of Richard Feverel* (1859), *The Way of All Flesh* (1884; 1903), *Father and Son* (1907), and *A Portrait of the Artist as a Young Man* (1916), all in one way or another find it essential to the continuance of their authentic existence that they resist the coercive systems they inherit and are expected to live within. Edmund Gosse, faced by his father's intransigent fundamentalism, clings "through thick and thin" to "a hard nut of individuality," refusing ever to resign a belief in his "innate and persistent self." Stephen Dedalus, declining to serve that in which he can no longer believe, "whether it call itself [his] home, [his] fatherland or [his] church," uses for his defense "silence, exile and cunning," as he sets out "to discover the mode of life or of art whereby [his] spirit [can] express itself in unfettered freedom." Yet the intense self-reliance of Gosse and Dedalus is, I think, a less typical response than one might expect and self-sufficiency is more often claimed than achieved even in "modern" works.[18]

[18] Quotations in this paragraph are from Edmund Gosse, *Father and Son* (London: William Heinmann, 1948), p. 191; James Joyce, *A Portrait of the Artist as a Young Man* (New York: Viking Press, 1964), pp. 247, 246.

The point may be supported by briefly considering the predicament of representative nineteenth century novel heroes. Like their predecessors in the eighteenth century, they are apt to find themselves isolated from society, but unlike a Tom Jones or a Crusoe, or even a Marianne Dashwood, their isolation is an immediate fact. They have been expelled from no initial paradise and their lives can in no sense be considered to repeat the fortunate fall of Adam. Like Pip in *Great Expectations* (1861), the nineteenth century hero is likely to come to consciousness "turned . . . upside down" in a hostile world. Facing such a world he has no choice but to be free; but it is a freedom he would, if he could, escape. At the end of the century, Jude Fawley in Hardy's *Jude the Obscure* (1895) seems to bring to a culmination the plight of the nineteenth century individual: "As you got older, and felt yourself to be at the centre of your time, and not at a point in its circumference, as you had felt when you were little, you were seized with a sort of shuddering." Man, who had once existed in a world whose dimensions were laid down and continuously sustained by God, now discovers that he is himself the sole legislator of order in an alien world. To be at the center of one's existence, rather than to exist in a world whose center is God, is a horrifying discovery that is made again and again in the nineteenth century novel. In a world whose center cannot hold, desperate strategies are undertaken to regain a sense of divine substance to existence. Jude, after his "shuddering" discovery, seeks to escape his existential freedom by investing Christminster with divine meaning; it becomes the center of the universe to him, a "city of light," the "Heavenly Jerusalem." Dorothea Brooke, victim of "soul hunger" in the godless society of *Middlemarch* (1872), tries to recline "in the lap of [Casaubon's] divine consciousness." Cathy, in *Wuthering Heights* (1847), tells Nelly that her "love for Heathcliff resembles the eternal rocks beneath." Jane Eyre sees in Rochester her "whole world . . . almost [her] hope of heaven," and he stands "between [her] and every thought of religion, as an eclipse intervenes between man and the broad sun." All such attempts to invest a person (or, in Jude's case, a place) with divine meaning are doomed to failure and, if unchecked, lead to destruction. No person can act as God for another person, or justify another's existence, or guarantee another's selfhood. These are among the salient lessons of the nineteenth century novel which, as a rule, reveals the difficulties involved in discovering a sense of personal equilibrium in a world where external order cannot be assumed.[19]

The positive aspects of individualism (suggested as early as *Crusoe* and fulfilled, seemingly, in *Portrait of the Artist*) are not, on the whole, discoverable in the nineteenth century novel. When Pip, finding that the self can have no great expectations that life will somehow be taken care of without individual effort, learns that he must take responsibility for his own future, he grows importantly in awareness, but his discovery hardly brings him joy. Existential freedom, indeed, seems seldom to be viewed after the Nietzschean fashion as a glorious opportunity for man to fulfill his human potential, and the discovery that self is prior to structure is more often a case for despair than for hope in the nineteenth century. The *Übermenschen* who begin to appear in English fiction as the century turns have negative value: one thinks of Kurtz in *The Heart of Darkness* (1899), the universal representative of Europe, an emissary of the European mind, appearing (as he thinks) as a god to the African savages; or, somewhat later, of Gerald Crich, in *Women in Love* (1921), with his burning ambition "to extend over the earth a great and perfect system in which the will of man ran smooth and unthwarted, timeless, a Godhead in process." The "horror" that both men discover is that man cannot be God, that ultimate value and order are not theirs to bequeath to the world. Crich, looking inward and finding, like Kurtz, hollowness at the center of his being, seeks "reinforcements" in the face of "universal collapse" in a relationship with Gudrun, making her (much as Cathy makes Heathcliff, and as Lovelace wished to make Clarissa) the guarantee and justification of his being: "If there weren't you in the world, then *I* shouldn't be in the world, either." (Compare Cathy's words: "If all else perished and *he* [Heathcliff] remained, I should still continue to be; and if all else remained, and he were annihilated, the Universe would turn to a mighty stranger.") But Crich, like Heathcliff and Lovelace before him, comes to recog-

---

[19] Quotations in this paragraph are from Charles Dickens, *Great Expectations*, chap. 1; Thomas Hardy, *Jude the Obscure*, Part First, chaps. 2, 3; George Eliot, *Middlemarch*, Book I, chap. 5; Emily Brontë, *Wuthering Heights*, chap. 9; Charlotte Brontë, *Jane Eyre*, chap. 24. For a brilliant and extended treatment of the argument made here, see J. Hillis Miller, *The Form of Victorian Fiction* (Notre Dame, Ind.: University of Notre Dame Press, 1968).

nize before his death the negative implications of subjectivity in a world which lacks a theological orientation.[20]

Such a brief and arbitrary notice of the theme of individualism in English novels after Jane Austen undoubtedly begs many questions. For example, not all Victorian and modern novelists are helpless before the nihilism that is often consequent upon the discovery of the death of God. In the Feuerbachian humanism of *Middlemarch* and the "star equilibrium" of *Women in Love*, positive and admirable solutions to a world without a transcendent origin of value are discovered and dramatized. Nevertheless, the anxiety and desperation that frequently attend the passage from an ontological world in later novels permit us, when we look back to Jane Austen and realize her own awareness of cultural instability, to view with understanding her distrust of excessive individualism and her affirmation of inherited structures.

IN THIS selective bracketing of Jane Austen's fiction I have attempted to suggest ways in which a persistent novelistic preoccupation with individualism over two centuries can usefully provide a large context for an examination of her novels. The eighteenth century novels which precede her fiction, though they occasionally contain troubling implications (at least for modern readers), generally testify to a world that is divinely structured. Behind the appearance of discontinuity and randomness that the fallen world presents, a divine order exists, so that even individual isolation is explicable in terms of universal Christian experience. Secure in the knowledge that the world is essentially ordered, the individual is also confident that it will—after much personal tribulation and a difficult process of education perhaps—provide him with a place. Usually this place is in society, but even when, as in *Clarissa*, his place is only to be found in the afterlife, the consolatory effect of knowing that his continued existence is guaranteed by God remains. In the nineteenth century, however, precisely this consolation is lacking. Many novels in that century testify to the loss of faith in

---

[20] Quotations in this paragraph are from D. H. Lawrence, *Women in Love*, chaps. 17, 24; Emily Brontë, *Wuthering Heights*, chap. 9.

any extrahuman foundation for society or individual existence, and, as I have argued, dramatize a situation in which the self is discovered as the only determinant of order and value. Far from rejoicing in his new-found freedom to structure his existence as he thinks fit, the typical nineteenth century hero is appalled by the burden of a responsibility he has not sought, and tries, in ways I have indicated briefly, to escape from an intolerable isolation.

It is not possible to provide satisfactory causal reasons why the nineteenth century novel was faced with a new metaphysical or theological situation. Sociological factors such as the continuing disruption of society from the effects of increasing industrialism; philosophical factors such as the idealistic course of British empiricism (leading to the epistemological subversion of the external world and the increasing isolation of the self); the loss of belief in such ordering structures as *concordia discors* and the great chain of being; an emerging historicism—these and other developments undoubtedly accompany, if they do not cause or explain, the shift from ontology to psychology, from public orders to private worlds, that recent scholars consider to have occurred between the eighteenth and nineteenth centuries.[21] Questions of cause aside, however, the point here to be emphasized is that Jane Austen's fiction is inter-

21 See, for example, A. O. Lovejoy, *The Great Chain of Being* (Cambridge, Mass.: Harvard University Press, 1936); Walter Jackson Bate, *From Classic to Romantic: Premises of Taste in Eighteenth-Century England* (1946; rpt. New York: Harper Torchbooks, 1961); M. H. Abrams, *The Mirror and the Lamp: Romantic Theory and the Critical Tradition* (1953; rpt. New York: W. W. Norton, 1958); Earl R. Wasserman, *The Subtler Language* (Baltimore: Johns Hopkins Press, 1959); Morse Peckham, "Toward a Theory of Romanticism: II. Reconsiderations," *Studies in Romanticism*, 1 (1961), 1–8; J. Hillis Miller, *The Disappearance of God* (Cambridge, Mass.: Harvard University Press, 1963), esp. pp. 1–16. As the romantic period is increasingly being thought of as the period of crucial change in English thought, so traditional aspects of the eighteenth century are being stressed. Paul Fussell, for example, in his *The Rhetorical World of Augustan Humanism* (Oxford: Clarendon Press, 1965), pp. 3–27, argues that the Augustan humanists (Pope, Swift, Johnson, Burke) resuscitated traditional Christian norms in the defense of an ethic and an ontology that were threatened by such developments as mechanism, relativism, commercialism, sensibility, and the conception of art "as an end-product of self-expression." Another sign of renewed respect for a Christian humanist tradition in the eighteenth century is to be seen in recent Burke scholarship. Cleared of nineteenth century charges of utilitarianism and political expediency, Burke is now, on the one hand, apotheosized as the great defender of the Natural Law, stemming from Cicero, Aquinas, and Hooker, and, on the other, considered as a political philosopher seeing in historical prescription the justification of the English constitution.

mediate, and in no way more importantly so than in her attitude to the problems of individual identity and morality. Existing at a point of transition between two centuries, she may also be seen as situated between two texts: "Therefore that ye shall rise, the Lord sends down" and *"Gott ist tot."*

In certain structural ways her novels follow in the tradition of eighteenth century fiction. The initial security, subsequent isolation, and final relocation in society that her heroines experience are stages reminiscent of the journey of the self in many previous novels. Occasionally, too, there are vestigial suggestions of the expulsion from the Garden theme, as when in *Mansfield Park* Maria Bertram breaks out of the gate into the park with Crawford at Sotherton. It can be argued further that Tom Bertram's disobedience of his father in the same novel (along with other sins against his father's house) invites something of a traditional suspicion of filial disobedience. Certainly *Mansfield Park*, by its very title, invites an allegorical reading. On the other hand, it is clear that Jane Austen's plots no longer work explicitly within the controlling theological framework of earlier novels; they do not secularize the pattern of *felix culpa*; and there are intimations that the isolation of the individual is no longer explicable in terms of universal Christian experience.

The last point may be supported by another reference to Mrs. Smith, whose "situation" could hardly be more "cheerless":

She had been very fond of her husband,—she had buried him. She had been used to affluence,—it was gone. She had no child to connect her with life and happiness again, no relations to assist in the arrangement of perplexed affairs, no health to make all the rest supportable. Her accommodations were limited to a noisy parlour, and a dark bed-room behind, with no possibility of moving from one to the other without assistance, ... (*P*, 154)

In such passages Jane Austen's last novel moves out of the eighteenth century and gives suggestions of Victorian *Angst*. "There is so little real friendship in the world" (156), Mrs. Smith tells Anne Elliot, and one is tempted sometimes to hear modern chords in the sad melody of *Persuasion*, and to sense in Anne's marriage to Wentworth at the end of this novel an anticipation of Matthew Arnold's existentialist response in "Dover Beach" to a world lacking value and consolation:

> Ah, love, let us be true
> To one another! for the world, which seems
> To lie before us like a land of dreams,
> So various, so beautiful, so new,
> Hath really neither joy, nor love, nor light,
> Nor certitude, nor peace, nor hope for pain;   (ll. 29–34)

As I argue in chapter five, however, the danger is not that we will miss the new directions of *Persuasion* but that we will grant them too much prominence. *Persuasion* brings into central focus what had been latent and peripheral in the other novels, but even here Anne Elliot's response to her reduced existence is in several respects nearer to Clarissa's than to that in "Dover Beach." Thus, while it is significant that Anne does not return to her father's house—either literally, or in the tropological sense Clarissa intends —it is also important that she remains, throughout her period of isolation, faithful to an inherited idea of conduct and that, in the end, she refuses to repudiate her early habit of obedience and sense of duty. In these respects Anne retains what other Austen heroines either possess or come to accept: a belief in the prior existence of certain imperatives for individual action.

Where are these imperatives located? Where does the individual in Jane Austen's world place his allegiance? Two important answers to these questions are not generally to be found in criticism. The first is that it is to religion that the individual owes his duty; the second and connected answer is that it is to society. Ultimately, I believe Jane Austen's morality is based in religious principle, and religious responses are not uncommon in her fiction. But I am not concerned here to argue for the dramatized presentation in her novels of a religious basis for individual behavior. Few novels may be properly termed "theological" (though in the eighteenth century they may look to theological sanctions for society and the self). As a form the novel's area of concern seems typically to be "ethical." This is perhaps to say with Angus Wilson that the English novel after Richardson deals with the question of "right and wrong" rather than with "good and evil."[22] Certainly most novels are more

---

[22] "Evil in the English Novel," *The Listener*, 68 (27 Dec. 1962), 1079–80.

interested in the relation of the individual to others in society than
in the relation of the individual to God, more interested in morality
than in theology.

A morality fit for man in society need not be, as Dickens and
other nineteenth century novelists reveal, a social morality, and
here perhaps we have another means of placing Jane Austen's novels
by setting them against certain tendencies that precede and follow
her fiction. Thus, whereas the eighteenth century novelist, generally
speaking, can accept society whole, as a given structure within whose
terms the individual must act, the nineteenth century novelist tends
to question the ethical constitution of society and to set against it a
morality generated by the interaction of two people or a small
group. On the one hand, to make the point quickly, we have the
man of the hill in *Tom Jones*, whose withdrawal is wrong both as
strategy and as morality; on the other, we have Wemmick's moated
"castle" at Walworth in *Great Expectations*, a pocket carefully
separated from the taint of surrounding London. From Fielding's
comprehensive affirmation of society, the English novel, we may say,
moves, no doubt through Sterne and the sentimental tradition, to
Dickens' circumscribed ethic in which a small enclave is purified
through love amid a world of wickedness. In this comparison, Jane
Austen's affiliation is with Fielding rather than Dickens (though
Persuasion will require qualifications at the proper time). Her fiction puts forward a positive vision of society, and although her great
novels, *Pride and Prejudice*, *Mansfield Park*, and *Emma*, each end
by describing the "perfect happiness" of hero and heroine in the
company of a "small band of true friends" (*E*, 484), this is not to be
read as a circumscription of Jane Austen's ethical concern, or as an
indication of her loss of faith in an inherited structure of morality.
In each case, society has been reaffirmed around the central union,
and the social fragmentation that initially threatened has been
reconstituted through individual commitment into a new whole. A
measure of Jane Austen's social affirmation may be gained from
comparing the final union of Knightley and Emma with the concluding marriages of Dickens' novels—with, for example, the muted
and circumscribed happiness of Arthur Clennam and Little Dorrit:
"They went quietly down into the roaring streets, inseparable and
blessed; and as they passed along in sunshine and shade, the noisy
and the eager, and the arrogant and the froward and the vain,

fretted and chafed, and made their usual uproar" (*Little Dorrit,* concluding sentence).

I wish to argue, then, that Jane Austen affirms society, ideally considered as a structure of values that are ultimately founded in religious principle, at the same time as she distinguishes it from its frequently corrupted form. The latter distinction permits one to oppose the charges (often made by critics favorably disposed to Jane Austen) that she disliked her society, that she was, in Lionel Trilling's phrase, "conscious of, or unconsciously aware of, not a good society but a bad one, a predominantly vulgar society," that she, in David Daiches's words, "expose[d] the economic basis of social behavior with an ironic smile."[23]

To answer the first charge, it is surely only necessary to admit that the discovery and depiction of viciousness within society need not lead to a rejection of society. Fielding's example is before us. At least as aware of the viciousness and corruption of society as Jane Austen, Fielding, working on the assumption of a fallen world, is able to define ways in which an individual can come to terms with an ubiquitous vanity and hypocrisy. Jane Austen, I would argue, especially in her early novels, not only takes over much of Fielding's ethical framework—his division of moral responses into opposed pairs which are exemplified in characterization—but she also comes to broadly similar ethical resolutions. The individual, by reconciling his benevolence and his prudence, his sensibility and his sense, can satisfy the claims of society without compromising his integrity. As Trilling insists, Jane Austen was indeed aware of "a predominantly vulgar society"; she calls it "the neighbourhood," or "the world," and the coercive power it may exert is recognized. But she is also aware, as Fielding was, of an ideal society behind corrupted forms, which provides in its manners and conventions, properly understood, a framework of morality and order to which the self can authentically respond.

To answer Daiches's charge, it is necessary to be clear about Jane Austen's attitude toward money. That she had an awareness of pressing economic factors in the society of her experience is no more to be denied than her awareness of widespread "vulgarity." *Sense*

[23] "A Portrait of Western Man," *The Listener,* 49 (11 June 1953), 971; "Jane Austen, Karl Marx and the Aristocratic Dance," *American Scholar,* 17 (Summer 1948), 289.

and Sensibility particularly, we will see, reveals the evil that may result from economically motivated conduct. But to suggest that she was "the only English novelist of stature who was in a sense a Marxist before Marx" is totally to misconceive the direction of her thought. In what sense is she Marxist? Daiches's own argument— that her heroines escape from the possibility of financial indigence into the "country house ideal"—is scarcely a satisfactory one. Clearly, he is not really arguing that Jane Austen is a Marxist author; what he is doing is to express a Marxist disapproval of the economy of a hierarchical social structure.[24]

A more extreme and influential argument, identifying (by implication, at least) Jane Austen's morality with the available means of economic survival, is to be found in Mark Schorer's much cited "Fiction and the 'Analogical Matrix.' " *Persuasion,* for Schorer, is a "novel of courtship and marriage with a patina of sentimental scruple and moral punctilio and a stylistic base derived from commerce and property, the country house and the inherited estate." The morality, that is, is explicit but superficial; the harsh economic reality, implicit in the "metaphorical substructure" of the novel, is basic and the real determinant of the novel's values. The comedy "lies in the difference between the two orders of value which the metaphors, like the characters, are all the while busily equating."[25] But can this be fairly argued? Would it not be truer to say that Jane Austen is aware of the confrontation between traditional and economic values in her society, and that, like Richardson before her, she resists any economic transvaluation of a traditional morality whose roots are ultimately religious? Schorer has been led by his hypothesis to overemphasize the importance of the "buried" metaphor. Not only are his "economic" derivations frequently false— such words as "credit," "figure," independence," and "prospect"

----

[24] ". . . there is a more important reason for our distaste for Mr. D'Arcy [*sic*] and what he stands for. However fine a life he might be able to lead himself, it was at tremendous cost to society as a whole. He represented the apex of a pyramid, and he flourished at the top of a social hierarchy which existed in order to maintain him. In other words, though the country house ideal represents a fine way of living, it has proved so far a socially wasteful way of achieving a good ideal for a very few" (Daiches, "Aristocratic Dance," p. 294).

[25] Schorer's essay is collected in *Critiques and Essays on Modern Fiction,* ed. John W. Aldridge (New York: Ronald Press, 1952); citations are from pp. 83–84, 85, 86.

may have quite other than economic meanings in given contexts—
but he also fails to realize that Jane Austen's use of economic words
is often conscious and thematic, that she is fully aware of the motivations which a financial vocabulary may reveal. It is a consistent
mark of moral integrity in her novels that solely financial considerations be excluded from personal decisions, though there are also
occasions on which it would be unwise, if not immoral, not to take
them into account. Frequently, "economic" words are employed intentionally to assert that possession of money entails a commensur-
ate moral responsibility. One example only need be given here.
When Maria Bertram, realizing that Henry Crawford will not
marry her, decides for purely expedient reasons to marry the very
rich Rushworth, we are told that "independence was more needful
than ever." Though Crawford has destroyed her happiness, Maria
determines that "he should not destroy her credit, her appearance,
her prosperity too" (*MP*, 202). Financially and socially she secures
her "independence" and "credit" through marriage, but the moral
content of these words is ironically present (or "buried") beneath
Maria's interpretation of their meaning, and what she loses by her
marriage is any claim to a moral "independence" or "credit." Her
consistent references to Rushworth as "Sotherton" are another indication of where her real "interest" lies.

Two other charges against Jane Austen's social vision may be
appropriately mentioned here. The first, argued forcibly and in
different ways by Arnold Kettle and Graham Hough, questions
whether Jane Austen's fiction is not limited by the "class basis" of
her moral standards. I try to come to terms with this, in my view
mistaken, charge in chapter four. The second charge, implicit in
criticism since Sir Walter Scott's favorable review of *Emma* in the
Quarterly, has to do with scale. How comprehensive is her society?
Is she limited by being, in Gilbert Ryle's witty phrase, "exempted
by the width of the Home Counties from having to try to portray
in her pastel-shades the ebony complexion of urban sin"?[26] The
answer to this perennial question has to be of the yes-and-no kind.
Quite clearly she is limited in respect to subject (and was well
aware of this, as her celebrated letters to the Prince Regent's

[26] "Jane Austen and the Moralists," in *Critical Essays*, ed. B. C. Southam,
p. 116.

librarian attest). When she describes "urban" life, it is either Bath, which has, at least in *Northanger Abbey*, little sign of the massive effects of the industrial revolution, Portsmouth (discussed in the next chapter), or London, which is wicked enough, but which owes more, one suspects, to theatrical stereotype than to felt experience. But against this kind of limitation, deliberately chosen in the interest of an aesthetic end, one has to emphasize her deep awareness of a transitional society and her special ability to invest the everyday occurrence—a walk in a garden, a visit to an estate, an outing to Box Hill or to Lyme Regis—with large and (though one hesitates to use the word) symbolic significance.

Jane Austen's serious concern over the state and continuity of the social structure is not, I think, to be doubted, and the novel which more than any other expresses this concern is *Mansfield Park*. Often considered a heresy to her early individualism, this novel seems to me central to Jane Austen's convictions, the work where her morality and ontology are most clearly in evidence, and for this reason I consider it first of all her novels. As its title implies, it is a novel concerned with place and tradition and with the relation of the individual to his inheritance, but it is not, as many critics have charged, a reactionary defense of the *status quo*. One of the crucial motifs of the work, indeed, discussed at some length in the next chapter, has to do with the "improvement" of estates, and in developing this motif Jane Austen is able to distinguish with precision and skill between proper and improper responses to an inherited culture. The "estate" in *Mansfield Park* is symbolic of a whole social and moral inheritance, a fact which explains, *inter alia*, why the theatricals are so distrusted.

In *Mansfield Park* the "moral autonomy" of which Harding speaks is rather a moral commitment to an ideal of conduct, which the heroine cannot discover in her vicinity, but which she nevertheless believes in as an ideal and attainable order, and which she is able by virtue of her fidelity and consistency to bring once more into being. Fanny's conduct suggests that, for Jane Austen, individual behavior must be in accordance with social principle, but this, I think, is a constant in her fiction. Those who undermine society are either entirely rejected (as Lady Susan is, *pace* the sympathetic reading of Marvin Mudrick), or they come to learn the necessary limits of human freedom and to affirm their moral "estate." It may be argued that this is an enclosure of individual choice, but it cannot be argued that this is bad faith. Quite consciously Jane Austen limits the individualism of her heroines from a recognition of the possibly destructive effects of excessive freedom. Something of the eighteenth century novelist's distrust of *curiositas* lingers in her novels, where a persistent theme treats of the dangers posed to the social fabric by the strongly subjective self.

In stressing a traditional rather than a "modern" or a "subversive" Jane Austen, I do not wish to ignore recent criticism and scholarship, much of it excellent, that has itself in one way or another taken this route. To the work of Trilling, Babb, Litz, Southam, and Moler I am particularly indebted, and—if the sentiment be not too suspiciously reminiscent of the gratitude of the Reverend Mr. Collins—future chapters will acknowledge the influence of these, and other, critics and scholars. Nor, in asking that Jane Austen be read as an author who affirms society, do I wish to ignore her keen awareness of the dangers of automatic formality and a complacent pride in status. Conscious of the possible weakening of external structures and of the possibility of an economic transvaluation of morality, however, she insists on individual commitment to, rather than mere acceptance of society. Her novels may be seen as the continuing record of a responsible woman concerned with right conduct in "such days as these" (*PP*, 38).

A final consideration of this introduction may be to notice how deeply Jane Austen was aware of her responsibilities as author. Conscious that of all human activities imaginative creation permits the greatest freedom, she quite consciously delimits her powers of expression. R. W. Chapman long ago noted how "exceptionally, and even surprisingly, dependent upon reality as a basis of imaginary construction"[27] she was in her novels, and the reason for this surely is that she is as aware of the dangers of unlimited imaginative freedom in authors as in heroines. Throughout her writing it is remarkable how meticulously careful Jane Austen is to ground her world in a precise temporal and spatial frame. The chronology and geography of her novels are exact. She uses almanacs and road books in

---

[27] Letter to the Editor, *Times Literary Supplement*, 10 Dec. 1931. A. Walton Litz also discusses Jane Austen's "acute need for some grounding in realistic detail," *Artistic Development*, pp. 93–94.

their construction and, ignorant of Northamptonshire, she enquires of her sister if it is a "country of Hedgerows" (*L*, 298). Learning that it is not, she probably altered a scene, later to include her original description in *Persuasion*, whose setting (Somersetshire) would permit its authentic introduction.[28]

In an interesting series of letters to her niece Anna Austen—the only extended literary criticism Jane Austen left—we meet this same demand for exact realistic fidelity:

Lyme will not do. Lyme is towards 40 miles distance from Dawlish & would not be talked of there.—I have put Starcross instead. If you prefer *Exeter*, that must be always safe. (*L*, 394)

Yes—Russel Square is a very proper distance from Berkeley S^t.—We are reading the last book.—They must be *two* days going from Dawlish to Bath; They are nearly 100 miles apart. (*L*, 395)

The last chapter does not please us quite so well, we do not thoroughly like the *Play*; perhaps from having had too much of Plays in that way lately. And we think you had better not leave England. Let the Portmans go to Ireland, but as you know nothing of the Manners there, you had better not go with them. You will be in danger of giving false representations. Stick to Bath & the Foresters. There you will be quite at home. (*L*, 395)

Twice you have put Dorsetshire for Devonshire. I have altered it.—Mr Griffin must have lived in Devonshire; Dawlish is half way down the County. (*L*, 396)

Accuracy as to geographical distances and traveling time (and in other passages as to the appropriateness of her niece's choice of names) points to more than the recognition that "an artist cannot do anything slovenly" (*L*, 30), or to the aim of the miniaturist concerned with a "little bit (two Inches wide) of Ivory" (*L*, 469). Her awareness of the "danger of giving false representations" in its adjacence to the mention of the play is not only a comment on the nature of the theatricals in *Mansfield Park*, but evidence of a concern that the novelist should describe things that are really there, that imagination should be limited to an existing order.

It is in this manner too that we should view her frequent require-

[28] R. W. Chapman's conjecture in a note to the Oxford edition of *Persuasion*, p. 271.

ments that her niece should pay attention to the minutiae of social decorum:

I have also scratched out the Introduction between Lord P. & his Brother, & Mr. Griffin. A Country Surgeon . . . would not be introduced to Men of their rank. (*L*, 394)

We are not satisfied with Mrs. F.'s settling herself as Tenant & near Neighbour to such a Man as Sir T. H. without having some other inducement to go there; she ought to have some friend living thereabouts to tempt her. (*L*, 400)

This kind of sentiment is probably what led D. H. Lawrence to accuse Jane Austen of a "sharp knowing in apartness,"[29] but it is perhaps fairer to discover in this ligature between fiction and reality a philosophic indication. It is inadvisable to follow the Portmans to Ireland because that would be to leave a location one knows in every detail of geography and social behavior and to enter an unknown realm, one of imagination without reference to fact. The strength of a novel is like that of Antaeus; it depends upon frequent contact with the ground. The ungrounded imagination is as dangerous for an author as it is for a character within the novel, and imaginative limitation is welcome, for it is proof that there is a center to reality other than the individual mind. In her close attention to physical fact Jane Austen declares her belief, not in man as the creator of order but in man's freedom to create within a prior order. Thus her individualism as author, like the individualism of her heroines, respects finally the given structure of her world. Her careful attention to topographical details, as found in *Mansfield Park*, takes on in this regard something of an ontological significance.

[29] *A Propos of "Lady Chatterley's Lover,"* reprinted in *Sex, Literature and Censorship*, ed. Harry T. Moore (1953; rpt. New York: Viking Press, 1959), p. 109.

Mansfield Park:
JANE AUSTEN'S
GROUNDS OF BEING

"I used to think Pride and Prejudice *best," she said, "but now I
like* Mansfield Park *better."*
*"You are quite right—it has a far deeper and truer experience of
life—it is a book for the adult."*

Joyce Cary, *To Be a Pilgrim*

*We found these old institutions, on the whole, favourable to moral-
ity and discipline; and we thought they were susceptible of amendment, without altering the ground.*

Edmund Burke, *Reflections on the Revolution in France*

*To us Jane Austen appears like one who inherits a prosperous and
well-ordered estate—the heritage of a prose style in which neither
generalization nor abstraction need signify vagueness, because there
was close enough agreement as to the scope and significance of such
terms.*

Mary Lascelles, *Jane Austen and Her Art*

⚜ DESPITE a great deal of critical attention in recent years, *Mansfield Park* continues to be received antagonistically by many readers, and the substance, if not the inimitable trenchancy of Reginald Farrer's views, is still to be heard: "alone of her books, *Mansfield Park* is vitiated throughout by a radical dishonesty;" Fanny Price is "the most terrible incarnation we have of the female prig-pharisee;" here, most clearly, the "official" censor intervenes on behalf of society to suppress insurgent individualism.[1]

Two factors, one external and one internal, explain the novel's continuing ability to antagonize. The external factor is that it follows, both in date of publication and in the experience of many readers, the "light and bright and sparkling" *Pride and Prejudice*, a novel that is often read (wrongly, I shall argue) as an unqualified celebration of the free spirit. The internal factor has to do with the novel's plot, which seems first to be moving in an accommodative direction, but which is then—so the argument runs—wrenched from its natural course in order that a morality of "cold, questionless

[1] Reginald Farrer, "Jane Austen," *Quarterly Review*, 228 (July 1917), 20–23. Much of the recent interest in the novel stems from Lionel Trilling's epochal essay, "*Mansfield Park*," collected in *The Opposing Self* (New York: Viking Press, 1955). Among the many interpretations of *Mansfield Park* since Trilling, the following seem to me especially valuable: Joseph W. Donohue, Jr., "Ordination and the Divided House at Mansfield Park," *ELH*, 32 (June 1965), 169–78; Joseph M. Duffy, Jr., "Moral Integrity and Moral Anarchy in *Mansfield Park*," *ELH*, 23 (March 1956), 71–91; Thomas R. Edwards, Jr., "The Difficult Beauty of *Mansfield Park*," *Nineteenth-Century Fiction*, 20 (June 1965), 51–67; David A. Lodge, "The Vocabulary of *Mansfield Park*," in his *Language of Fiction* (New York: Columbia University Press, 1966); Kenneth Moler's chapter in *Jane Austen's Art of Allusion* (Lincoln: University of Nebraska Press, 1968); Charles Murrah, "The Background of *Mansfield Park*," in *From Jane Austen to Joseph Conrad*, ed. Robert C. Rathburn and Martin Steinmann, Jr. (Minneapolis: University of Minnesota Press, 1958); Tony Tanner, "Introduction," *Mansfield Park* (Baltimore: Penguin Books, 1966). In addition to these articles, Avrom Fleishman's comprehensive monograph, *A Reading of "Mansfield Park": An Essay in Critical Synthesis* (Minneapolis: University of Minnesota Press, 1967), is both useful and provocative.

obedience" may be imposed.[2] Any attempt to consider the novel as central to Jane Austen's thought—not the "counter-truth" that even such a sympathetic critic as Walton Litz feels it to be—must take these two factors into account. It must understand, that is, why the rejected Mary Crawford is not "in every detail the exact counterpart of Elizabeth Bennet" in *Pride and Prejudice,* and why the endogamous marriage of Fanny and Edmund is justified.[3] A critic need not seek to defend a certain lack of aesthetic tact that is to be marked in the concluding chapters: Mary Crawford's underlying viciousness, foreshadowed in her earlier words and actions, is somewhat too crudely brought to the surface, her "evil" is given too infernal a guise. But to go beyond a recognition of a certain artistic failure, as Farrer and others have done, and discover moral dishonesty at the center of the book, is to misunderstand Jane Austen's fundamental intuitions about individual character and society and to fail to realize that her moral fervor in this novel is called forth (and largely justified) by the seriousness of her fictional issues.

The issues at stake in *Mansfield Park,* though they are of more crucial moment, are not different in kind from those treated in the earlier novels. Here, as elsewhere, Jane Austen is concerned with defining a proper relation between the individual and society, but whereas in a novel like *Pride and Prejudice* this relation could be expressed in terms of a positive marriage between characters whose initial attitudes were widely opposed, in *Mansfield Park* such a union would have negative force. In *Pride and Prejudice* the representatives of individuality (Elizabeth) and of society (Darcy) are both fundamentally right-minded, however much danger initially exists that their respective positions may become intractable. Mutual concessions and contributions permit a dynamic integration of self and society, of energy and culture. In *Mansfield Park,* by contrast, those who represent individuality (the Crawfords) are shown to be crucially suspect, while those who represent, or should

---

[2] Marvin Mudrick, *Jane Austen: Irony as Defense and Discovery* (Princeton: Princeton University Press, 1952), p. 165. Following Farrer, Mudrick sees *Mansfield Park* as the "triumph of gentility." But even devoted Janeites share the wish that the novel had ended with a double wedding. See, for example, G. B. Sterne, "The *Mansfield Park* Quartette," in *Speaking of Jane Austen* (New York: Harper, 1944).

[3] Quoted phrase from Lionel Trilling, "A Portrait of Western Man," *The Listener,* 49 (11 June 1953), 970.

represent, society in the novel (the Bertrams) are without exception deficient. Far from describing a mutual growth of education on the part of opposed individuals, the plot of *Mansfield Park* reveals an increasing moral confusion in the minds of everyone except Fanny Price, and there can be little support adduced from the text to argue for a dialectical ending of the kind that is found in *Pride and Prejudice*. Not only would marriages between Edmund Bertram and Mary Crawford and between Fanny Price and Henry Crawford make nonsense of all the symbolic foreshadowing of the actual ending, but, thematically, they would require a traditional morality to capitulate to relativism, and "society" to surrender to "self."[4]

What are the threats posed by the Crawfords, and how are they revealed? In answering these questions one is able, I believe, not only to justify the resolution of *Mansfield Park* but to identify the persistent concerns of Jane Austen's fictional career. One may begin, not with the symbolically resonant episode of the theatricals but with an examination of a motif of nearer application to the title of the novel, the motif of estate improvements. Only in the context of "improvement" can the larger significance of the play be understood and the function of Fanny Price, a curiously atypical heroine in many respects, be appreciated.

THROUGHOUT Jane Austen's fiction, estates function not only as the settings of action but as indexes to the character and social responsibility of their owners. Thus in *Pride and Prejudice* the aesthetic good sense that is evident in the landscape of Pemberley ("neither formal, nor falsely adorned" [245]) permits the reader (and Elizabeth) to infer the fundamental worth of Darcy's social and ethical character, while in *Emma* Donwell Abbey, with its

---

[4] The point is strengthened when one recalls that Edmund, in urging Fanny to accept Crawford's proposal, argues for a union of opposites: "Your being so far unlike, Fanny, does not in the smallest degree make against the probability of your happiness together. . . . I am myself convinced that it is rather a favourable circumstance" (348–49). But Edmund is, of course, morally blind at this point, and in arguing for a *concordia discors*, he is also unconsciously arguing his own suit with Mary. For perceptive analyses of Jane Austen's method of symbolically foreshadowing her resolution, see Duffy, "Moral Integrity," and Murrah, "Background."

"suitable, becoming, characteristic situation" (358), is the appropriate expression of Knightley's firm sense of stewardship. *Persuasion* provides a negative example, the renting of Kellynch Hall pointing to Sir Walter Elliot's abandonment of his social trust. Landscape improvements, too, figure incidentally in all the novels, but it is in *Mansfield Park* that Jane Austen chooses to make them a recurring motif and, in so doing, to suggest an attitude to the process of social change that is central to all her fiction.[5]

The motif is raised early in the novel during a conversation in the Mansfield dining parlor (I, vi). Rushworth, the rich but stupid owner of Sotherton Court, has just returned from a visit to Smith's place, Compton, which has recently been improved by Humphry Repton, the controversial heir of Capability Brown in landscape gardening: "I never saw a place so altered in my life. I told Smith I did not know where I was" (53). His own place Rushworth now considers "a prison—quite a dismal old prison," which "wants improvement . . . beyond any thing" (53). Maria Bertram, his fiancée, suggests that he too employ Repton, and the officious Mrs. Norris, learning that Repton charges five guineas a day, is quick to support

[5] With a few exceptions, literary critics have ignored the motif of estate improvements in Jane Austen's fiction. Frank Bradbrook's chapter on the picturesque (in *Jane Austen and Her Predecessors* [Cambridge: Cambridge University Press, 1966]), for example, is largely concerned with Jane Austen's relationship to Gilpin. R. W. Chapman, however, has an interesting appendix on improvements in the Oxford edition of *Mansfield Park*; Tony Tanner recognizes the thematic importance of "improvement" in his fine introduction to the Penguin edition of *Mansfield Park*; and Avrom Fleishman in *A Reading* has not only noted the "cultural implications of Fanny's Romantic taste" (p. 31) but has also anticipated my own view of the function of improvements in the novel by seeing them in the context of Burkean conservatism: "The discussions of landscape 'improvement' in the novel therefore sound a note prophetic of the gentry's political weakening and decline" (p. 32). Most suggestively, perhaps, Martin Price, "The Picturesque Moment," in *From Sensibility to Romanticism*, ed. Frederick W. Hilles and Harold Bloom (Oxford: Oxford University Press, 1965), relates "zealous improvement" in Jane Austen to "the readiness to impose self upon the world about one" and to a "failure of moral sympathy" (see esp. pp. 265–68). Historians of taste have more often given extended treatment to Jane Austen's use of landscape in *Mansfield Park*. See especially Elizabeth W. Manwaring, *Italian Landscape in Eighteenth Century England* (1925; reissued New York: Russell and Russell, 1965), pp. 221–24; and Edward Malins, *English Landscaping and Literature: 1660–1840* (London: Oxford University Press, 1966), pp. 129–39. Nikolaus Pevsner provides a great deal of information about the houses in Jane Austen's art and life in "The Architectural Setting of Jane Austen's Novels," *Journal of the Warburg and Courtauld Institutes*, 31 (1968), 404–22.

her favorite niece and to seize the opportunity of spending someone else's money: "Well, and if they were *ten* [guineas], . . . I am sure *you* need not regard it. The expense need not be any impediment. If I were you, I should not think of the expense. . . . Sotherton Court deserves every thing that taste and money can do" (53).

Interestingly, in view of her well-established viciousness in other respects, Mrs. Norris is (or was) something of an improver herself, having done a "vast deal in that way at the parsonage" (54):

> "[W]e made it quite a different place from what it was when we first had it. You young ones do not remember much about it, perhaps. But if dear Sir Thomas were here, he could tell you what improvements we made; . . . If it had not been for [Mr. Norris's sad state of health], we should have carried on the garden wall, and made the plantation to shut out the churchyard, just as Dr. Grant has done." (54)

I shall later argue that Jane Austen is using the technical vocabulary of improvements in a symbolic way; here it is sufficient to note that while Mrs. Norris says she has done a "vast deal," Henry Crawford is the true expert in this matter. Though the original condition of his own estate, Everingham, seemed "perfect" to his sister, Mrs. Grant, with "such a happy fall of ground, and such timber" (61), Crawford has nevertheless "improved" it: "My plan was laid at Westminster—a little altered perhaps at Cambridge, and at one and twenty executed" (61).[6] Henceforward he becomes the acknowledged expert on improvements and is urged by Mrs. Grant and by Julia Bertram to lend his practical aid at Sotherton Court. Mary Crawford, it is true, finds "improvements *in hand* . . . the greatest of nuisances" (57), but she has no objections to them once "complete": "had I a place of my own in the country, I should be most thankful to any Mr. Repton who would undertake it, and give me as much beauty as he could for my money" (57).[7]

---

6 Edward Malins (*Landscaping and Literature*, p. 134) finds "illogical" Mrs. Grant's remark about the "perfect" condition of Everingham before improvement, "for if Everingham was 'perfect' before he improved it, what would be the point of altering it?" Precisely! Crawford should *not* have altered it. Now, doubtless, its trees have been cut down and its appearance altered beyond recognition.

7 Mary's propensity for "improving" is also evident in her opinion that Mansfield wants "only to be completely new furnished" to suit her taste (48).

Against this group of enthusiasts only Fanny Price and Edmund Bertram offer any opposition to improvements. Fanny, quoting Cowper, expresses her concern for the fate of the avenue at Sotherton which Rushworth plans to "improve" (he has already cut down "two or three fine old trees" which blocked the prospect[55]). Her sentiments, while sufficiently romantic, are not to be read ironically. Unlike the subverted enthusiasm of the heroine in *Northanger Abbey*—Catherine "cared for no furniture of a more modern date than the fifteenth century" (182)—Fanny's respectful attitude to the traditional aspects of the estate, like her later regret over the disuse of the chapel, is largely underwritten by her author. Edmund, for his part, though willing to admit the need of "modern dress" (56) at Sotherton, argues against the employment of an improver: "had I a place to new fashion, I should not put myself into the hands of an improver. I would rather have an inferior degree of beauty, of my own choice, and acquired progressively" (56).

Why Repton, and the figure of the improver generally, should so divide the characters in *Mansfield Park* is a question that seems, initially, easy to answer. Throughout Jane Austen's writing life Humphry Repton (1752–1818) was a figure of controversy, the butt of satire, and a man whose name must frequently have been on the lips of anyone connected with the land. As R. W. Chapman notes, she would have come across Repton's celebrated Red Books in some of the houses she visited, and she must have been aware of the "paper war" in which he upheld his principles of landscaping against the attacks of Sir Uvedale Price and Richard Payne Knight, the chief proponents in their different ways of the new picturesque.[8] The context of the paper war, however, is only a partial explanation of Jane Austen's intentions in *Mansfield Park*, and to the

---

[8] For an account of the "paper war," see Manwaring, *Italian Landscape*, pp. 156–62; Malins, *Landscaping and Literature*, pp. 123–41, 147–53; and Christopher Hussey, *The Picturesque: Studies in a Point of View* (1927; reissued, with a new preface by the author, London: Frank Cass, 1967), pp. 161–85. The major documents of the controversy (at least in the initial phase) were Richard Payne Knight's "didactic" poem "The Landscape" (London, 1794); Uvedale Price's *Essay on the Picturesque* (London, 1794); and Humphry Repton's *Sketches and Hints on Landscape Gardening* (London, 1795). Open letters passed between Repton and Price; other interested parties entered the fray; and the controversy was taken up in the reviews of the time. Though Repton defended Capability Brown, his own work often differed in important ways from Brown's; see Malins, *Landscaping and Literature*, pp. 123–25.

degree that it suggests that her distaste for Repton was merely aesthetic, implying a preference for the more naturalistic styles of Price and Knight, it can be misleading. However "enamoured of Gilpin on the Picturesque" she may have been, Jane Austen commonly treats an enthusiasm for this style with some irony in her fiction—not everyone has Marianne Dashwood's passion for dead leaves. As the tone of Fanny's and Edmund's dissenting remarks in the Mansfield dining parlor suggests, moreover, she is less occupied with the aesthetic merits of different styles of landscape than with the negative social implications of a particular mode of "improvement." The important question, then, is why she chose to cast Repton as a negative social example.

A glance at Repton's *Sketches and Hints on Landscape Gardening* (1795) and *Observations on the Theory and Practice of Landscape Gardening* (1803) introduces something of a problem here, for these works reveal him to be not only an engaging, if occasionally sycophantic, writer but a theorist whose principles of landscaping often seem close to Jane Austen's own views. His emphasis on "utility," his insistence, in the first chapter of *Sketches*, upon a "due attention to the character and situation of the place to be improved" align him with, for example, Edward Ferrars in *Sense and Sensibility*, whose "idea of a fine country . . . unites beauty with utility" (97) and who finds "more pleasure in a snug farm-house than a watch-tower" (98). In his celebrated debate with Marianne (I, xviii), Ferrars' rational view of the countryside does not, of course, wholly invalidate Marianne's enthusiasm for the picturesque; like Marianne, Jane Austen was as sensitive to the "beauties of nature" as she was aware that "admiration of landscape scenery [had] become a mere jargon" (97). But as in ethical matters Jane Austen gives priority to Elinor's sense over Marianne's sensibility, so in landscape she favors Edward's humanized, social settings to Marianne's romantic scenes. After a temporary enthusiasm for "rocks and mountains," Elizabeth Bennet in *Pride and Prejudice* settles for Darcy's tastefully improved estate.

Not all of Repton's principles of landscaping are close to Jane Austen's implied views, of course, nor was his practice always consistent with his theoretical principles. His theory, moreover, written in the midst of debate, often has an apologetic air, giving rise to the suspicion of rationalizations after the fact. Undoubtedly some of Repton's improvements fully merited the criticisms they received. While it may be true, therefore, as Donald Pilcher argues, that Repton was made "the scapegoat for the sins of [a] flock of fashionable 'improvers'," and that Jane Austen, in singling him out, both capitalized upon his notoriety and, somewhat unfairly, made him a representative of a much wider movement, it is also possible that she had a reasoned dislike of Repton's methods. Why this should be is perhaps suggested by the radical improvements Repton made at his own cottage in Essex (pictured in the frontispiece). What he has "shut out" and "screened off" may have improved his view, but it has also removed him from any participation in the community. One wonders, in particular, what happened to the beggar (veteran, evidently, of many wars) after Repton's "improvement."[9]

Repton's association with Capability Brown's methods accounted for much of his disrepute, for inevitably he became heir not only to Brown's practice but to the criticism that had long been directed at the "omnipotent magician" and at the figure of the improver generally. As early as Garrick's play *Lethe or Esop in the Shades* (1740), Brownian improvements had been subject to satire (Brown is here satirized when Lord Chalkstone takes exception to the layout of the Elysian fields as viewed from the shores of the Styx). Even earlier, in the country house poem of the seventeenth century, expensive innovations in estates had been castigated for their extravagance, selfishness, and disregard of "use." Thus, when Jane Austen used Repton as a negative figure, and Thomas Love Peacock cruelly satirized him as Marmaduke Milestone in *Headlong Hall* (1816),

[9] The frontispiece to this study reproduces Repton's "View From My Own Cottage, in Essex," from his *Fragments on the Theory and Practice of Landscape Gardening* (London, 1816), facing p. 232. Somewhat speciously, in his commentary on his "appropriation" here, Repton claims not to be excluding himself from "the cheerful village, the high road, and [the] constant moving scene" (p. 235). For appreciations of Repton's work, see John Nolen's introduction to *The Art of Landscape Gardening*, ed. John Nolen (Boston and New York: Riverside Press, 1907); Dorothy Stroud, *Humphry Repton* (London: Country Life, 1962); and Donald Pilcher, *The Regency Style* (London: B. T. Batsford, 1948), pp. 17–46, from which work I have taken the opinion quoted in the text. Whether or not Jane Austen had personal reasons for disliking Repton, she clearly intended him to be a representative figure—as Mary Crawford's phrase, "any Mr. Repton," and Edmund's general distrust of the improver make evident.

they took their places in a long tradition of anti-improvement literature.[10]

Jane Austen's own treatment of improvements, I suspect, owes much to Cowper's *The Task*. In Book III ("The Garden"), her favorite author castigates "improvement" as the "idol of the age" in a passage that continues the traditional complaints of the country house poem against the ostentation and hostility to tradition of the vain trustee. Here too is an awareness of the enormous transformation that improvements could bring about in a landscape:

> The lake in front becomes a lawn;
> Woods vanish, hills subside, and vallies rise:
> And streams, as if created for his use,
> Pursue the track of his directing wand.... (ll. 774–77)

With her knowledge of Cowper alone Jane Austen would have been well prepared to point up the insidious implications of extreme landscaping, but she was also undoubtedly aware of Richard Payne Knight's vituperative poem "The Landscape" (London, 1794), in which Repton is bidden to "follow to the tomb" his "fav'rite Brown":

> Thy fav'rite Brown, whose innovating hand
> First dealt thy curses o'er this fertile land. (Book I, ll. 287–88)

Even without Cowper and Knight, it is likely that Jane Austen's own experience would have led her to a dislike of the drastic alterations to landscape which frequently attended Brownian or Reptonian improvements. The radical nature of such improvements, even more pronounced in the work of less talented imitators, was everywhere evident at the time. Often involving not only the indiscriminate cutting down of trees and the magical creation of rivers and lakes but, on occasions, the relocation of whole villages which

---

10 For a detailed treatment of the anti-improvement literature of the eighteenth century, see Manwaring, *Italian Landscape*, pp. 140–55, and Malins, *Landscaping and Literature*, pp. 97–122. For an examination of even earlier expressions of dislike of excessive changes in an estate, see G. R. Hibbard, "The Country House Poem of the Seventeenth Century," *Journal of the Warburg and Courtauld Institutes*, 19 (Jan. to June 1956), 159–74; Charles Molesworth, "Property and Virtue: The Genre of the Country-House Poem in the Seventeenth Century," *Genre*, 2 (April 1968), 141–57.

blocked the prospect and the redirection of roads by special acts of Parliament, such projects could hardly fail to strike her as emblems of inordinate change. If Edmund Burke in his political prose following the French Revolution could use the imagery of excessive estate improvements to illustrate the horrors of the revolution, we need not be surprised that Jane Austen should suggest in the adoption of Reptonian methods dangerous consequences for the continuity of a culture.

The example of Burke may be usefully extended here, not because he necessarily had a direct influence on Jane Austen's thought, but because his dislike of radical change, again and again expressed in terms of injuries done to an estate or house, suggests an appropriately serious context for her own treatment of improvements.[11] Examples could be multiplied of Burke's employment of house and estate metaphors in the *Reflections*.[12] Often, indeed, in speaking of the state, Burke is clearly using the image of the estate to control the construction of his thought:

...one of the first and most leading principles on which the commonwealth and the laws are consecrated, is lest the temporary possessors and life-renters in it, unmindful of what they have received from their ancestors, or of what is due to their posterity, should act as if they were the

11 I am aware, of course, of the curious biographical connection between Jane Austen and Edmund Burke. The Austen family was connected with Warren Hastings, who was the godfather of Eliza Hancock, Jane Austen's romantic cousin. Eliza married the Comte de Feuillide, who was guillotined in 1794; she then married Henry Austen (Jane's favorite brother) in 1797. When Hastings was acquitted of the charges which Burke and others had brought against him, Henry wrote to him in fulsome terms, congratulating himself and England on the triumph of justice in the case. Hastings was later to express warm approval of *Pride and Prejudice*. (See William Austen-Leigh and R. A. Austen-Leigh, *Jane Austen: Her Life and Letters* [London: Smith, Elder, 1913], pp. 31–45, 79.) The general family liking for Hastings the man need not, of course, deny Jane Austen's predilection for the philosophic stance of his great opponent. It is perhaps worth mentioning an early expression of "Burkean" sentiments by Jane Austen. In the margins of her copy of Oliver Goldsmith's *History of England*, the young Jane wrote, "Every ancient custom ought to be Sacred, unless it is prejudicial to Happiness" (see Mary Augusta Austen-Leigh, *Personal Aspects of Jane Austen* [London: John Murray, 1920], pp. 28–29).

12 For a close examination of Burke's imagery in *Reflections*, including an attention to the metaphor of the "noble house," see James T. Boulton, *The Language of Politics in the Age of Wilkes and Burke* (Toronto: University of Toronto Press, 1963), pp. 97–134.

entire masters; that they should not think it amongst their rights to . . . commit waste on the inheritance, by destroying at their pleasure the whole original fabric of their society; hazarding to leave to those who come after them, a ruin instead of an habitation—and teaching these successors as little to respect their contrivances, as they had themselves respected the institutions of their forefathers. By this unprincipled facility of changing the state as often, and as much, and in as many ways as there are floating fancies or fashions, the whole chain and continuity of the commonwealth would be broken.[13]

Constantly the need of a stable "ground" structure is stressed, as in his expressed "prejudice" in favor of church establishment:

For, taking ground on that religious system, of which we are now in pos-session, we continue to act on the early received, and uniformly continued sense of mankind. That sense not only, like a wise architect, hath built up the august fabric of states, but like a provident proprietor, to preserve the structure from prophanation and ruin . . . hath solemnly and for ever con-secrated the commonwealth, and all that officiate in it. (*R*, 111)

But it is not only in his veneration of traditional structures and dislike of excessive alteration that Burke serves as a useful gloss for *Mansfield Park*. His concept of "improvement," where this is neces-sary, is also relevant to Jane Austen's motif.

As he was fond of stating, Burke was no enemy to change and improvement, and the unimproved existence of institutions is a condition against which he constantly warns in the *Reflections*. "A state without the means of some change is without the means of its conservation" (*R*, 23). An even greater danger for Burke, however, lies in the overthrow or destruction of establishments sanctioned by time and custom. Thus Burke is led, as Father Canavan has shown, to distinguish carefully between what is necessary improvement and what is more properly to be considered destruction. Burke would agree with Charles James Fox in this matter that "improvements were not to be confounded with innovations; the meaning of which was always odious, and conveyed an idea of alterations for the worse." To "improve" was to treat the deficient or corrupt parts of an established order with the character of the whole in mind; to

---

[13] *Reflections on the Revolution in France*, ed. William B. Todd (New York: Rinehart, 1959), p. 115. All subsequent references will be to this edition and will be made in parentheses in the text, the page number being preceded by *R*.

"innovate" or "alter," on the other hand, was to destroy all that had been built up by the "collected reason of the ages." The difference is, of course, the difference between the two revolutions: the English had introduced "improvement" with their revolution, the French "innovation" and "alteration" with theirs.[14]

It is perhaps worthwhile emphasizing the consistent antonymy of "improvement" and "innovation," or "alteration," at this period. A further passage from Burke will make the point, while a passage implicitly critical of Burke's viewpoint by William Godwin will provide the kind of exception that proves the rule. Burke writes: "A spirit of innovation is generally the result of a selfish temper and confined views. People will not look forward to posterity, who never look backward to their ancestors. Besides, the people of England well know, that the idea of inheritance furnishes a sure principle of conservation; . . . without at all excluding a principle of improvement" (*R*, 38). Godwin, on the other hand (surely with this precise passage in mind), writes of "government" that it is the "perpetual enemy of change." Among other abuses, governments "prompt us to seek the public welfare, *not in alteration and improvement,* but in a timid reverence for the decisions of our ancestors . . ." (my italics). Interestingly, this passage from the third edition of *Enquiry Concerning Political Justice* (1798) is a revision of a passage in the first edition (1793), in which "innovation" is phrasally associated with "improvement." The point is clear: Godwin's association of both "innovation" and "alteration" with "improvement" is an intentional dig at Burke, as well as an indication of his diametrically opposite political ideology.[15]

In the context of the anti-improvement literature of the time and of the political prose that frequently makes use of metaphors drawn from the practice of estate improvements, Jane Austen's motif takes on a serious meaning. In her view, radical improvements of the kind Repton made were not improvements at all but "innovations" or "alterations" of a destructive nature. No less than a political consti-

[14] See Francis P. Canavan, *The Political Reason of Edmund Burke* (Durham, N.C.: Duke University Press, 1960), esp. the chapter on "The Process of Social Change." Fox's distinction was made in the Commons, 29 April 1792 (*The Speeches of the Right Honourable Edmund Burke in the House of Commons and in Westminster Hall,* IV, 42. Cited in Canavan, p. 168).

[15] See *Enquiry Concerning Political Justice,* ed. F. E. L. Priestley (Toronto: University of Toronto Press, 1946), I, 245, and III, 247.

tution, an estate, with the immaterial systems of religion, morality, and manners that it contains and upholds, will need improvement from time to time. Cultural atrophy, resulting from neglect, is to be avoided. Even more serious, however, is a too active and thoughtless response on the part of an heir. Thinking to introduce improvement, he may well destroy the "whole original fabric" of his inheritance. What has been "acquired progressively" should not be radically changed. Not to know where one is in an estate that has been "altered" is hardly the cause for pleasure that Rushworth considers it, and Mrs. Norris's "vast" improvement at the Mansfield parsonage, which made it "quite a different place from what it was when [the Norrises] first had it" (54), strikes an insidious note in the context of Burke's prose.

Following the conversation at Mansfield there are two main episodes in the novel in which the improvements theme is taken up. The first is the visit to Sotherton, expressly made by the party from Mansfield for the purpose of assessing its "capabilities." The second occurs when Crawford proposes improvements to Thornton Lacey, the parsonage that Edmund is to occupy on ordination. The two extreme responses that are evident in these episodes help negatively to define Jane Austen's own view of what constitutes the proper improvement of a cultural inheritance.

Sotherton Court, an "ancient manorial residence of the family, with all its rights of Court-Leet and Court-Baron" (82), is "one of the largest estates and finest places in the country" (38). Its status as a representative estate is stressed. Edmund notes that the "house was built in Elizabeth's time, and is a large, regular, brick building— heavy, but respectable looking . . ." (56). Mary Crawford, while dismissing its owner, sees that "a man might represent the county with such an estate" (161). Heavy with the air of tradition and history, Sotherton is, however, aesthetically out of date. When the party from Mansfield arrive, they find the house as Edmund described it—"ill placed . . . in one of the lowest spots of the park" (56). With its brick construction, avenues, walls, palisades, and iron gates, it is self-evidently an estate that has largely missed the "improvements" of the great eighteenth century gardeners.[16] Altogether

16 Malins observes in *Landscaping and Literature*, p. 135, that "we do not hear of the faults which Crawford is presumed to have found," but they are surely everywhere evident. For example, Crawford finds "walls of great promise"; they will be soon knocked down, if he has his way.

it is a "good spot for fault-finding" (90). The interior of the house echoes the old-fashioned condition of the park, for it is "furnished in the taste of fifty years back" (84), and though "of pictures there were abundance . . . the larger part were family portraits, no longer any thing to any body but Mrs. Rushworth" (84–85). As for the chapel, built in James II's reign and "formerly in constant use both morning and evening" (86), its function has ceased, prayers having been discontinued by the late Mr. Rushworth. Fanny, who had wished to see Sotherton in its "old state" (56), is disappointed: "There is nothing awful here, nothing melancholy, nothing grand. Here are no aisles, no arches, no inscriptions, no banners" (85–86). Like her response to the avenue earlier, Fanny's remarks are somewhat romantic (on this occasion she quotes from Scott), and Edmund gently rebukes her by describing the original modest function of the chapel. Again, however, Fanny's instinctive response is in some measure valid, for Sotherton as a functioning estate has clearly fallen into a state of desuetude. In Burkean terms "the idea of inheritance" which "furnishes a sure principle of conservation" has been lost. Here it is less important that Rushworth has come to his inheritance out of the direct line than that he has utterly no awareness of his duty as trustee. Well aware of the aesthetic deficiencies of his estate, he is ignorant of far worse ills. We gather what these are from the complacent description given by Maria Bertram, as the party from Mansfield approaches Sotherton in the barouche:

"Now we shall have no more rough road, Miss Crawford, our difficulties are over. The rest of the way is such as it ought to be. Mr. Rushworth has made it since he succeeded to the estate. Here begins the village. Those cottages are really a disgrace. The church spire is reckoned remarkably handsome. I am glad the church is not so close to the Great House as often happens in old places. The annoyance of the bells must be terrible. There is the parsonage; a tidy looking house, and I understand the clergyman and his wife are very decent people. Those are alms-houses, built by some of the family. To the right is the steward's house; he is a very respectable man. Now we are coming to the lodge gates; but we have nearly a mile through the park still . . . it would not be an ill-looking place if it had a better approach." (82)

Rushworth's improvements will clearly have nothing to do with his run-down cottages. His attention to the road leading to his house, like his admiration of Smith's "approach" at Compton and his later delight in wearing a "blue dress, and a pink satin cloak" (139) for the play, reveal his character to be grounded in vanity. Nor will his marriage to Maria be the "improvement" (53) which Mrs. Grant predicts. Maria's pride in the handsome spire shows a love of display equal to her husband's, while the pleasure she takes in discovering that the church and great house are not close is nicely ambiguous. The propinquity of house and church, common in English estates and often emphasized in Jane Austen's fiction, signifies the necessary interdependence of the clerical and landed orders. Here the physical distance between the two need have no significance, but with Maria as mistress the bells are unlikely to summon the family to regular worship, and the threat is implied that the physical gap will become a spiritual gap—a spatial correlative of a gap between, in Lord Lindsay's terms, a morality of grace and a morality of station.[17] Rushworth and Maria will become the antitypes of the landed ideal proposed by generations of English poets:

> The Lord and Lady of this place delight
> Rather to be in act, than seeme in sight.[18]

Their disregard of religion, as evident in Maria's remarks as in the present disuse of the chapel, will deny the religious dimension of landed ownership, and the displacement of their concern from the function to the appearance of Sotherton will neglect the traditional emphasis on "use" as the basis of landed existence:

> 'T is Use alone that sanctifies Expence
> And Splendour borrows all its rays from Sense.[19]

If the condition of Sotherton serves as a negative emblem of cultural atrophy, stemming from the neglect of its trustees, a second estate, Thornton Lacey, faces the even greater danger of excessive "alteration." The threat exists in Crawford's plans for its "improvement." Aware that the parsonage is to be Edmund's home on ordination, Crawford predicts that "there will be work for five summers at least before the place is live-able" (241):

17 *The Two Moralities: Our Duty to God and Society* (London: Eyre and Spottiswoode, 1948).
18 Thomas Carew, "To My Friend G. N. from Wrest," ll. 31–32.
19 Alexander Pope, "Epistle to Burlington," ll. 179–80.

"The farm-yard must be cleared away entirely, and planted up to shut out the blacksmith's shop. The house must be turned to front the east instead of the north. . . . And *there* must be your approach—through what is at present the garden. You must make you a new garden at what is now the back of the house. . . . The ground seems precisely formed for it. I rode fifty yards up the lane between the church and the house in order to look about me; and saw how it might all be. Nothing can be easier. The meadows beyond what *will be* the garden, as well as what now *is* . . . must be all laid together of course; . . . They belong to the living, I suppose. If not, you must purchase them. Then the stream—something must be done with the stream; but I could not quite determine what. I had two or three ideas." (242)

What is remarkable here is how closely Crawford's proposals resemble Repton's plans for Harlestone Hall, the house most frequently considered the model of Mansfield Park. In Fragment VII of his *Fragments on the Theory and Practice of Landscape Gardening* (1816), Repton describes his method at Harlestone:

The House was formerly approached and entered in the south front, which was encumbered by stables and farm yards; the road came through the village, and there was a large pool in front; this pool has been changed to an apparent river, and the stables have been removed. An ample Garden has been placed behind the house, the centre of the south front has been taken down, and a bow added with pilasters in the style of the house: the entrance is changed from south to north side, and some new rooms to the west have been added.[20]

Disarmed by Repton's tasteful improvements at Harlestone (pictured on the dust jacket of this book and in the frontispiece to Chapman's Oxford edition of *Mansfield Park*), we may be unwilling to grant negative significance to Crawford's "Reptonian" pro-

[20] Quoted by R. W. Chapman in the Oxford edition of *Mansfield Park*, p. 552. Harlestone Park has been considered the model for Mansfield Park by, among others, F. Alan Walbank in *The English Scene*, ed. F. Alan Walbank, 2nd ed. (London: B. T. Batsford, 1946), p. 8. Chapman, however, seems persuaded by Sir Frank MacKinnon's argument in favor of Cottesbrook as a possible model (see R. W. Chapman, *Facts and Problems* [Oxford, At the Clarendon Press, 1948], p. 84, and R. W. Chapman, *Jane Austen: A Critical Bibliography*, 2nd ed. [Oxford, At the Clarendon Press, 1955], item 148). Whether Harlestone or Cottesbrook is Jane Austen's model for Mansfield seems to me of little importance; what is important is her clear association of Crawford's methods with those of Repton. Cf. Malins, *Landscaping and Literature*, pp. 138–39.

posals.[21] Given Jane Austen's symbolic mode, however, Crawford's suggestions are insidious enough. His plans to "clear away," "plant up," and "shut out" features of the landscape are to be read as a rejection of a traditional shape of reality, while his wish to re-orient the front of the house suggests a desire for complete cultural re-orientation. Furthermore, if Repton is indeed echoed in Crawford's prose, it can be argued that Jane Austen has the latter go beyond Repton's stated practice in the *Fragments*. Whereas Repton—in the paragraph preceding the passage above—was careful to insist upon "unity of character" at Harlestone, arguing that "where great part of the original structure is to remain, the additions should doubtless partake of the existing character," Crawford is intent on completely changing the condition of Thornton Lacey; he wishes to give it a "higher character," "raise it into a *place*" (243–44). (There is, of course, an additional irony in his grandiose plans for what is, after all, a parsonage.) In other respects, however, Crawford is reminiscent of Repton. His "before and after" description of the garden is the verbal equivalent of the splendid selling device Repton invented in his Red Books. There Repton masked his illustration of the scene as it would be *after* improvement with a flap depicting the *present* (and of course unfashionable) appearance of the landscape. By merely lifting up the flap a prospective customer discovered a transformation.

Edmund Bertram, however, is not tempted by Crawford's picture of a transformed Thornton. He too has "two or three ideas," and

---

[21] In the Oxford first edition (1923) Chapman accurately reproduced in color Repton's before and after illustration of the south front of Harlestone Park from the *Fragments on the Theory and Practice of Landscape Gardening*. Superimposed ingeniously on the water color representation of the improved scene is a flap (or "slide") which has the effect of showing the house and grounds before improvement. In the Oxford second edition (1926) this frontispiece was replaced by two facing full-page half-tones showing Harlestone Park before and after improvement, an arrangement which continued in the third edition and in reprints of the third edition up to the 1953 impression. In the 1960 impression, however, the before improvement plate was dropped. Subsequent impressions have not reintroduced it, but the editor of the Oxford University Press has informed me that the before improvement plate will be reinstated in the next impression. Readers owning copies of recent impressions may consult the dust jacket of this study, the front of which pictures Repton's "improvement" of Harlestone Park, the back his illustration of the house and park before improvements. Jane Austen's distaste for Repton notwithstanding, few would deny that Repton's alterations here are tasteful and in keeping with the original character of the house.

"one of them is that very little of [Crawford's] plan for Thornton Lacey will ever be put in practice" (242). He admits that the yard should be removed in the interests of a "tolerable approach" (242) —once again he is not averse to "modern dress"—but he will not permit the wholesale redisposition of the structure that Crawford has in mind. He would agree, one might suggest, with Burke's "prejudice" in favor of an established commonwealth—that it is "with infinite caution that any man ought to venture upon pulling down an edifice which has answered in any tolerable degree for ages the common purposes of society, or on building it up again, without having models and patterns of approved utility before his eyes" (*R*, 73).

At Sotherton, where Crawford's help was invited, his schemes may at least have helped to bring an old-fashioned landscape up to date (though, even here, there would have been misplaced priorities and emphases); but at Thornton Lacey, uninvited, his plans are not only extravagant and ostentatious, they are also supererogatory. In terms of a value system that is to be found throughout Jane Austen's fiction, Thornton is a substantial and healthy estate. The house is surrounded by yew trees and the glebe meadows are "finely sprinkled with timber" (242). The church (unlike that at Sotherton) is "within a stone's throw" (241) of the house; and the house itself, with its air of having been "lived in from generation to generation, through two centuries at least" (243), is an instructive contrast to Rushworth's moribund home. One is reminded of the healthy conditions of other estates in Jane Austen's fiction and of the signs of essential soundness which she consistently provides. An abundance of timber is one such sign; the nearness of church and house another.

Trees, of course, have provided an emblem of organic growth throughout English literature. One thinks, for example, of the wych elm in *Howards End*, which, in surviving the excavations of the Wilcox men, gives some hope for social continuity. On the other hand, the cutting down of trees has suggested a radical break with the past, at least from the time of Donne's Satire II ("Where are those spred woods which cloth'd heretofore/Those bought lands?") to Ford Madox Ford's *Parade's End*, where the loss of the great tree at Groby signals the end of an order. In the light of this tradition, Fanny's objections to the cutting down of the avenue at Sotherton have deeper meaning.

In Jane Austen's fiction it is remarkable how often the presence of trees betokens value.[22] Pemberley has its "beautiful oaks and Spanish chestnuts" (*PP*, 267), Donwell Abbey (noticeably "with all [its] old neglect of prospect") has an "abundance of timber in rows and avenues, which neither fashion nor extravagance had rooted up" (*E*, 358), and there is no "such timber any where in Dorsetshire, as there is now standing in Delaford Hanger" (*SS*, 375). It is a sign, in *Sense and Sensibility*, that the Norland estate is secure at the beginning of the novel that safeguards have been taken against "any charge on the estate, or . . . any sale of its valuable woods" (4). Equally it is a sign of the present owner's corrupted values that, when the old owner dies, he should cut down "the old walnut trees" in order to build a greenhouse (226).

If trees suggest organic growth and continuity, the nearness of church and house stresses the religious content of landed life, and precisely this would be lost at Thornton if Edmund were to accede to Crawford's plans and give in to the temptation that is posed by Mary Crawford. While her brother paints his picture of an improved Thornton, Mary, hoping to transform Edmund into a man of fashion, is able imaginatively to "shut out the church" and "sink the clergyman" (248). Like Mrs. Norris's improvements at Mansfield which, we are told, were intended to "shut out the churchyard" (54), like Maria's pleasure in the "distance" between church and house at Sotherton, and like Mary's own response to the leaving off of prayers in the Sotherton chapel—"every generation has its improvements" (86)—Mary's view of a future Thornton entirely excludes any sense of religious responsibility.

This, then, is why improvements of the kind the Crawfords favor are distrusted in *Mansfield Park*: they signal a radical attitude to a cultural heritage; they take no account of society as an organic structure; they effect, and indeed seem to favor, a widening of the gap between church and house, religion and the landed order. With the contrast that is implied between proper "improvement"

22 And not only in her fiction. Her letters frequently reveal her love of trees. Writing to Cassandra (8 Nov. 1800), she tells of a "dreadful storm," which destroyed "highly valued Elms" and various other trees. She regrets that the "three Elms which grew in Hall's Meadow & gave such ornament to it, are gone" (*L*, 86). In another letter (6 June 1811), her dislike of a certain Mr. Tilson becomes evident: "Mr. Tilson admired the trees very much, but greived [*sic*] that they should not be turned into money" (*L*, 289).

and improper "innovation" or "alteration," we may be in a position to understand why all the fuss is made about the theatricals.

IF THE ESTATE is symbolic of an entire inherited culture, the Mansfield house plays a similar role in the novel, thus, I believe, explaining why the episode of the theatricals carries such a crucial weight of significance. What is endangered during the rehearsals of *Lovers' Vows* is not merely the reputations of Maria and Julia, or the decorum of an establishment; when the Honourable John Yates brings the theatrical "infection" (184) from Ecclesford, and an "inclination to act" (123) is awakened in almost everyone, a whole cultural orientation comes under collective attack. In trying to turn the Mansfield house into a theater, the Crawfords, from outside, and the Bertrams, from within, attempt to replace a stable world, in which the self relates to a pre-existing order, with a world of process, in which the self extemporizes and directs. Once we understand that the physical structure of the Mansfield house gives body to the less tangible existence of a traditional ethos, then the rehearsals of Kotzebue's play give every reason for concern.

Beginning modestly—"a few yards of green baize for a curtain, and perhaps that may be enough" (123)—the enterprise soon gathers momentum, invading more and more of the house's space and altering the disposition of its furniture. As Mary Crawford gleefully exults at one point, "we are rehearsing all over the house" (169). The plaster work of a room is damaged by the construction of a stage; a scene painter is called in to replace the estate carpenter; the billiard room adjoining Sir Thomas's bedroom is appropriated for, and soon begins to be called, *the Theatre*; and Sir Thomas's bedroom becomes the green room.

One of Edmund's early objections is thus clearly justified. Arguing against "innovation" he had said, "I think a theatre ought not to be attempted.—It would be taking liberties with my father's house" (127). But Tom had then replied with some hauteur:

"His house shall not be hurt. I have quite as great an interest in being careful of his house as you can have; and as to such alterations as I was suggesting just now, such as moving a book-case, or unlocking a door, or even as using the billiard-room for the space of a week . . . you might just as well suppose he would object to our sitting more in this room, and less in the breakfast-room, than we did before he went away, or to my sisters' pianoforte being moved from one side of the room to the other." (127)

For Tom, the "alteration" of his "father's house" is a matter of small moment. Yet when Sir Thomas returns home so unexpectedly at the very end of the first volume and on the night of the first full "rehearsal"—a splendidly melodramatic *coup de théâtre*, this—the first thing he notices, as he goes to his room, is the "removal of the book-case from before the billiard room door" (182). But the whole passage deserves quotation, for it describes the extent of the transformation that has taken place at Mansfield:

Sir Thomas had been a good deal surprised to find candles burning in his room; and on casting his eye round it, to see other symptoms of recent habitation, and a general air of confusion in the furniture. The removal of the book-case from before the billiard room door struck him especially, but he had scarcely more than time to feel astonished at all this, before there were sounds from the billiard room to astonish him still further. Some one was talking there in a very loud accent—he did not know the voice—*more* than talking—almost hallooing. He stept to the door . . . and opening it, found himself on the stage of a theatre, and opposed to a ranting young man, who appeared likely to knock him down backwards. (182)

Jean Rousset has described the Baroque ethos in seventeenth century France as one in which the world was felt to be a theater and life a comedy in which one had to assume a role.[23] It was an age that made a reality out of metaphor and invested all existence with theatricality. Houses were frequently surprise boxes, walls opened like doors, and theaters were suddenly discoverable in houses. Something akin to such a "baroque" world is surely what Sir Thomas confronts on his return from the West Indies. But it is a world that is granted no validity in *Mansfield Park*. The "general air of confusion in the furniture" marks both the moral confusion of the actors and the confusion that their acting has introduced

[23] *La Littérature de l'Age Baroque en France: Circé et le Paon* (Paris: José Corti, 1953), esp. pp. 13–31.

into an ordered social structure. Whatever failings Sir Thomas will reveal in other acts during the novel, his response on discovering the theater is exemplary. He immediately sets about returning Mansfield to its "proper state" (187). The stage is dismantled, the bookcase is returned to its former position, all the copies of *Lovers' Vows* are burnt, and the scene painter, who has "spoilt only the floor of one room, ruined all the coachman's sponges, and made five of the under-servants idle and dissatisfied" (190–91), is dismissed.[24] Henry Crawford, learning that "very little will remain of the theatre to-morrow" (193), departs for Bath, and Yates, finding Sir Thomas "so unintelligibly moral" (191), leaves also, but not before seeing "the destruction of every theatrical preparation at Mansfield" (194). It turns out that Sir Thomas would indeed object to Tom's sisters' pianoforte "being moved from one side of the room to the other."

Jane Austen's strategy in the theatricals episode, as in her description of landscape improvements, has clearly been to expose the dangers to the "estate" of excessive and unprincipled change. Her metonymy extends beyond simple metaphorical convenience, for by locating traditional systems in the fabric of the house, or in the landscape of the park, she has affirmed her faith in the substantial existence of certain pre-existing structures of morality and religion, and, in a way that might be of interest to structural anthropologists, has suggested how essential to the continuity of an ethos is the actual physical disposition of its setting. When the Salesian missionaries wished to convert the Bororo Indians, they tried to make them abandon their circular villages to live in huts laid out in parallel rows. Then, they knew, the Indians would be "in every sense, dis-oriented. All feeling for their traditions would desert them, as if their social and religious systems . . . were so complex that they could not exist without the schema made visible in their ground-plans and re-affirmed to them in the daily rhythm of their lives."[25] A similar recognition of the cultural importance of locality is implied in *Mansfield Park*, where a traditional religious and moral ethos is, in a real sense, embodied in the estate's fabric and where the changes

[24] Avrom Fleishman has described the revolutionary implications of *Lovers' Vows* in *A Reading*, pp. 24–29.

[25] See Claude Lévi-Strauss, *Tristes Tropiques: An Anthropological Study of Primitive Societies in Brazil*, trans. John Russell (New York: Atheneum, 1964), p. 204.

effected or proposed by Henry Crawford in house and landscape carry strong overtones of the disorientation of a whole culture.

It is, therefore, quite insufficient to regard Sir Thomas' restoration of the house to its "proper state" as merely a reactionary defense of the *status quo*. Like Edmund's later refusal to accept Crawford's "improvements" for Thornton Lacey, his actions are in response to a specific attack. They do not mean that Mansfield is a perfect structure (even before the play, this is hardly so), or the baronet a perfect trustee. Nor are they meant to suggest that Jane Austen views the social structure as an immutable configuration whose integrity would be destroyed by the introduction of the slightest change. As her attitude to proper improvement has already suggested, Jane Austen does not propose the inherited estate as an absolute structure existing out of time. Given the fallibility of human nature, an estate can never be a perfectly exemplary social model. In something of the same manner we should not expect always to discover that manners will incorporate moral intentions which are themselves based in the Natural Law.

Yet, if the estate for Jane Austen must always be to a greater or lesser degree an imperfect embodiment of a natural moral order ultimately based in God, it remains a saving structure of great importance in her thought. Like Darcy's well-stocked library at Pemberley, which puts to shame the poor collection of books of the *nouveau riche* Bingley, it "ought to be good," since it is the "work of many generations" (*PP*, 38). An estate is the appropriate home of what Burke terms the "collected reason of the ages" or the "wisdom of our ancestors;" and for Jane Austen as for Burke, historical prescription is an important basis for social and moral behavior. For this reason the individual does well to respect the topography of his inherited landscape and the "furniture" of his "house."

Precisely because the estate is a structure in time, however, it will need improvement on occasion, as the example of Sotherton sufficiently attests. There is a constant need for the individual not only to preserve but properly to improve his inheritance, which means, as we have seen, that he should respect the character of the whole while repairing the deficiency of the part. Those who automatically assume that status confers value (the Bertram sisters), or that a life of privilege precludes the need for activity (Lady Bertram), or that the responsibilities of an heir may be lightly regarded (Tom) promote the atrophy and permit the "alteration" that are the dangers they should prevent. The estate as a structure in time is valid only as it is actively supported by the individual.

These truths the episode of the play conveys in a number of subtle ways, and one finds it difficult to understand those critics who have asked with Henry Crawford, "What signifies a theatre?" In the light of studies by Trilling, Litz, Fleishman, and others, the episode stakes its claim to be one of the most successful integrations of theme and action in English fiction.[26] All of the characters are revealed by their conduct during the play and by the parts they choose or are persuaded to take. In many cases, indeed, the casting of *Lovers' Vows* accurately prefigures the future careers of the players. Thus, for example, Tom Bertram's willingness to "descend a little," to "take any part . . . so as it be comic" (131) reflects his failure to take seriously his role in life, that of heir to the estate and, in his father's absence, of "master of the House" (123). His extravagance has already cost Edmund the Mansfield living, and his continued irresponsibility and loose living will lead him to a near fatal illness. The Bertram sisters, each vying for Henry Craw-

[26] Trilling, *Opposing Self,* considers that the "decisive" objection to the theatricals is a "traditional, almost primitive, feeling about dramatic impersonation" (p. 218); and Jonas Barish, "The Antitheatrical Prejudice," *Critical Quarterly,* 8 (Winter 1966), 329–48, provides the kind of detailed history of a persistent distrust of theatricality—in Plato, the Church fathers, the English puritans, and others —to support Trilling's contention. Moreover, although Barish is not concerned with Jane Austen, his essay illuminates aspects of theatricality in *Mansfield Park* and identifies the nature of the opposition over the play. For Barish, the antitheatrical prejudice is "antepredicative," going before all attempts to rationalize it (p. 342); it is connected with "a conservative ethical emphasis in which the key terms are those of order, stability, constancy and integrity, as against a more existentialist view that prizes exploration, process, growth, flexibility, variety and versatility of response" (p. 342). For arguments placing the theatricals episode in social, religious, and historical contexts, see Avrom Fleishman, *A Reading,* pp. 24–29; David Spring, "Aristocracy, Social Structure, and Religion in the Early Victorian Period," *Victorian Studies,* 6 (March 1963), 263–80; Sybil Rosenfeld, "Jane Austen and Private Theatricals," in *Essays and Studies: 1962,* ed. Beatrice White (London: John Murray, 1962), pp. 40–51; and William Reitzel, "*Mansfield Park* and *Lovers' Vows,*" *Review of English Studies,* 9 (Oct. 1933), 451–56. A. Walton Litz, *Jane Austen: A Study of Her Artistic Development* (London: Chatto & Windus, 1965), pp. 117–27, sets the theatricals in convincing biographical and social contexts and has an interesting discussion of the significance of the casting. Litz's association of Mary Crawford with Eliza de Feuillide (so often denied by Austen critics and scholars) is convincing, as is his association of Fanny Price with Philadelphia Walter.

ford's attentions, reveal their selfish and jealous natures in their competition for the part of Agatha, the abandoned mother of Frederick, which role is to be played by Crawford. Maria's delight in securing the role is partly due to her triumph over Julia, partly to her pleasurable anticipation of acting a scene of tearful reunion with her stage son, a scene which—as all are aware—involves outward manifestations of affection. But her willingness to play the part of a fallen woman is not only culpable in light of her engagement to Rushworth, it also appropriately foreshadows her own later fall with Crawford in London. As it is, Maria's conduct during rehearsals is so blatant that even the vacuous Rushworth is excited to jealousy. Mary Crawford finds it necessary on one occasion to excuse their conduct:

"By the bye, I looked in upon [Henry and Maria] five minutes ago, and it happened to be exactly at one of the times when they were trying *not* to embrace, and Mr. Rushworth was with me. I thought he began to look a little queer, so I turned it off as well as I could, by whispering to him, 'We shall have an excellent Agatha, there is something so *maternal* in her manner, so completely *maternal* in her voice and countenance.' " (169)

Julia Bertram, for her part, finds solace for her disappointment over Henry in a growing acquaintance with Yates, whose role as the seducer (Baron Wildenhaim) is appropriate in view of his later elopment with Julia.

The attitudes of the older generation are no less revealing. Lady Bertram's complete lack of interest in the scheme denotes her indolent withdrawal from any sense of personal responsibility for the behavior of her children—just as her exaggerated concern for her lap dog Pug testifies to the displacement of her ethical duty. Mrs. Norris is "exceedingly delighted with the project" (129); not only will she be pleasing her favorite nephew and niece, but she will also be able, at no expense to herself, to play the "executive part" (166), a role she enjoys throughout the novel. To the degree that the whole house is caught up in the scheme, Mansfield Park is endangered. But two characters, Edmund and Fanny, oppose the scheme, though with different consistency, and the nature and quality of their opposition provides a focus for a further consideration of the conflict of orientations that the theatricals reveal.

WHETHER or not the subject of *Mansfield Park* is "ordination," there can be no doubt that Edmund's choice of profession is a matter of continuing importance throughout the book.[27] By electing to be ordained, Edmund has committed himself to a vocation, and though any profession is in effect the assumption of a role, his especially is "a permanent impersonation which makes virtually impossible the choice of another. It is a commitment which fixes the nature of the self."[28] This understood, his decision to act in the play is not the "ridiculous belly flop" Kingsley Amis charges but a denial of a chosen identity.[29]

One should, perhaps, underscore the seriousness with which Edmund views his duties as a clergyman, since it is possible to assume that he, like other representatives of the cloth in Jane Austen's fiction who display few signs of vocation—Henry Tilney, Mr. Collins, Mr. Elton—is becoming a member of a spiritually dry Anglican church. Despite recent attempts to impugn Edmund's professional sincerity, however, it is clear that the novel establishes the authenticity of his initial commitment. Only if Edmund's choice is firmly based may the crucial nature of his actual compromise during the play, and his near compromise when he goes to London half intending to ask Mary to marry him, be properly understood. I see no evidence to show that his "improperly executed" induction or his pluralism (if this can, indeed, be proved) are held against him. On the contrary, both the sincerity of his motivation and Jane Austen's subscription to his serious conception of professional role seem fully stressed.[30]

---

[27] Trilling has recently been shown to have misquoted from the letter in which Jane Austen speaks of "ordination," and it now seems doubtful that "ordination" refers explicitly to the subject of *Mansfield Park.* For a series of letters exhausting aspects of the debate, see *Times Literary Supplement,* 19 Dec. 1968; 2 Jan. 1969; 9 Jan. 1969; 16 Jan. 1969; and 30 Jan. 1969.

[28] Trilling, *Opposing Self,* p. 219.

[29] "What Became of Jane Austen? [*Mansfield Park*]," *The Spectator,* 199 (4 Oct. 1957), 339.

[30] Following Clarence L. Branton's "The Ordinations in Jane Austen's Novels," *Nineteenth-Century Fiction,* 10 (Sept. 1955), 156–59, Avrom Fleishman argues that Edmund, like other clergymen in Jane Austen's fiction, is ordained without first becoming a deacon. He goes on to notice that Sir Thomas, after arguing

Edmund's professional philosophy is most seriously propounded in the chapel at Sotherton. Mary Crawford has just discovered to her surprise and embarrassment (since she has been treating religion and clergymen with levity) that Edmund is to become a clergyman; nevertheless, she persists in her low opinion of his future career: "A clergyman is nothing" (92). Edmund's reply reply follows:

"The *nothing* of conversation has its gradations, I hope, as well as the *never*. A clergyman cannot be high in state or fashion. He must not head mobs, or set the ton in dress. But I cannot call that situation nothing, which has the charge of all that is of the first importance to mankind, individually or collectively considered, temporally and eternally—which has the guardianship of religion and morals, and consequently of the manners which result from their influence. No one here can call the *office* nothing. If the man who holds it is so, it is by the neglect of his duty, by foregoing its just importance, and stepping out of his place to appear what he ought not to appear." (92)

Through Edmund's sentiments we see one of the few explicitly articulated presentations of what I take to be Jane Austen's own view of an ideally constituted society—a society in which the primary social gestures (manners) incorporate moral intentions, which are themselves founded in religious principles. That Edmund

---

against plurality, nevertheless acquires the Mansfield living for Edmund after his marriage to Fanny, Edmund being then already in possession of Thornton Lacey. From these discoveries of irony on Jane Austen's part, Fleishman seeks to modify the opinions of those critics who have seen an Evangelical influence at work in *Mansfield Park*: "Jane Austen's primary interest seems, then, to be not in the purification of the Church—the Evangelicals' prime target—but rather in the moral criticism of the gentry" (p. 22). I fail to see ironies of the kind Fleishman discovers. Neither Edmund nor his father is a consistent character; both have the unfortunate habit of not always practicing what they preach; but their fundamental sincerity with respect to their notion of the clergyman's role is not in question. Had Jane Austen intended us to see irony in the process of Edmund's ordination, or in his acquisition of the Mansfield living at the end of the novel, she would have made it adequately clear in the "fabric of her dialogue," to borrow a phrase from Howard Babb. Why must we assume in any case that the Edmund Bertrams retained Thornton Lacey when they came to Mansfield? It seems more reasonable to argue that Edmund and Fanny are housed in the Mansfield living for other than ironic reasons: they will undoubtedly fulfill their pastoral duties more responsibly than the epicurean Grants (or the selfish Norrises before them), and as they return "within the view and patronage of Mansfield Park" (*MP*, 473) they also meet the requirements of Jane Austen's affirmative, "comic" conclusion.

should shortly after distinguish his idea of manners (*"conduct . . .
the result of good principles"* [93]) from the common meaning of
the word ("refinement and courtesy . . . the ceremonies of life")
provides additional support for believing that the voice we hear in
this scene is Jane Austen's, for in all her novels—with certain qualifications to be made of *Persuasion*—social behavior is ideally
rooted in a natural moral order that is itself divinely sanctioned.

While the passage testifies to Edmund's firm notions of professional role, it also deposits evidence that will soon condemn him
for inconsistency. Despite all his reasoning, his agreement to act in
the play marks his surrender to Mary Crawford's sexual attraction;
moreover, by agreeing to act the part of a clergyman rather than
be one, he has in effect admitted the possibility that his role may
be temporary, his office "nothing;" he has "stepp[ed] out of his
place to appear what he ought not to appear." Well aware that
"the man who chooses the profession itself, is, perhaps, one of the
last who would wish to represent it on the stage" (145), he finds
himself in a dilemma that will recur throughout the novel. Just
before the ball at Mansfield, for example, he is "deeply occupied
in the consideration of two important events . . . which were to fix
his fate in life—ordination and matrimony" (254–55), and David R.
Carroll is surely right to see Edmund's agreement to act as a wish
fulfilment in which he can reconcile his profession and his love of
Mary: Anhalt, the part he plays, permits him to be both a clergyman and the accepted lover of Amelia, who is played by Mary.[31]

That these roles may not be so easily reconciled in life is evident
enough from Mary's attitudes to profession and to marriage. Adopt-
ing the "true London maxim, that every thing is to be got with
money" (58), she is no less convinced that a future life without
money would be, like the profession of a rural parson, "nothing."
During her stay at Mansfield, we are told, "matrimony was her
object" (42)—in this she appropriately resembles the husband-hunting Amelia in *Lovers' Vows*—and when her regard shifts from Tom
Bertram, the eldest son, to Edmund, the problem of his profession
becomes of concern to her, especially after she has established that
Edmund has no fortune from an uncle or grandfather (92). Mary's

---

[31] *"Mansfield Park, Daniel Deronda,* and Ordination," *Modern Philology,* 62
(Feb. 1965), 218.

solution is that Edmund must change his profession, become a soldier or go into the law: "You really are fit for something better. Come, do change your mind. It is not too late" (93).

Edmund's professional commitment comes perilously close to being subverted by Mary Crawford, and had Fanny succumbed to Henry Crawford's courtship at Mansfield or at Portsmouth, the marriage of Mary and Edmund, we may assume, would soon have followed, with inevitably destructive consequences for the estate. The opposition of Fanny and Crawford, in this light, becomes of first importance in the novel; it is a contrast not only of attitudes to life but in conceptions of social role and of personal identity. And since Fanny is a more consistent character than Edmund, and Henry poses an even greater threat than his sister, the juxtaposition of their characters most clearly illustrates Jane Austen's thematic intentions.

In the opposition of Crawford and Fanny, the twin themes of improvements and theatricality appear as opposite sides of the same coin. Crawford, the "capital improver" (244), is also "considerably the best actor of all" during rehearsals (165); Fanny, who is consistently opposed to Crawford's style of improvement, finds it "absolutely impossible" (146) to act. On the one hand, we have a character who views his "estate" as manipulable and who opts for a variable conception of self; on the other, a character who holds to a permanent sense of place and a stable idea of personal identity.

Like his "Circean" propensities with regard to landscape, Crawford's "Protean" nature with regard to self is much in evidence.[32] Of all the would-be actors, he is most excited by the prospect of "rais[ing] a little theatre at Mansfield" (123):

"I really believe ... I could be fool enough at this moment to undertake any character that ever was written, from Shylock or Richard III. down to the singing hero of a farce in his scarlet coat and cocked hat. I feel as if I could be any thing or every thing, as if I could rant and storm, or sigh, or cut capers in any tragedy or comedy in the English language. Let us be

---

[32] The combination of Circean and Protean tendencies in the same figure was a feature of the *ballets de cour* of seventeenth century France, an era in which Crawford would have been much more at home. Cf. Jean Rousset's description: "Le magicien de soi-même et la magicienne d'autrui étaient destinés à s'associer pour donner figure à l'un des mythes de l'époque: l'homme multiforme dans un monde en métamorphose" (*L'Age Baroque*, p. 22).

doing something. Be it only half a play—an act—a scene; what should prevent us? Not these countenances I am sure ... and for a theatre, what signifies a theatre?" (123)

As in a later scene (III, iii), where his remarkable ability to read from Shakespeare is displayed, Crawford's polymorphic nature and ambitions are evident. He can "undertake any character that ever was written;" but his choice of at least one role is ironically indicative of the threat he poses. Shakespeare's Richard III is not only the supreme dissimulator, the diabolical shape-changer; he is also the usurper king who brings dissension to a country:

> I'll play the orator as well as Nestor,
> Deceive more slily than Ulysses could,
> And, like a Sinon, take another Troy.
> I can add colours to the chameleon,
> Change shapes with Proteus for advantages,
> And set the murd'rous Machiavel to school.
> Can I do this, and cannot get a crown?
> (*3 Henry VI*, III. ii. 188–94)

Crawford's histrionic abilities seem not in themselves objectionable. When "with the happiest knack, the happiest power of jumping and guessing," he reads in turn the speeches of the "King, the Queen, Buckingham, Wolsey, Cromwell," Fanny is properly impressed by his "capital" reading (337). What makes his wish and ability to act a multiplicity of parts dangerous, however, is that these are not his avocation, but his vocation, not his recreation, but his profession. Lady Bertram is unwittingly perceptive, though perhaps after the fact, when she suggests that on account of his "turn for acting" he will have a theater at Everingham (338).

Throughout the novel the temporary and specious nature of Crawford's enthusiasms is exposed. If he has "dignity or pride, or tenderness or remorse" (337), the qualities are not his intrinsically but those of the temporary part he is playing. If he is "pre-eminent" (240), the adjective will be found to describe his skill at cards, and if he does "honour" to anything, it is misplaced, as when, with "playful impudence," he does "honour to the game" (240). Like his sister (who excels as actress, horsewoman, harpist, cardplayer), Crawford is hugely talented, but his talents are of short duration or wrongly directed. In a novel where the word "act" carries a good deal of meaning, only once, during his courtship of Fanny, is he described as "acting as he ought to do" (404). His role of faithful lover and responsible landowner, however, has no more permanence than any of his other roles, and he will soon forsake it for another part—already suggested by his actions at Sotherton and during the play scenes—that of seducer.

Crawford is not, of course, the only character whose attitudes show no awareness of social responsibility. Within the park, and especially in the person of Tom Bertram, a similar refusal to commit the self to a social role is abundantly evident, and David Spring is right to discover in the novel intimations of a Victorian sense of responsibility, perhaps even to see the novel as symptomatic of a general moralizing of the English landed order.[33] Crawford's variability is the most heinous, however, precisely because he is the most gifted, and, rightly directed, his energies would be of most benefit to society. His given role is that of landowner, but his estate is hardly ever seen by him, for "to any thing like a permanence of abode . . . Henry Crawford had, unluckily, a great dislike" (41). Given the implication that residency is as important for a landlord as for a parson in *Mansfield Park*, this is a telling mark against him. But if his geographical mobility is suspect, his refusal to opt for a single role is even more so. In *Pride and Prejudice*, Wickham will burn through three careers—clergyman, lawyer, and soldier—in as many years. Crawford, much more solidly established at Everingham, with a considerable £4,000 a year, need look to no professional career for his support; yet, as the novel reveals, many roles attract him, though "not for a constancy" (341), and in all cases his allegiance is "rather eager than lasting" (236). Hearing William Price's account of his adventures at sea, Crawford is for a moment attracted by the role of naval officer:

He longed to have been at sea, and seen and done and suffered as much. His heart was warmed, his fancy fired, and he felt the highest respect for a lad who, before he was twenty, had gone through such bodily hardships and given such proofs of mind. The glory of heroism, of usefulness, of exertion, of endurance, made his own habits of selfish indulgence appear in shameful contrast; and he wished he had been a William Price, distin-

[33] "Aristocracy," 270.

guishing himself and working his way to fortune and consequence with so much self-respect and happy ardour, instead of what he was! (236)

Somewhat later, the role of preacher appeals to him: he "should like to be such a man" (341). But his imagined picture of his role as a London clergyman reveals, as we shall see, the insincerity of his professions and the suspect theatricality of his idea of preaching.

In Crawford's conversation with Edmund on the subject of pulpit delivery (III, iii) we have perhaps the most subtle exposure of his variability. In this scene the motifs of improvement and theatricality are again brought together in an exchange which permits Fanny, in her usual position of "quiet auditor" (136), to judge between the characters and outlooks of the two men. Crawford's remarks follow his "truly dramatic" reading from Shakespeare's *Henry VIII*, a performance which has impressed Fanny in spite of herself (337). Now, however, as he turns to comment upon Edmund's profession, she finds further grounds for disapproval. The topic in question has to do with the failure of "sensible and well-informed men" to read aloud in public (339). Edmund speaks first:

"Even in my profession . . . how little the art of reading has been studied! how little a clear manner, and good delivery, have been attended to! I speak rather of the past, however, than the present.—There is now a *spirit of improvement* abroad; but among those who were ordained twenty, thirty, forty years ago, the larger number, to judge by their performance, must have thought reading was reading, and preaching was preaching. It is different now. The subject is more justly considered. It is felt that distinctness and energy may have weight in recommending the most solid truths. . . ." (339–40; my italics)

Crawford is deferential in response (conscious that he is under the gaze of Fanny), and his subsequent remarks on the delivery of sermons seem to accord with Edmund's views:

"A sermon, well delivered, is more uncommon even than prayers well read. . . . It is more difficult to speak well than to compose well; that is, the rules and trick of composition are oftener an object of study. A thoroughly good sermon, thoroughly well delivered, is a capital gratification. . . . The preacher who can touch and affect such an heterogeneous mass of hearers, on subjects limited, and long worn thread-bare in all common hands; who can say any thing new or striking, any thing that rouses the attention, without offending the taste, or wearing out the feelings of his hearers, is a man whom one could not (in his public capacity) honour enough. I should like to be such a man." (341)

Behind both passages one senses Jane Austen's awareness of discussions of sermon delivery and public speaking in the works of the elocutionists and rhetoricians of the late eighteenth century. Thomas Sheridan, for example, in his first lecture on elocution, observes that "good public reading, or speaking, is one of the rarest qualities to be found, in a country, where reading and speaking in public, are more generally used, than in any other in the world; where the doing them well is a matter of the utmost importance to the state, and to society"; and Hugh Blair, writing on "Eloquence of the Pulpit," sounds like Crawford when he notes that the subjects of the "Pulpit Orator," though noble and important in themselves, are "subjects trite and familiar":

They have, for ages, employed so many Speakers, and so many pens . . . that it requires more than an ordinary power of genius to fix attention. Nothing within the reach of art is more difficult, than to bestow, on what is common, the grace of novelty. No sort of composition whatever is such a trial of skill, as where the merit of it lies wholly in the execution; not in giving any information that is new, not in convincing men of what they did not believe; but in dressing truths which they knew, and of which they were before convinced, in such colours as may most forcibly affect their imagination and heart.

Both theorists, of course, advocate "improvement" in public reading and pulpit delivery, Sheridan going so far as to see improvement in elocution as necessary "to the support of our constitution, both in church and state."[34]

That Jane Austen also advocated improvement in pulpit delivery is clear enough from Edmund's measured remarks. But that not all improvements in the pulpit were acceptable to her is suggested by a

[34] Quotations in this paragraph are from Thomas Sheridan, *A Course of Lectures on Elocution*, ed. R. C. Alston (Menston: The Scolar Press, 1968); pp. 1, 5; and Hugh Blair, *Lectures on Rhetoric and Belles Lettres*, ed. Harold F. Harding (Carbondale, Ill.: Southern Illinois University Press, 1965), II, 102. Sheridan's *Lectures* (London, 1762) were reprinted eight times in the eighteenth century; Blair's *Lectures* (London, 1783), often reprinted, were of course very influential.

passage in *The Watsons* (1805?), in which Mr. Watson not only praises a sermon read by Mr. Howard "with great propriety . . . [and] without any Theatrical grimace or violence," but also expresses dislike for the "studied air & artificial inflexions of voice, which your very popular & most admired Preachers generally have" (*MW*, 343–44). Crawford's preaching, one suspects, would be of the latter variety. The "capital gratification" he expects from delivering a sermon reminds us of his reaction, "in all the riot of his gratifications" (123), to the idea of the theatricals, and his imagined picture of a future career as clergyman not only contradicts Edmund's repeated insistence on the duties of office, at Sotherton (92) and during the conversation about Thornton Lacey (247), but reveals an entirely different, histrionic conception of the preacher's role, in which the clergyman is an actor, his pulpit a stage, and the sermon a play script:

"I must have a London audience. I could not preach, but to the educated; to those who were capable of estimating my composition. And, I do not know that I should be fond of preaching often; now and then, perhaps, once or twice in the spring, after being anxiously expected for half a dozen Sundays together; but not for a constancy; it would not do for a constancy." (341)

Jane Austen could have found grounds for her negative attitude to theatricality in the pulpit in the works of the elocutionists; another possible source is Cowper's *The Task*. In Book II, Cowper has a long section on the pulpit (ll. 326–573) in which he expresses an abhorrence of "all affectation" in a minister of God. The "theatric" preacher

> mocks his Maker, prostitutes and shames
> His noble office, and, instead of truth,
> Displaying his own beauty, starves his flock! (ll. 427–29)

Crawford is not, of course, satirically exposed in the way Cowper's "vain pastor" is, but it is implied that he too would let down "the pulpit to the level of the stage" (l. 564). As Cowper's *The Task* provides a possible source for Jane Austen's treatment of the false improver Rushworth, so here his poem may lie behind her description of the would-be preacher Crawford. Rather than pursue further the parallels that exist between Cowper's "theatrical clerical coxcomb" and Jane Austen's own actor, it will be more to the point of my argument to show how in the conversation about pulpit delivery Jane Austen not only exposes Henry but permits through Edmund's remarks a proper correction of existing practices. The difference of emphasis between the two men thus recapitulates their differences over estate improvements.

Edmund's remarks are cautious; he admits the need of improvement in reading as he had admitted the need of "modern dress" at Sotherton. But the distinctness and energy of an improved delivery must always be in the recommendation of the "most solid truths." Edmund might here be following the advice of Hugh Blair's chapter on "Eloquence of the Pulpit." "Embellish truth," says Blair, "only, with a view to gain it the more full and free admission into your hearers' minds." Crawford's arguments in favor of pulpit eloquence, by contrast, subordinate "truth" (i.e., the biblical text) to delivery, and, close as his attitudes sometimes seem to those of the rhetorician, he would be open to Blair's strictures, for the latter not only distinguishes between "truth" and "mode" in delivery, he stresses the priority of text to style: the preacher is never to employ "strong figures or a pathetic Style except in cases where the subject leads to them."[35] Crawford's description of "subjects limited, and long worn thread-bare in all common hands" reminds us of his view of the liturgy, which he considered to possess "redundancies and repetitions" (340). In both cases, clearly, the inadequacy of the given text is to be compensated for by the theatricality of Crawford's presentation: "nineteen times out of twenty I am thinking how such a prayer ought to be read, and longing to have it to read myself" (340). Here, however, as Fanny recognizes, Crawford's "improvement" is no more acceptable than at Sotherton, which he had considered a "good spot for fault-finding." In his conversation with Edmund, no less than at Sotherton and Thornton Lacey, Crawford shows his attitudes to be potentially destructive of inherited structures.

[35] *Lectures*, ed. Harold F. Harding, pp. 125, 114–16. Like other writers on pulpit delivery, Blair stresses the "dignity of the Pulpit"; "affected smartness and quaintness of expression . . . give to a Preacher that air of foppishness, which he ought, above all things to shun" (*ibid.*, p. 116).

So FAR I have considered the estate a metonym of an inherited culture endangered by forces from within and from without. The novel's title, the motifs of landscape improvement and theatricality, have, I believe, justified this emphasis. In conclusion, it is necessary to consider more fully the role of Fanny Price and to examine the paradox of *Mansfield Park* which, simply stated, is that the estate is preserved not by its trustees but by the one character who is initially, and later for a time again, an outsider. As David Lodge insists, all the inhabitants of Mansfield Park, Fanny excepted, are "deficient according to the novel's own system of values."[36] Edmund, who argues for the importance of "office," who insists upon residency, who voices a philosophy of "proper improvement," fails in ways we have examined. Sir Thomas, for his part, despite his actions on his return, is by no means consistently the "first defender of Mansfield Park," as has been claimed.[37] Against the responsible speeches and actions which mark him as aware of his trust must be set his failures as father. In his too easy acceptance of Maria's expedient marriage to Rushworth, and in his later attempt to coerce Fanny into a similar financially rewarding match with Crawford, he shows his values to have a mercenary tinge. His greatest failure, however, as he himself comes to learn, lies in the education of his children: "Here had been grievous mismanagement" (463). While they had been taught "elegance and accomplishments" and "had been instructed *theoretically* in their religion" (my italics), they "had never been properly taught to govern their inclinations and tempers, by that sense of duty which can alone suffice" (463).[38]

As a direct result of Sir Thomas's failure in the education of his children, the estate is endangered by those who should properly improve it. Only Fanny possesses the instinctive "sense of duty"

[36] *Language of Fiction*, p. 96.

[37] Mudrick, *Irony as Defense*, p. 175. On the other hand, Sir Thomas is by no means the villain of the piece. For example, even as he mistakenly upbraids Fanny for her refusal of Crawford, he ensures that a fire will be provided for her in the East room.

[38] For an excellent description of the contemporary context of Sir Thomas's educational failures, see Kenneth L. Moler's chapter on *Mansfield Park* in *Art of Allusion*.

necessary for the continuance of the traditional culture of Mansfield. An enemy both to excessive estate improvements and to theatricals, she is the "only one who has judged rightly throughout, who has been consistent" (187). That the initially deracinated individual, the adopted daughter of the house, should be the true trustee of its traditions is the instructive irony of the novel, an irony whose meaning requires careful interpretation.

Unlike all the other heroines of Jane Austen's novels, Fanny does not begin her fictional existence in security—in the center of her family's property, to echo the opening description of *Sense and Sensibility*. As the daughter of an impecunious Lieutenant of Marines, she is adopted at the age of ten into the Bertram family, Lady Bertram being her mother's sister. Only later, when she has come to think of Mansfield as her home, will she, at the age of eighteen, be forced to leave her center of existence and, like Catherine Morland and the Dashwood sisters before her, find herself amidst a hostile new environment, the irony in her case being that this environment is her previous home at Portsmouth. From there in turn she will be recalled to Mansfield and, like all the heroines except Anne Elliot, will fulfill her fictional career in a social role as the effective mistress of the Mansfield estate.

How, in the face of such a journey, are we to account for Fanny's instinctive morality, her innate qualities? Unlike Elizabeth Bennet, or Emma, Fanny does not discover the rightness of social principles after recognizing how close she has come to betraying or rejecting them; her "right conduct" is consistent from the beginning. Clearly, given the manifest inadequacy of her parents, no "genetic" explanation can be put forward for her social and moral worth. Nor, in spite of Joseph Wiesenfarth's persuasive reading, is it wholly convincing to argue that Fanny's principled conduct stems from her adoptive environment and the education she receives there.[39] True, Jane Austen is explicit throughout the novel concerning the crucial importance of an early education: to the failure of parents or guardians in this area is attributed not only the irresponsibility of the Bertrams but the ill discipline of the Price children and the amorality of the Crawfords. Further, Jane Austen takes care to distinguish

[39] See Wiesenfarth's chapter in *The Errand of Form* (New York: Fordham University Press, 1967).

Fanny's early education from the "accomplishments" of the Bertram sisters; Fanny is "the antitype to the merely accomplished
woman."[40] Edmund is established as her mentor: "his attentions
were . . . of the highest importance in assisting the improvement of
her mind . . . he recommended the books which charmed her leisure
hours, he encouraged her taste, and corrected her judgment; he
made reading useful by talking to her of what she read, and
heightened its attraction by judicious praise" (22). In just such a
way Fanny at the end will direct Susan's education at Mansfield
Park. But, when all is said, there is a quality—an impulse—in
Fanny which cannot be contained within the educational hypothesis.

We must, I think, see Fanny in this respect (and however different she may otherwise appear from the character of her creator) as
the representative of Jane Austen's own fundamental commitment
to an inherited culture—not merely to the "ceremonies of life," but
to the "conduct . . . the result of good principles" of which Edmund
Bertram speaks (93), to a social order founded in religion, which
the country house can in fact embody, but which, more importantly,
it can be made aesthetically to represent. To support the point,
Fanny's outlook and actions may be briefly followed through the
novel, and especially in her stay at Portsmouth.

During the theatricals Fanny first comes into prominence as a
moral force, her earlier concern over the fate of the Sotherton avenue
and the disuse of the chapel now being underscored by her personal
resistance to the play. When the "bustle" (129) of the preparations
becomes oppressive to her, she retires to the East room, formerly the
school room, which she has gradually taken over following the ter-
mination of formal education at Mansfield. Though Mrs. Norris has
"stipulated for there never being a fire in it on Fanny's account"
(151), Fanny has been able to order her small and modest space to
the best effect (an ability Captain Harville will later show at Lyme):
"Her plants, her books—of which she had been a collector, from
the first hour of her commanding a shilling—her writing desk, and
her works of charity and ingenuity, were all within her reach" (151).
While the Crawfords and the Bertrams rehearse, Fanny retires to
her "nest of comforts" (152), there to pursue "useful" tasks which

[40] Moler, *Art of Allusion,* p. 124.

foster growth and respect the wisdom of the past. In contrast to all the movement of furniture that is taking place elsewhere, Fanny preserves the East room as it always was: she "would not have changed its furniture for the handsomest in the house" (152). Her room becomes the still point in a moving house, a sanctuary of consolation, but also of responsibility. Edmund admires her "little establishment" exceedingly (156).[41]

Fanny's withdrawal from "any thing unpleasant below" (151) is not, perhaps, to the modern taste; it savors too strongly of a concern for salvation of self to the exclusion of a concern for others. But if Fanny's withdrawal is the strategic withdrawal of the moral self from the corruption of its environment, it is also a search inwards for a purity of moral intention:

[S]he had begun to feel undecided as to what she *ought to do*; and as she walked round the room her doubts were increasing. Was she *right* in refusing what was so warmly asked, so strongly wished for? . . . Was it not ill-nature—selfishness—and a fear of exposing herself? . . . It would be so horrible to her to act, that she was inclined to suspect the truth and purity of her own scruples. . . . (152–53)

Such inner searchings distinguish Fanny from all the other characters in the novel, and help to account for the role of judge and moral counselor she finds herself reluctantly assuming in the eyes of others. Edmund comes to the East room during the theatricals episode to externalize his misgivings in dialogue with Fanny (I, xvi), and in rejecting her views seems almost to be going against his own conscience. Later at Portsmouth Crawford will try to make Fanny's judgment his "rule of right" (412), but she refuses to take on the role, arguing that "we have all a better guide in ourselves . . . than any other person can be" (412).

It is important to stress Fanny's role as judge of what is right in the novel, for recent criticism has accused Fanny of not knowing herself, of unconsciously using her moral rectitude as an offensive weapon against those more vital than she. Avrom Fleishman, for example, has argued that she "is presented not as a paragon of virtue

41 For an examination of Fanny's domestic progress at Mansfield, including an attention to the symbolic significance of rooms, see Sister M. Lucy Schneider, C.S.J., "The Little White Attic and the East Room: Their Function in *Mansfield Park*," *Modern Philology*, 63 (Feb. 1966), 227–35.

but as a weak woman with self-defensive and self-aggrandizing impulses who, because of her economic dependency and her social inferiority, is forced to adopt what Alfred Adler has called a feminine, submissive style of life."[42] I confess to reading Jane Austen's intention and achievement in her portrait of Fanny somewhat less subtly. To see a complex irony subverting Fanny's moral character is, I believe, as misguided as to consider her occasional enthusiasms—bookish and poetically mediated as these usually are—subject to ironical undercutting. Some irony there may be directed toward Fanny; she speaks, as Kenneth Moler has convincingly demonstrated, in the tones and vocabulary of Hannah More;[43] but, whatever qualifications are to be made to the somewhat sententious nature of her expression on occasions, the strength, not weakness, of her moral character and the purity of her motivations are surely more in evidence.

Not a deep psychological irony but an overall structural irony characterizes Fanny's journey in *Mansfield Park*. As the novel progresses, Fanny moves closer to the center of the house, her inward journey marking her rising worth. During the second volume, and in part because of her known opposition to the play, Fanny rises in Sir Thomas's estimation and becomes indispensable to Lady Bertram's comfort. She finds herself invited "out" to the Grants' parsonage for dinner and cards. Her modesty and quiet manners gain her prestige in the eyes of everyone except the vindictive Mrs. Norris, whose continual reminders to her—"Remember, wherever you are, you must be the lowest and last" (221)—become an inverse index to Fanny's rising importance and value, at the same time as they testify to Mrs. Norris's own sense of social insecurity. From a childhood without prospects in Portsmouth, via the little white attic and the East room, to a ball at which she is treated just "like her cousins" (275)—this is Fanny's journey from circumference to center, from limited to primary significance. And with Crawford's proposal of marriage that follows, her virtue, like Pamela's, seems about to be given its reward. From being "dependent, helpless, friendless, neglected, forgotten," she can acquire "the consequence so justly her due" (297). But precisely at the end of the second

42 Fleishman, *A Reading*, p. 45.
43 Moler, *Art of Allusion*, pp. 124–25.

volume, Jane Austen begins to disappoint expectations in order correctly to fulfill the thematic impulses she has already set in motion.

Fanny refuses Crawford's proposal (III, i), thereby inviting general disapproval. Sir Thomas, who stands *in loco parentis*, assures her she is on "safe ground" in accepting Crawford (331); Lady Bertram goes so far as to promise her a puppy from pug's next litter if she consents; Edmund himself urges her to "let [Crawford] succeed at last" (347); and Mary Crawford adds her arguments from the "world at large" (359) by citing her friend, Janet Fraser, who, when proposed to, "could not do otherwise than accept . . . for he was rich, and she had nothing" (361). In face of these arguments, Fanny's continued refusal of Crawford takes on something of the quality of Clarissa's refusal to marry Solmes in face of a relatively similar coercion; in thematic terms, her resistance upholds the traditional character of the "house." Were she to accept Crawford, then Edmund would marry Mary, Tom eventually accede to the Park, and theatricality and radical improvements destroy the estate.[44]

Fanny's lonely decision reaffirms her decision not to act in the play at the end of the first volume. As then there were multiple reasons for her to accede to the general desire, so now, but with this difference. Then Fanny's position had been peripheral, that of a critical but necessarily ineffective observer, and she could find support for her decision in the authority of the absent father; here her position is central and authority itself favors what she feels to be wrong. Can we doubt that this is Jane Austen's own position, that even when the self is alone and unsupported by human example of approval, it must still imperatively act in accordance with what is "right," must still support what is valid in its moral inheritance?

The immediate consequence of Fanny's continued refusal is her

----

[44] Joseph Wiesenfarth compares Sir Thomas's speech to Fanny, on discovering she means to refuse Crawford, with Mr. Harlowe's speech to Clarissa in Richardson's novel: "At this point in *Mansfield Park* . . . we see that Jane Austen has gone to school to Richardson, the master of moral pressure, in an effort to dramatize the relation of education to the resilience of the Christian heroine. Fanny holds out against pressure, just as Harriet Byron and Clarissa Harlowe did, because her freedom and integrity demand it. Fanny, in her enlightened obstinacy, supports the meaning of life that she has been educated to respect. Sir Thomas's position as a counterforce is therefore richly ironic" (*Errand of Form*, p. 103).

banishment to Portsmouth; in terms of the spatial journey of the novel, she is expelled from the center to the circumference. Sir Thomas, wrongly attributing to Fanny "wilfulness of temper, self-conceit, and every tendency to that independence of spirit, which prevails so much in modern days" (318), intends the trip to Portsmouth as "a medicinal project upon his niece's understanding" (369). And in one sense Fanny does learn; she finds, against her sentimental expectations, that her parents' home is "the abode of noise, disorder, and impropriety" (388), that her father is loud and vulgar, her mother incompetent, her brothers and sisters lacking in discipline. "The smallness of the house, and thinness of the walls" oppress her (382); the "narrowness of the passage and staircase" leading to the room she must share with her sister Susan strike her imagination (387); "in almost every respect" her home is the "very reverse of what she could have wished" (388). Not until *Persuasion* and the description of Mrs. Smith's lodgings will we again encounter this sense of claustrophobia suggesting the limitations of a way of life.[45] Even so, it will not do to emphasize the squalor of Portsmouth at the expense of other themes. Noise, discomfort, relative poverty —these, after all, tell more against Fanny's parents than against her, and what is disclosed is not so much a social condition that has been economically determined as a social disorder that has stemmed from factors other than economic (however much it is aggravated by these), from the very selfishness and indolent failure to fulfill the requirements of role which endanger Mansfield. In Fanny's "review of the two houses," then, we discover not the rejection of her home by one who has acquired gentility, but the recognition of a contrast between a cultural space which—in spite of the deficiencies of its inhabitants—retains order, stability, and harmony, and a cultural space which, through gross parental indolence and indifference, has become a Hobbesian state of incivility. "The elegance, propriety, regularity, harmony—and perhaps, above all, the peace and tranquillity of Mansfield, were brought to her remembrance every hour

45 Though one also recalls Miss Bates's warning in *Emma*, "ours is rather a dark staircase" (239). Had the situation of Jane Fairfax been brought into the foreground in *Emma*, we should have had something of the Portsmouth situation in this novel. For an interesting argument connecting the smallness of the rooms at Portsmouth with Jane Austen's own reduced expectations at Chawton, see Brigid Brophy, "Jane Austen and the Stuarts," in *Critical Essays on Jane Austen*, ed. B. C. Southam (London: Routledge & Kegan Paul, 1968), pp. 28–30.

of the day, by the prevalence of every thing opposite to them *here"* (391).[46]

Of more importance than what Fanny discovers at Portsmouth is the response she makes to what she discovers. As she had retired from the "bustle" (129) of the theatricals at Mansfield, so now she "remove[s] . . . up stairs" to her room from the disorder below (399); like the East room, her bedroom at Portsmouth has no fire. Here, however, Fanny takes her sister with her, assuming for the first time "an office of authority" and endeavoring "to exercise for [Susan's] advantage the juster notions of what was due to every body" (396). As at Mansfield, her actions, though done in privacy, are "useful" (390) and affirmative:

Fanny found it impossible not to try for books again. There were none in her father's house; but wealth is luxurious and daring—and some of hers found its way to a circulating library. She became a subscriber—amazed at being any thing *in propria persona*, amazed at her own doings in every way; to be a renter, a chuser of books! And to be having any one's improvement in view in her choice! (398)

The situation of Fanny at Portsmouth is the situation which will be more fully explored in *Persuasion*, when Anne Elliot finds herself compelled to leave her "estate," Kellynch Hall, and the question that the Portsmouth chapters ask is the question of the later novel: How should the culturally deprived individual respond? What does she do (in terms of the above passage) when she finds herself in a home without books? Fanny's answer anticipates Anne's response at Uppercross; within the limitations of her environment, she seeks to preserve the shape of a culture.

But if the Portsmouth experience prefigures Anne's dilemma in *Persuasion*, it has another function in *Mansfield Park*, for ultimately Fanny's presence in Portsmouth is less important than her absence from the Park. While Fanny is at Portsmouth, the Bertrams and the Crawfords fulfill the destinies foreshadowed by their previous actions during the play. Lady Bertram, with a misplaced con-

---

[46] The point is delicate, and one cannot deny that Jane Austen achieves a new, almost Dickensian, realism in the Portsmouth chapters. Moreover, she will return to a consideration of relative poverty in *Persuasion* where, however, in the character of Captain Harville, she will illustrate an affirmative and competent response quite lacking in Fanny's parents.

cern for epistolary technique which vitiates her concern for her son, informs Fanny that Tom has contracted a fever as a consequence of "a neglected fall, and a good deal of drinking" (426). The news of his illness causes Mary to reveal herself to Fanny when she admits that the sound of "Sir Edmund" is a welcome one (434). Another letter from Mary denies Henry's culpability in a matter which, it is soon discovered, is his elopement with Maria. Julia meanwhile, during a visit to her sister in London, has eloped with Baron Wildenhaim (as Mary Crawford now calls Yates). Amid all this disorder, Edmund has not escaped his troubles: further London acquaintance with Mary reveals to him her venal nature. Without Fanny, it becomes clear, the structure of the Mansfield world is crumbling, and it is not only fitting but necessary that her return be sought at the Park. She has become the guardian of a debased heritage.

Fanny's return from "exile" (393) to the "beloved place" (446) completes the ironical pattern of the novel's structure. At the beginning of the novel, the problem facing Sir Thomas and Mrs. Norris (not, significantly, Lady Bertram) had been where Fanny should be "placed." The answer reached was that Fanny should be placed in the "little white attic . . . so near Miss Lee, and not far from the girls, and close by the housemaids" (9–10). Her spatial position was clearly a definition of her intermediate social status, and Sir Thomas's intention was to make it clear to her that she was "not a *Miss Bertram*" (10). But at the end of the novel, "where [Maria] could be placed, [becomes] a subject of most melancholy and momentous consultation" (464), and Sir Thomas has come to discover that "Fanny was indeed the daughter that he wanted" (472). As Fanny becomes the mistress of Mansfield parsonage, "an establishment . . . in another country" is found for Maria, where she is joined by Mrs. Norris (465). The Portsmouth "experiment" (369) may have taught Fanny to view life somewhat less idealistically (it does not, however, teach her Sir Thomas's intended lesson, the value of a financially rewarding marriage), but the real lesson of Fanny's visit is that learned by Sir Thomas and Edmund. They learn the imperative need for the social order to be informed by individual worth. If "situations formerly supported persons," it is now necessary, in Burke's words, that "personal qualities should support situations."[47]

[47] From "A Letter to William Elliot, Esq." (1795), *The Works of Edmund Burke* (London: George Bell, 1906), V, 77.

That there is a natural moral order stemming from God, that this order may ideally be incorporated into the historical structure of the estate, that the role of education is to call the individual to an awareness of his duty to God and to his social trust—all these beliefs are present in *Mansfield Park*, but with one further recognition. From the individual himself must come the affirmative response, and the courage to maintain faith in "principles" and "rules of right" even when these are everywhere ignored and debased. Such qualities, represented quietly but firmly in Fanny's nature, are either inherently possessed by Jane Austen's heroines (Elinor and Anne) or they are ultimately learned (Elizabeth and Emma); in any case they suggest an author whose deepest impulse was not to subvert but to maintain and properly improve a social heritage.

CHAPTER 2

ASPECTS OF
Northanger Abbey
AND *Sense and Sensibility*

I see clearly that the principal ties which kept the different classes of society in a vital and harmonious dependence upon each other have, within these 30 years, either been greatly impaired or wholly dissolved. Everything has been put up to market and sold for the highest price it would buy. . . . All . . . moral cement is dissolved, habits and prejudices are broken and rooted up, nothing being substituted in their place but a quickened self-interest. . . .

Wordsworth, Letter to Daniel Stuart, 1817

It is surely mistaken to assume that the affirmative elements in her morality and her humor are not as real as the subversive ironies which occasionally accompany them.

Ian Watt, Introduction to *Jane Austen: A Collection of Critical Essays*

✦✦✦ To TURN from *Mansfield Park* to a consideration of *North-*
✦✦✦ *anger Abbey* and *Sense and Sensibility* is to move back in
terms of chronology of composition and down in terms of literary
quality, but it is not to move into an entirely different world.
Though the tones, textures, and literary contexts of these "early"
novels are evidently different, they exhibit the same underlying
social and ethical assumptions as the mature work.[1] True, their
ironic content is greater, and they seem to give to the individual a
larger freedom to define his own world, but Jane Austen's irony is
not here the aloof and secretly critical irony in face of a vulgar and
acquisitive society that it has been considered, nor does she grant
to, or even unconsciously desire for, her characters an unlimited
power of self-definition. To withdraw from society and place faith in a
passionate relationship, as Marianne does with Willoughby, is to take
a direction to be censured even as its appeal is admitted. Society
remains in these novels the necessary context of individual action.

This is not to say that the "grounds" on which an individual is
to act are always to be discovered in the setting of his experience.
The Bath society of Catherine Morland's adventures, the London
into which the Dashwood sisters are introduced, are hostile, vulgar,

[1] In describing *Northanger Abbey* and *Sense and Sensibility* as "early" novels,
I am aware that there have been objections to the view which sees a division in
Jane Austen's work between early (Steventon) fiction and late (Chawton) fiction.
Q. D. Leavis, in a series of articles in *Scrutiny*, 10 (June 1941; Oct. 1941; Jan.
1942), argues that Jane Austen's mature fiction is the reworking of early drafts.
Recent criticism, however, has found this theory unsound. See B. C. Southam,
"Mrs. Leavis and Miss Austen: the 'Critical Theory' Reconsidered," *Nineteenth-
Century Fiction*, 17 (June 1962), 21–32, and the same author's appendix to his
*Jane Austen's Literary Manuscripts: A Study of the Novelist's Development
through the Surviving Papers* (London: Oxford University Press, 1964). Whatever changes were later made to the three novels begun in the second half of the
1790's (and the changes in *Sense and Sensibility* and *Pride and Prejudice* seem
to have been extensive), the basic structures and themes of these works remain
within the conventions of eighteenth century fiction. For this reason alone they
may be described as "early" works, though in the case of *Northanger Abbey* and
Sense and Sensibility there is also evidence of artistic immaturity. For a judicious
chronology of Jane Austen's fiction, see appendix in A. Walton Litz, *Jane
Austen: A Study of Her Artistic Development* (London: Chatto & Windus, 1965).

and acquisitive environments, whose selfish and economic principles
it would be immoral to accept. Nothing is more noteworthy in
these works than the incisive ways in which economic motivations
are exposed. Yet there remains behind the perversions of moral
conduct everywhere described a steady vision of ideal social modes.
Jane Austen is deeply aware of a threatened change from a stable
society based on Christian principles to a society in which money,
or the appearance of money, is all that counts, but her irony works
to locate and reveal those elements in society subversive of traditional norms.

It is important to insist upon the positive nature of her fictional
response. As is true of all her major fiction, with the exception of
Persuasion, these novels suggest through the controlling presence of
an affirmative narrative voice and the developing careers of their
heroines, acceptable *social* alternatives to the largely corrupt worlds
described. Both novels fail ultimately to find a convincing artistic
shape for the moral and social vision proposed, but the failure is
artistic—in Wayne Booth's terms a failure of aesthetic rhetoric—
and not a covert indication of Jane Austen's unconscious dislike of
her world.

To a far greater degree than her mature fiction, these novels find
their origin in other novels and fulfill their impulse by correcting,
qualifying, or reconstituting the fictional "shapes" of previous
works. That they are "parodic" is not, of course, to their discredit.
All fiction (and art, too, if we accept E. H. Gombrich's persuasive
argument in *Art and Illusion*) is parodic in the sense that authors
do not present a wholly original picture of life, but create out of an
existing fund of characterization and design. Far from diminishing
the quality of Jane Austen's novels, indeed, careful studies of her
alterations of motifs in other novels reveal the superiority of her
moral and aesthetic achievement to that of the Gothic and sentimental fiction on which she was bred, and we may now see *Northanger
Abbey* and *Sense and Sensibility* as the products of a continuing effort
on her part to capture in fictional form a satisfying personal resolution of real moral questions, already raised but unsatisfactorily
answered in the fiction of her experience.[2]

My purpose in this chapter is not, however, to examine *North-*

[2] See especially the relevant chapters of Kenneth Moler, *Jane Austen's Art of
Allusion* (Lincoln: University of Nebraska Press, 1968), and Walton Litz, *Artistic
Development*.

anger Abbey and *Sense and Sensibility* against their fictional predecessors. Rather, I wish to consider certain aspects of these works as
they contribute to an understanding of Jane Austen's social and
ethical attitudes, and to suggest briefly the developing manner in
which she came through these early efforts to a wholly convincing
aesthetic expression, in *Pride and Prejudice*, of an original and positive view of the individual's relation to society.

Of first importance to this approach is a recognition of the particular structure of these works. Behind the parodic aspect is the pattern of the heroine's effective disinheritance, followed by the
need to formulate a response to a new, less certain existence, which
I have considered to underlie much of Jane Austen's work. In
Northanger Abbey, of course, the insecurity of Catherine is itself a
matter of irony. This "mirror-image of the 'standard' heroine" is
compelled by the premises of models to be satirized to be separated
from the serenity of her Fullerton home and to encounter, in a
suitably deflationary way, "the violence of such noblemen and
baronets as delight in forcing young ladies away to some remote
farm-house" (18).[3] The stolid Mrs. Allen is a comic version of the
villainous chaperon (we compare *and* contrast, for example, Mrs.
Jewkes in *Pamela*), and when the grotesquely comic anti-villain,
John Thorpe, carries her off to Blaize Castle, and when she wishes
to stop, "only laughed, smacked his whip, encouraged his horse,
made odd noises, and drove on" (87), we see the joke and hardly
consider him another Gothic tyrant. But the atmosphere changes in
the second volume, where General Tilney's conduct does indeed
approach a Gothic tyranny, and it is not unreasonable to suggest
that, as readers, we have been lulled into a false sense of security,
only to have our complacency dislodged at the abbey. Certainly one
of the effects of the General's brutal domestic conduct is to lead
us to question not only the "placid indifference" (61) of Mrs. Allen
but also the "philosophic" composure (234) of the Morland parents
and the "common feelings of common life" (19) which were apparently at first set up as normative against the "thousand alarming
presentiments of evil" to be expected (18). Jane Austen has her
cake and eats it too. The novel subverts the falsities of such works

---

[3] The first quoted phrase is from Litz, who argues—correctly in my view—
against any single model for Jane Austen's parody (*ibid.*, pp. 60–61).

as *The Mysteries of Udolpho,* but it also retains enough of the extrarational probing of the Gothic novel to put into question any easy acceptance of a rationally grounded existence.[4]

An even more critical awareness of the possible insufficiency of inherited grounds is present in *Sense and Sensibility.* Unlike Catherine Morland's experience, the isolation of the two heroines in *Sense and Sensibility* is not, even initially, simply a matter of following a fictional formula, and the novel as a whole, though it is obviously a version of the novel of sentiment, contains a surprising amount of direct social observation. The early chapters of this uneven work have a sureness of tone and a precision of statement that qualify them to be ranked with the best chapters Jane Austen ever wrote, and as the Dashwoods are expelled from their seemingly secure and timeless "estate," the possibilities of social fragmentation, of increasing distances among social groups, and of an economic transvaluation of traditional morality seem to be strongly present in Jane Austen's mind. A rather close attention to these chapters is warranted, since they reveal concerns never far from her thought throughout her career.

The story opens with an estate changing hands. Held for many generations in the same family, Norland Park has been managed with respect, and its trustees have over the years gained the "general good opinion of their surrounding acquaintance" (3). As we encounter it, however, Norland is passing out of the direct line, for the late owner had been a single man. He leaves the estate to his nephew, but attaches strings to the bequest: the estate is entailed on Henry Dashwood's son and, beyond this, on his grandson. Though such provisions were not unusual in a society anxious to secure the continuity of the land, they present something of a problem, for Henry Dashwood has married twice, and though John Dashwood, the son of his first marriage, is provided for by the inheritance of his mother's fortune (half of which is his now, the other half to be his when his father dies), the three daughters of

---

4 Cf. Lionel Trilling: "We are quick, too quick, to understand that *Northanger Abbey* invites us into a snug conspiracy to disabuse the little heroine of the errors of her corrupted fancy—Catherine Morland, having become addicted to novels of terror, has accepted their inadmissible premise, she believes that life is violent and unpredictable. And that is exactly what life is shown to be by the events of the story; it is we who must be disabused of our belief that life is sane and orderly" (*The Opposing Self* [New York: Viking Press, 1955], p. 207).

his second marriage are less well situated, the present Mrs. Henry Dashwood having no fortune whatsoever. Thus when Henry Dashwood survives his uncle a bare twelve months, and to the £7,000 at his own disposal and the £3,000 that his uncle provided for the girls, can add nothing but a dying request to his son to look after his wife and daughters, the Dashwood sisters find themselves in a somewhat reduced and dependent condition. John Dashwood, meanwhile, inherits the estate (worth £4,000 per annum) and the rest of his mother's fortune ("which had been large"). Having married a woman with £10,000, he is financially very well situated.

The solidity of financial specification evident in these scenes is found throughout Jane Austen's work, marking an awareness on her part, which is only now beginning to be recognized, of an economically fluid contemporary society.[5] It will be useful briefly to ask what thematic implications her attention to incomes have. How well off, for example, is John Dashwood? Assuming his mother's fortune to have been as low as £20,000, we can estimate his annual income, conservatively, as between £5,000 and £6,000, compared with a total of £500 for Mrs. Dashwood and her three daughters; but what does this mean in contemporary terms? Glancing at other novels, how rich is Fitzwilliam Darcy with his £10,000 a year, his park ten miles round, and his house in London? What shall we say of Bingley with his inheritance of £100,000, but with no inherited estate? Then, what of Emma Woodhouse with her fortune of £30,000, Mary Crawford with £20,000, her brother with a yearly income of £4,000 and his estate at Everingham? Rushworth has £12,000 a year, making him, as far as we know, the richest of her characters. Sir Thomas Bertram's income is not specified, but he has a considerable country seat, an overseas estate, and two livings at his disposal. But his Antigua interests are in some trouble and he has an extravagant eldest son, reasons enough, perhaps, for the too quick acceptance he grants to Maria's union with Rushworth and Sotherton. When we look to the less well situated characters, similar

[5] See F. G. Gornall, "Marriage, Property & Romance in Jane Austen's Novels (1)," *Hibbert Journal*, 65 (Summer 1967), 151–56; and the continuation of this article in *Hibbert Journal*, 66 (Autumn 1967), 24–29. Avrom Fleishman has given careful attention to the sociology and economy of Jane Austen's fiction. See *A Reading of "Mansfield Park": An Essay in Critical Synthesis* (Minneapolis: University of Minnesota Press, 1967), esp. pp. 14–18 and the Appendix to Chapter III, pp. 40–42.

questions arise. How necessitous is Willoughby with his income of £600 a year? Does he really need to marry an heiress with £50,000? How unmarriageable are the five Bennet girls with the share of £5,000 which is all that they can expect? It is clearly ironical that Mrs. Bennet should consider that "if a smart young colonel, with five or six thousand a year, should want one of my girls, I shall not say nay to him" (*PP*, 29), but why should Jane Austen set her unjustifiable optimism at this figure?

One indication of the contemporary value of these and other carefully described incomes is given in G. E. Mingay's *English Landed Society in the Eighteenth Century*.[6] Mingay proposes three large categories of great landowners, lesser landowners, and freeholders. Great landowners are defined as having a great house, a London residence, at least £5,000 a year, and about 10,000 to 20,000 acres. Only Darcy of the major characters is of this group. Bingley, with his £4,000 to £5,000 a year is rich enough, but his family's money has been made in trade and he is seeking entry into the land. Most of Jane Austen's families can be placed in Mingay's second group, which he subdivides into three categories: wealthy gentry (£3,000 to £5,000 per annum), Squires (£1,000 to £3,000). and Gentlemen (£300 to £1,000). Assuming this to be roughly correct, several of Jane Austen's incomes become significant. As I have already noted in the introduction, the Bennet family, on the death of Mr. Bennet and with the entailment of their estate on Mr. Collins, face degradation. They are already living to the limit of the Longbourn income (£2,000) and should their father die, their £5,000 will provide a mere £250 a year, a sum scarcely capable of keeping a smaller family in a position of gentility. Returning to *Sense and Sensibility*, it is equally clear that Mrs. Henry Dashwood and her three daughters, with their £500 a year, are confronted with a critical reduction in expectations.[7] There is, therefore, good reason for Henry Dashwood to urge his son to do something more for them. John Dashwood, for his part, finds himself favorably situated for

---

6 London: Routledge and Kegan Paul, 1963. Mingay's estimates are for 1790, but it is reasonable to suppose that Jane Austen's fiction reflects the incomes of this period, rather than the inflated economy of the decade in which her novels were published.

7 Everything has to be seen in relative terms, of course. The Dashwoods retain two maids and a manservant after their "degradation."

climbing. Solidly placed among the wealthy gentry as he is by virtue of the Norland income, Dashwood's inheritance from his mother and his prudential marriage to Fanny Ferrars have substantially increased his income and his social horizon.

What conclusions are we to draw from these facts? One persistent line of interpretation would, I think, see in Jane Austen's concern over income, status, and the rise and fall of families an autobiographical relevance, and it is true that Jane Austen's existence after her father's death in 1805, as she moved from Bath to Southampton and finally to Chawton, was a "reduced" one.[8] The family income, before Mrs. Austen's sons came to the rescue, was a mere £210 a year, and even after annuities from Edward (£100) and James, Henry, and Frank (£50 each), this only reached a relatively meager £460 a year, £40 less than the Dashwoods. In her visits to such great houses as Stoneleigh Abbey and Godmersham Park, moreover, Jane Austen would have had ample opportunity to contrast her habitual life with a more luxurious and spacious existence. But while there are intriguing biographical comparisons suggesting a personal predicament behind her interest in an economically fluid world, it would be a mistake to read her life too closely into her fiction. As I have argued in my introduction, Jane Austen ironically exposes mercenary conduct in her novels not in order to come to terms with her own "reduced" position but because she fears that economic considerations will outweigh and overcome moral considerations in human conduct. Throughout her fiction the most amoral characters —Wickham, Mary Crawford, Mr. Elliot—are also the most economically motivated. In *Northanger Abbey*, of course, Catherine's attraction for John Thorpe and the General, like her brother's attraction for Isabella, is purely mercenary. When the General discovers she is not an heiress, his attitude becomes hostile in the extreme. But it is in *Sense and Sensibility* that the vicious cancer of economically motivated conduct is most searchingly analyzed.

The brilliant second chapter describes the diminution of John Dashwood's generosity, as, abetted by his wife, he progressively re-

---

8 Cf. Brigid Brophy, "Jane Austen and the Stuarts," in *Critical Essays on Jane Austen*, ed. B. C. Southam (London: Routledge and Kegan Paul, 1968), and Geoffrey Gorer, "Poor Honey—Some Notes on Jane Austen and her Mother," in his *The Danger of Equality* (New York: Weybright and Talley, 1966). For details of the reduction in the family income, see William Austen-Leigh and Richard A. Austen-Leigh, *Jane Austen: Her Life and Letters* (London: Smith, Elder, 1913), pp. 182–83.

duces the size of his financial aid. At first he considers giving his sisters
£1,000 each, but Mrs. Dashwood points out that this will be the
"ruin" of him and his son, and so by degrees this sum is diminished
by half and then considered unnecessary in view of the £10,000 that
his sisters will share on their mother's death. An annuity of £100
while the mother lives, John Dashwood thinks, is to be preferred,
but his wife has other ideas:

> "To be sure," said she, "it is better than parting with fifteen hundred
> pounds at once. But then if Mrs. Dashwood should live fifteen years, we
> shall be completely taken in."
> "Fifteen years! my dear Fanny; her life cannot be worth half that
> purchase."
> "Certainly not; but if you observe, people always live for ever when
> there is any annuity to be paid them; and she is very stout and healthy,
> and hardly forty. An annuity is a very serious business; it comes over and
> over every year, and there is no getting rid of it. You are not aware of
> what you are doing. I have known a great deal of the trouble of annuities;
> for my mother was clogged with the payment of three to old super-
> annuated servants by my father's will, and it is amazing how disagreeable
> she found it. . . ." (10–11)

From an annuity to a "present of fifty pounds now and then," from
this to occasional "presents of fish and game," these are easy steps,
and, with barely a break in the logic, the John Dashwoods move on
to a recognition of how "comfortable" their relations will be on
five hundred a year. Then, in this economic *reductio ad absurdum*,
they end with a feeling of injury that the Norland china, plate and
linen have been left to Mrs. Henry Dashwood and not to themselves.

What had been a center of order and morality has in the change
of ownership become the home of the most grasping covetousness.
Ties, not only of family affection, but, as Mrs. Dashwood's remarks
about superannuated servants imply, between landlord and tenant,
master and servant, are excluded from the reckoning. In such a society, as Wordsworth would soon phrase it, "everything has been
put up to market and sold for the highest price it would buy."[9]

London especially is permeated by this transvaluation of traditional assumptions. It is a world in which Miss Steele "was never

[9] *The Letters of William and Dorothy Wordsworth*, ed. Ernest de Selincourt
(Oxford: Clarendon Press, 1937), II, 783–84.

easy till she knew the price of every part of Marianne's dress" (249), in which value words acquire new and economic meanings. Thus John Dashwood construes Edward's action to remain true to his engagement to Lucy Steele, rather than accept the heiress his mother has found for him, as a disregard of "duty, affection, every thing" (266), and he finds Mrs. Jennings "a most valuable woman" because "her house, her style of living, all bespeak an exceeding good income" (226). A little later, when he hears of Colonel Brandon's gift of a living to the now disinherited Edward Ferrars, Dashwood is astonished; since there is not even the excuse of "relationship" or "connection" (294), Brandon has no reason for being "so improvident in a point of such common, such natural, concern" (295). Learning that the living is worth £200 per annum, he immediately calculates its "value" (£1,400) and is then the more astonished at the improvidence of the Colonel's action. Dashwood's most vicious expression of a totally economic outlook occurs, however, when he sees how sick Marianne is (she is grief-stricken on account of Willoughby's infidelity). He can only express his concern to Elinor in terms of the fall in Marianne's market value: "I question whether Marianne *now*, will marry a man worth more than five or six hundred a-year, at the utmost" (227).[10]

The economic cancer has spread from the city (traditionally the home of greed) to the country, and at Norland Park is marked by the enclosure of the Common and by the land purchases that Dashwood has made in the name of "duty":

"...I have made a little purchase within this half year; East Kingham Farm, you must remember the place, where old Gibson used to live. The land was so very desirable for me in every respect, so immediately adjoining my own property, that I felt it my duty to buy it. I could not have answered it to my conscience to let it fall into any other hands. A man must pay for his convenience; and it *has* cost me a vast deal of money." (225)

The kind of "conscience" shown in this action will not keep the Dashwood family in that "general good opinion of their surrounding acquaintance" (3) which it had enjoyed for generations. Within the park, Dashwood's improvements (in anticipation of the theme

10 This is ironical in two ways. First, if we accept Mingay's groupings, Dashwood is placing her in a class below her inherited station; second, his figure of "five or six hundred a-year" corresponds to Willoughby's income from Combe Magna.

in *Mansfield Park*) have already altered the structure of the landscape at the same time as they have ignored the provisions of old
Dashwood's will. A greenhouse is being built for Mrs. John Dashwood
upon the knoll behind the house, and the "old walnut trees are all
come down to make room for it. It will be a very fine object from
many parts of the park . . ." (226).

More than a decade before Cobbett took his rural rides, Jane
Austen seems to have sensed the rise of the economically motivated
landed gentry which he (and Wordsworth) disliked so much, and
the implicit distinction she makes between a morally based and an
economically based country society anticipates Cobbett's distinction between a "resident *native* gentry, attached to the soil, known
to every farmer" and "a gentry only now-and-then residing at all . . .
looking to the soil only for its rents, viewing it as a mere object of
speculation . . . and relying, for influence, not upon the good will
of the vicinage, but upon the dread of their power."[11]

Sense and Sensibility may not be a total artistic success, but in
its cool exposure of economically motivated behavior it gives
powerful expression to Jane Austen's persistent apprehensions about
the possible course of society. In face of these recognitions, two
directions seem possible to her: disaffection and withdrawal from a
manifestly imperfect world, or commitment to society, properly defined as a morally founded structure. Jane Austen takes the second
direction, though the temptation of the first is strong. Before supporting the argument with an analysis of *Sense and Sensibility*, I
shall first examine Jane Austen's attitude toward society in *Northanger Abbey*, the least artistically mature of her novels.

Northanger Abbey, while it does not reflect the same persistent awareness of an economically debased society, takes its
own close look at the conditions of social existence. As well as
being a response to the Gothic novel, it is, to borrow Malcolm
Bradbury's phrase describing E. M. Forster's fiction, a "socio-
moral" novel, and in her description of Catherine, Jane Austen
provides an early attempt at defining proper moral behavior in the

[11] See David Thomson, *England in the Nineteenth Century* (1950; rpt. Baltimore: Penguin Books, 1966), pp. 14–15, for this quotation at length and for a
discussion of the rise of a "purely profit-making class of landed gentry."

face of a largely immoral world. In describing Catherine's journey from Fullerton to Bath, to Northanger, and then back to Fullerton, Jane Austen follows the pattern of the English novel of education in which, from Defoe and Fielding onward, movement through space has accompanied a moral enlightenment on the part of the protagonist. In Catherine's case, there is little psychological development, and while this is not a *sine qua non* of the novel of education—Tom Jones undergoes little psychological change—it becomes in *Northanger Abbey* a matter of dissatisfaction both for the reader and, I think, for the author. As W. A. Craik has said, Catherine seems younger than the reader or the author, and she is too naive "to work out her own disillusionment like Emma."[12] What mental change does occur in the heroine is unsatisfactorily prepared: we are not convinced by her suddenly acquired susceptibility to lurid Gothic imaginings at Northanger, and, as Alan McKillop has argued, there is a break in imaginative continuity between the volumes. Catherine changes from an antiheroic ingenue to an unabashed Gothic heroine without sufficient preparation.[13] Neither her reading of Gothic fiction nor Henry's extemporaneous recipe for horrors on the ride to Northanger can adequately explain the psychological shift, though Henry's invented story (II, v) does quite skilfully provide the schedule for Catherine's later "Gothic" adventures.

But if Jane Austen fails structurally and thematically to combine a novel of manners and a literary response to the Gothic novel, we should nevertheless be aware of her positive moral intentions in *Northanger Abbey*. An examination of the heroine's experience in Bath with the Thorpes and at Northanger with Henry Tilney reveals Jane Austen's direction, even if the moral journey is not completed satisfactorily.

In Bath the conduct of the Thorpes is all too plainly outrageous to need much in the way of comment, and in depicting them (especially the boorish brother) Jane Austen may be doing little other than catching "the grotesque shapes toward which the human form and

12 *Jane Austen: The Six Novels* (London: Methuen, 1965), p. 10.
13 "Critical Realism in *Northanger Abbey*," in *From Jane Austen to Joseph Conrad*, ed. Robert C. Rathburn and Martin Steinmann, Jr. (Minneapolis: University of Minnesota Press, 1958), p. 44.

the world are being forced under the weight of stupidity."[14] It would be to break a butterfly upon a wheel, for example, to draw the didactic conclusion that it is immoral to treat one's mother as Thorpe does on his first meeting with her in Bath: "Ah, mother! how do you do? . . . where did you get that quiz of a hat, it makes you look like an old witch?" (49); or to condemn his version of "fraternal tenderness" as cruel, in his treatment of his younger sisters: "he asked each of them how they did, and observed that they both looked very ugly" (49). Nevertheless, beyond our amused recognition of the barbaric energy of Thorpe's portrait, we cannot be unaware of how invariably his actions violate decorum, and how they are, beyond this, occasionally vicious.

If John Thorpe's behavior exhibits a brazen disregard for decorum, his sister Isabella's apparent observation of decorous standards is the hypocrite's recognition that it pays to simulate propriety. Aware that there are public norms of behavior, Isabella seeks to justify her conduct by seeming to observe them. In something of the same manner she appeals to the norms of fiction, pretending to be a heroine of sensibility. But though her sentimental behavior is occasionally coincident with propriety, it is more frequently at variance, and the "easy gaiety," immediate friendship, and "lengthened shake of hands" (34) on her first meeting with Catherine indicate at one and the same time her conformity to the behavior of romantic novels and her insincerity.[15] Isabella's pose as a heroine of sensibility (evident, for example in her specious remembrance of her first meeting with Catherine's brother [118]) is no more sincere than her pose of decorous conduct. Her apparent acceptance of the sentimental attitude conceals a hard-hearted realism in money matters as is revealed when, on learning of the modest income of the Morland family, her enthusiasm for her brother's courtship of Catherine diminishes considerably: "You have both of you something to be sure, but it is not a trifle that will support a family now-a-days; and after all that romancers may say, there is no doing without money" (146).

In the meeting of Catherine and Isabella we have that encounter

[14] Quotation from Alvin Kernan, *The Plot of Satire* (New Haven: Yale University Press, 1965), p. 5.

[15] Jane Austen herself distrusted too quick friendships. Cf. her description of Miss Armstrong in a letter to Cassandra, 14 Sept., 1804: "She seems to like people rather too easily" (*L*, 142).

between innocence and experience, between benevolence and prudence, which the eighteenth century novel took such delight in exploiting. Until Catherine can add a touch of percipience to her "simplicity" she is doomed to be duped and misled. However worthy her ingenuous attitudes are, they militate against her coming to terms with her society. That Jane Austen intended some growth of moral perception in Catherine may be seen through an examination of the three "schemes" in which she is invited to participate while in Bath.

On the first occasion, when John Thorpe arrives at Pulteney Street and rudely bids Catherine accompany him to Claverton Down, her innocence, undirected by her habitually placid chaperon, is imposed upon. She is permitted by Mrs. Allen to perform a dubious moral action by accompanying Thorpe, but at least the trip teaches her to doubt whether he is "altogether completely agreeable" (66). On the second occasion, the invitation to Blaize Castle is of equally short notice, and Catherine's acceptance is, despite extenuating circumstances, morally reprehensible. Her excuses for going are: (1) Mrs. Allen makes no objection, (2) since it has been raining, the Tilneys will probably not fulfill their engagement anyway, and (3) according to Thorpe, the Tilneys are out driving in a phaeton. In addition to these excuses from outside there are also some internal promptings in favor of the trip, for it is to the romantic Blaize Castle, "the oldest in the kingdom," with "dozens" of "towers and long galleries" (85). Catherine's internal conflict between right conduct and self-gratification suggests a certain growth of conscience: "Thorpe talked to his horse, and she meditated, by turns, on broken promises and broken arches, phaetons and false hangings, Tilneys and trap-doors" (87). And she is deservedly punished for her wrong decision by the appearance of the Tilneys walking to meet her soon after the start of the drive, by Thorpe's refusal to stop the horse, and by Mrs. Allen's criticism on her return of the "strange, wild scheme" (89). In addition, she has to suffer apparent rejection from Eleanor when she goes to apologize, and coolness from Henry at the theater.

Catherine's moral progress is most clearly evident when she is invited to take part in the "Clifton scheme" (97). Already engaged for a walk with the Tilneys, she is determined not to break her word again. The pressure that is put on her in this scene anticipates the pressure Fanny Price will resist in her determined refusal to act in the play. As Edmund in *Mansfield Park* first degrades himself by adding his voice to the chorus of cries that Fanny should act, so in this novel "this was the first time of [Catherine's] brother's openly siding against her" (99). The scene reaches an appropriate climax when Thorpe returns after a short absence to announce that he has "been to Miss Tilney, and made [Catherine's] excuses" (100). When Catherine reacts by saying she "must run after Miss Tilney directly and set her right" (100), the emotional coercion of the Thorpes and her brother becomes physical: "Isabella . . . caught hold of one hand; Thorpe of the other; and remonstrances poured in from all three" (100). But Catherine's determination resists even this attack, and she runs off to Milsom-street, secure in the knowledge that "she had attended to what was due to others, and to her own character in their opinion" (101).

By the end of the first volume, then, Catherine has gained enough in the way of moral discrimination to resist immoral pressures and to act on a moral basis. Her education along these lines will culminate in the second volume when she finally comes to see through the "shallow artifice" of Isabella's letter requesting her intercession with James (218). But in the second volume—and because she is required to be the agent of Jane Austen's complex response to the Gothic novel—Catherine's progress as a moral heroine is interrupted, and she is made to become a figure of simplicity again as she figures, first, in the low Gothic parody of the locked cabinet, and then in the more serious misapprehension over the fate of Henry Tilney's mother. Henry's famous rebuke on this occasion has become something of a crux in critical discussion, but before considering whether it serves as a legitimate criticism of the undisciplined imagination, or is itself subject to authorial irony, something must be said of Tilney's role in the novel.

As much the anti-hero initially as Thorpe is anti-villain, Tilney's function in the first volume is to expose to Catherine various modes of triviality and affectation. His first act is to ridicule the conduct of the Assembly rooms by imitating the "simpering" manners of a Bath beau (26). Later, with a lexicographer's discrimination, he calls Catherine's attention to her inaccurate, Thorpe-derived, use of language, particularly to her misuse of "nice" (108). Then, with the confidence of a man who has studied his Gilpin—and his Uvedale

Price—he lectures her on the picturesque, to such good effect that "when they gained the top of Beechen Cliff, she voluntarily rejected the whole city of Bath, as unworthy to make part of a landscape" (111).[16]

Tilney's love of Gilpin and the picturesque, together with his likeable vitality and ironic power of discrimination, have led many readers to consider him as effectively an authorial surrogate within the novel.[17] This is only partly true, for his opinions, as recent critics have recognized, are often undercut, and his vision is far from being coincident with Jane Austen's. In his taste for the picturesque, for example, Henry (unlike Marianne Dashwood) seems unaware of the artificial nature of this cult, of any distinction between natural and acquired taste. A more serious and certainly "prepared" instance of his vulnerability, however, occurs on the occasion when his sister takes Catherine's remark that "something very shocking indeed, will soon come out in London" (112) to refer to an impending riot, rather than to the latest Gothic publication Catherine intends. Henry has great delight in exposing both his sister's overimaginative response ("My dear Eleanor, the riot is only in your own brain" [113]) and the ill-chosen language of Catherine. Apparently acting as a center of rationality equidistant from points of excessive imagination and linguistic impropriety, his lesson for the day is that it is irrational both to speak and to think hyperbolically. But there is a further irony present. Henry's lurid description of "a mob of three thousand" (113), which is apparently his ironical reconstruction of Eleanor's irrational fears, is actually—as the reference to St. George's Fields confirms—a description of a real event, the Gordon Riots of 1780. The effect of the passage, therefore, is not that it is unreasonable to conceive of "expected horrors in London" (113) in terms of a popular uprising but, on the contrary, that it may be perfectly reasonable so to construe such a phrase.[18]

16 Uvedale Price first argued that Bath was not picturesque in his "On Buildings and Architecture" (1798), an essay supplemental to his *Essay on the Picturesque* (1794).

17 Cf. Marvin Mudrick, who, while acknowledging some irony directed towards Tilney's "youthful pedantry," goes on to argue that "he is allowed to know about as much as the author does, to pass similar judgments, to respond with a similarly persistent and inviolable irony toward all characters and events that come within his range" (*Jane Austen: Irony as Defense and Discovery* [Princeton: Princeton, University Press, 1952], p. 51).

18 Walton Litz has also interpreted the irony of this passage (*Artistic Development*, p. 64).

Since Henry has himself introduced the detailed description of
the Riots (113), the effect is that of dramatic irony in that the necessary information is conveyed from author to reader through the
medium of a character's speech, but without that character's awareness of the implications of what he says. But it is important to
recognize that the deeper irony here does not entirely destroy the
character's irony. Though Henry's brief for rational attitudes is
undercut, all of his ironical censure of Catherine's linguistic hyperboles, and some of his ironical censure of Eleanor's imagination,
remain. (It would be an alarming world if all hyperbolic expressions were to be taken literally.) Henry's function as teacher is
limited but important in this passage which anticipates in the com-
plexity of its irony the crucial and much misunderstood scene at
Northanger, where Henry discovers to his horror that Catherine suspects General Tilney of having murdered his wife. Here is his rebuke:

"Dear Miss Morland, consider the dreadful nature of the suspicions you
have entertained. What have you been judging from? Remember the country and the age in which we live. Remember that we are English, that we
are Christians. Consult your own understanding, your own sense of the
probable, your own observation of what is passing around you—Does our
education prepare us for such atrocities? Do our laws connive at them?
Could they be perpetrated without being known, in a country like this,
where social and literary intercourse is on such a footing; where every man
is surrounded by a neighbourhood of voluntary spies, and where roads and
newspapers lay every thing open? Dearest Miss Morland, what ideas have
you been admitting?" (197–98)

This is the point at which readers are apt to take different directions. For some, Henry's remarks are the "thematic climax" of the
novel, the proper censure of the undisciplined imagination. For
others, the scene reveals the fallibility of the rational outlook, and,
taken with the violence of the General's later conduct, provides
sanction for the validity of the "sympathetic imagination." For
D. W. Harding, the clause, "where every man is surrounded by a
neighbourhood of voluntary spies," is the unconscious revelation of
Jane Austen's dislike of a society on which, nevertheless, she felt
compelled to rely.[19] As in the case of his "riot" speech, however,

19 "Regulated Hatred: An Aspect of the Work of Jane Austen," *Scrutiny*, 8
(March 1940), 348–49.

Henry's remarks here are partly fallible and partly correct. There is a double irony present. Catherine's imaginative fantasy is undercut, but given the nature of her actual experiences with the General, Tilney's rational rebuke is also insufficient. It is, after all, shortly following the rebuke that Catherine experiences the very real violence of the General, when, having discovered in London that she is not the heiress he thought her, he returns with dramatic suddenness to the Abbey and orders her immediate dismissal on the morrow.

Clearly, in the second volume of *Northanger Abbey* Jane Austen was trying to translate into characterization and action a complex response to Gothic fiction and the attitudes it embodied. To subvert the false and excessive reactions of a Radcliffe heroine was easy —too easy—as she revealed in the burlesque of Catherine and the mysteriously locked cabinet. But wholly to affirm a life without terrors, wholly to reject the function of the imagination, was not part of her intention. Thus, as she was preparing for the subversion of Catherine's "dreadful suspicions" concerning the General, she was also, I believe, depositing evidence which would give to Catherine's "sympathetic imagination" a certain, carefully limited, validity. A brief glance at Adam Smith's *Theory of Moral Sentiments* (1759) will help make the point. For Smith, moral judgments involve the individual's sympathetic participation, not only in the feelings of the person who is affected by a certain act, good or bad, but also (and this is relevant to *Northanger Abbey*) in the feelings of the executor of the act, and in the motives or promptings which led him to the act. Though the sympathetic faculty is not to be identified with the imagination for Smith, it cannot in fact function without the imagination: "Though our brother is upon the rack, as long as we are at our ease, our senses will never inform us of what he suffers. They never did and never can carry us beyond our own persons, and it is by the imagination only that we can form any conception of what are his sensations."[20] With Smith's distinction in mind, Catherine's "Gothic" misconceptions are to some degree excused. Throughout her relationship with the Tilneys, Catherine has intuited the General's habitual domestic tyranny. By her sym-

---

[20] *The Theory of Moral Sentiments* (London, 1759), p. 2. For an excellent general discussion of the sympathetic imagination, see Walter Jackson Bate, *From Classic to Romantic: Premises of Taste in Eighteenth-Century England* (1946; rpt. New York: Harper Torchbooks, 1961), pp. 129–60.

pathetic participation in the feelings of his children (especially Eleanor) she has reached an intuitional knowledge of their unease in their father's company, and by her imaginative responses to the General's occasional fits of anger she has come to an undefined recognition of his violence.

The General's actual domestic tyranny has been revealed in his obsessive attitude toward time. Even as Catherine upbraids herself after Henry's rebuke, the partial justice of her suspicions asserts itself, without her knowledge, when in spite of her grief she goes down to dinner as "the clock struck five" (199). On her departure from Bath for the Abbey the "clock struck ten while the trunks were carrying down," for the "General had fixed to be out of Milsom-street by that hour" (155). When they stop at Petty France, "his angry impatience at the waiters, made Catherine grow every moment more in awe of him" (156); when they arrive at the Abbey, Eleanor's manner suggests that "the strictest punctuality to the family hours would be expected at Northanger" (162), and she later "gently hints her fear of being late," a fear which is not unfounded, for on the "very instant of their entering" the General pulls the bell "with violence" and orders "Dinner to be on table *directly*!" Catherine trembles "at the emphasis with which he spoke" (165).

In such instances of his autocratic severity Catherine's intuitions have a credible basis. Though there are other instances of his selfishness and vanity, his violent egotism is particularly apparent in his psychotic demand that his household, and that of Henry's at Woodston, be regulated according to his habits. As long as he considers Catherine a financial catch, he feels a "pressing solicitude . . . of making Miss Morland's *time* at Northanger pass pleasantly" (209; my italics), but it is only during his absence in London that Catherine is aware of the "happiness with which their *time* now passed" (220; my italics). And when the General returns, of course, it is to order her to leave the next morning at seven o'clock, without a servant, "not even the hour . . . left to [her] choice" (224).

If we now return to Henry's reprimand, it is with the knowledge that Catherine has a real foundation for her suspicions. She has been imagining from actual behavior and not from Gothically structured fancies. In contrast, Henry's passivity in face of his father's selfish and violent habits is hardly commendable.

Jane Austen's implied brief for the sympathetic imagination

should not, however, be exaggerated. As *Sense and Sensibility* will again stress, Jane Austen requires of any mode of moral vision that it contain a rational awareness. When Henry bids Catherine to consult her "understanding," her "sense of the probable," therefore, he is speaking for his author. The General is a domestic tyrant, but he is not a murderer, and the distinction is not a small one. Catherine's sympathetic imagination is both valuable and dangerous. When it leads her to consider, on seeing the late Mrs. Tilney's portrait, that the General " must have been dreadfully cruel to her" (181), her opinion does not exceed a "sense of the probable." But when it leads her to speculate that because a husband does not take his exercise along his late wife's favorite walk, because the wife's death occurred after an "illness . . . sudden and short" (186), and because the husband stays up late at night, *therefore* he must have murdered her, or have her now imprisoned, it goes beyond the probable, it leaves an "observation of what is passing around" her and enters a fictional realm of unlimited imaginative error.

By some such devious and, ultimately, unsatisfactory way, Jane Austen has brought her heroine, and her hero, to the moral recognitions which are the necessary preliminaries to their union. Catherine has had to learn that moral action is no simple matter, that its grounds have to be discriminated from the grounds of a number of unacceptable responses. Common sense without suspicion—the assumption of her parents at Fullerton that life has no real dangers—has to be rejected, as well as the innocence which is born from it, for however benevolently intentioned the ingenuous self is, it may, without prudence, be led by the Thorpes of this world into immoral actions and situations. On the other hand, it may not be sufficient to stand back, as Tilney does, and rationally disassociate oneself from hypocrisy in a pose of superior awareness of discrepancies. There is a place for the sympathetic imagination in social intercourse: fellow feeling and moral intuition are, indeed, necessary parts of both social and ethical attitudes; but the role of sympathy is to be carefully limited and continually grounded in fact, examined against the laws of probability.

Such a summary describes the framework on which the moral discriminations of *Northanger Abbey* rest, but it has to be admitted that the ironic mode of the novel, though it is not the subversive weapon it has been considered, is ultimately unsatisfactory, not only for the reader, but also for the author. Jane Austen has progressed by a series of *nons*. Her ideal society is *not* Fullerton complacency, *not* Bath duplicity. Her ideal moral outlook is *not* Tilney's rationalism, *not* Catherine's benevolent ingenuousness, *not* her undisciplined imagination. Somewhere between Fullerton and North-anger, and necessarily by way of Bath, an ideal locus is discover-able, in which ingenuousness and acuity, sympathy and logic are reconciled, and from which both complacency and alarmism are banished. But the locus of this ideal—the grounds—is not in the novel.[21] It is implied, and affirmatively implied, but it remains out-side, or behind, the characterization, as a property of the narrative consciousness. The reader comes to perceive the presence of stand-ards of behavior and a fixed point of moral outlook, but he is apt to feel that his arrival at such a perception has left Catherine far behind. In *Emma*, to look ahead, though the reader has a con-stantly greater awareness than Emma of the disparity between her conduct and ideal behavior, Emma herself eventually comes to an equal awareness. At the end her awareness is total, and the norms continually implied in the narrative consciousness (and there dis-coverable by the reader) are finally accepted and understood by Emma, the central intelligence of the novel. A perfect coincidence of morality and art has been achieved, and this, I take it, is one mean-ing of F. R. Leavis's opinion that Jane Austen does not offer us "an 'aesthetic' value that is separable from moral significance."[22]

In *Northanger Abbey*, by contrast, Jane Austen fails to dramatize a moral outlook in the novel's resolution. In recognition of this, I believe, as much as from a desire to reintroduce a parody of the romantic novel, she had her narrator enter the novel in person in the last two chapters to ask, "what probable circumstance could work upon a temper like the General's?" (250), and then provide

[21] A word should be said, however, about the splendidly appointed, superbly organized estate at Northanger. Were it not for the General's character, his house—with its "old trees," "luxuriant plantations," not to mention its "village of hot-houses," "unrivalled" gardens, and Rumford fireplace—would be an appropriate emblem of a structured society (177–78). For all its Gothic connota-tions in Catherine's mind, Northanger provides us with a detailed picture of a progressive English estate of the period. Cf. Nikolaus Pevsner's discussion in "The Architectural Setting of Jane Austen's Novels," *Journal of the Warburg and Courtauld Institutes*, 31 (1968), 407–8.

[22] *The Great Tradition* (London: Chatto & Windus, 1948), p. 7.

the most hackneyed of devices to unravel the plot: a Viscount is introduced, whose fortune and title are sufficient in his marriage to Eleanor to remove the objections to the marriage of Henry and Catherine.

The introduction of the narrator into her work in these last pages may be illuminated from Robert C. Elliott's work on satire.[23] Elliott has shown the dual nature of all satiric works, their social value and their dangerous power. As the genre develops, he argues, the author often detaches himself from his persona, who is allowed to do the dirty work but is then himself satirized by the author. This procedure we have already seen working with Henry Tilney, and something of like nature is also happening at the end of the novel. The self-conscious appearance of the narrator is a recognition that her creation, too, is a work of fiction. The entry is as much a wry self-criticism as a criticism of other fictional works. Like Elliott's honest satirist, Jane Austen recognizes that she is part of the folly of mankind and that her subjective vision is not necessarily any greater than that of the very authors she has from time to time parodied. But as in Elliott's view, though the persona is himself undercut, much of what he says remains valid. As with Tilney, so now within the self-admitted fallibility of the narrator, there is a measure of valid outlook, a criticism of aberrant social behavior, and a requirement for objective values. Jane Austen's later fiction will, however, require a narrative procedure other than a progression by *nons*, will require that standards be dramatically externalized in characterization, that public norms be discovered in the actions and internal development of her characters, and in the setting of her novels.

Sense and Sensibility takes a step in this direction. Its twin heroines are much deeper characters than Catherine, and in their developing careers and relationships Jane Austen defines more convincingly than in *Northanger Abbey* her notion of the proper relation between the individual and society. This is not to say that the novel is without flaws. Two mediocre heroes who fail to realize

[23] *The Power of Satire* (Princeton: Princeton University Press, 1960), esp. pp. 220–22.

the dramatic investment their author has placed in them; the wretched episode of the miserable Eliza; a failure wholly to overcome what Walton Litz has called the "tyranny of antithesis"— these are among the fairly obvious artistic limitations of the novel. Against such limitations, however, one places an incisive exposure of economic motivation and the fact that the novel is, after all, the finest example of the sub-genre in which it takes its place.

As many scholars have shown, Jane Austen is here working within inherited terms of aesthetic and ethical debate. Mrs. Inchbald's *Art and Nature* (1796) and Maria Edgeworth's *Letters of Julia and Caroline* (1795) are only two of many novels, in the decade in which *Sense and Sensibility* had its genesis as *Elinor and Marianne*, to anticipate Jane Austen's treatment of familiar dualities of prudence and benevolence, reason and passion, discipline and freedom. While Mrs. Inchbald is Godwinian in her dislike of institutions and Rousseauesque in her affirmation of the natural virtues, Maria Edgeworth is nearer the norm of the genre and Jane Austen's own position in recognizing the potential excesses of sensibility and the need for the temporizing effect of reason. Another novel, Mme d'Arblay's *Camilla* (1796), suggests in its description of the heroine a common view of the "wayward" faculty:

[H]er every propensity was pure, and, when reflection came to her aid, her conduct was as exemplary as her wishes. But the ardour of her imagination, acted upon by every passing idea, shook her Judgment from its yet unsteady seat, and left her at the mercy of wayward Sensibility—that delicate, but irregular power, which now impels to all that is most disinterested for others, now forgets all mankind, to watch the pulsations of its own fancies.[24]

Jane Austen is listed among the subscribers to the first edition of *Camilla*, and she would, on the whole, subscribe to these reflections.

[24] *Camilla* (London, 1796), IV, 399. For studies treating the literary background to *Sense and Sensibility*, see the relevant portions of Henrietta Ten Harmsel, *Jane Austen: A Study in Fictional Conventions* (The Hague: Mouton, 1964); Walton Litz, *Artistic Development*; Kenneth Moler, *Art of Allusion*; also Alan D. McKillop, "The Context of *Sense and Sensibility*," *The Rice Institute Pamphlet*, 44 (April 1957), 65–78. J. M. S. Tompkins, " 'Elinor and Marianne': A Note on Jane Austen," *The Review of English Studies*, 16 (Jan. 1940), 33–43, suggests Jane West's *A Gossip's Story* (London, 1796) as a single model of *Sense and Sensibility*, but Kenneth Moler, while not denying Jane West's influence, is one of several critics to see affinities with a number of other sentimental novels.

Her achievement in *Sense and Sensibility* is not, however, to be assessed merely in terms of her ability to reveal the dangers of excessive sensibility, or, for that matter to modify a strictly rational outlook. Given her awareness of the widespread corruption of traditional moral assumptions, more than a mere accommodation of her inherited—almost hackneyed—terms was needed. The resolution of the novel was intended, I believe, not merely to discover the private happiness of the central characters, but to reconstitute around these unions the grounds of a moral society. It cannot be said that this intention is convincingly achieved—Marianne's marriage to the rheumatic Colonel Brandon is a gross over-compensation for her misguided sensibility—but it is wrong to imply, as Marvin Mudrick does, that the novel's failure reveals bad faith on Jane Austen's part, that Marianne's vitality and enthusiasm are betrayed not by Willoughby, but by an author who has here substituted for a personal commitment to feeling a dull conformity to social conventions.[25]

Marianne is one of the most interesting characters in Jane Austen's fiction. More than Emma even, she anticipates the tragically Quixotic heroines of the nineteenth century novel, whose visions of existence can find no fulfilment within the limitations of their societies. But while Jane Austen permits Marianne's quixotism to act as an implicit criticism of what is limited and pedestrian in her society, she also, quite convincingly, reveals the deficiencies of her idealism.

Nothing is clearer initially than that we are to view Marianne with a good deal of sympathy: she has "a life, a spirit, an eagerness which could hardly be seen without delight" (46). At first it seems she is to exhibit "heroic" qualities, conspicuous by their absence in the young Catherine Morland. Like her mother, she "can feel no sentiment of approbation inferior to love" (16); she is passionately fond of music and drawing; she objects to Elinor's friend, Edward Ferrars, because "he has no real taste" (17); and when they leave

[25] For an excellent brief rebuttal to Mudrick's view contained in *Irony as Defense*, see Walton Litz, *Artistic Development*, pp. 81–83. Litz argues that "the alternative to Willoughby is Colonel Brandon *not* because this was Jane Austen's heritage from life, but because it was her heritage from the broad antitheses of moralistic fiction," and that Jane Austen in *Sense and Sensibility* was "the victim of conventions, but these were primarily artistic, not social."

Norland, she sheds tears for a "place so much beloved" (27). But although her enthusiasms are occasionally those of the romantic heroines Jane Austen had delighted in burlesquing in her juvenilia, the parodic satire here is not harsh. What vindicates Marianne in the early scenes is the sincerity behind her enthusiasms, the personal quality present even when her sensibility is mediated through her reading. That she is not merely fashionable is shown in her dislike of Gilpinesque "jargon," indeed of "jargon of every kind" (97). During her conversation with Edward about landscape scenery she observes: "sometimes I have kept my feelings to myself, because I could find no language to describe them in but what was worn and hackneyed out of all sense and meaning" (97). And when Sir John Middleton suggests that she "will be setting [her] cap" at Willoughby, her caustic reply, though somewhat outspoken from a seventeen-year-old, is no less than his use of cliché deserves (45).

Strongly individualistic, Marianne's attitudes are often without egoism, and her disregard of "every common-place notion of decorum" (48) is on occasions magnificent. When Mrs. Ferrars, in the drawing room of her home in Harley Street, ignores the painted screens of Elinor to praise the absent art of the absent Miss Morton, Marianne's reaction is superb:

"This is admiration of a very particular kind!—what is Miss Morton to us?—who knows, or who cares, for her?—it is Elinor of whom *we* think and speak."
And so saying, she took the screens out of her sister-in-law's hands, to admire them herself as they ought to be admired.
Mrs. Ferrars looked exceedingly angry, and drawing herself up more stiffly than ever, pronounced in retort this bitter phillippic; "Miss Morton is Lord Morton's daughter." (235-36)

Given the mercenary and mediocre world in which she lives, Marianne's responses are often admirable, and one can understand why Mudrick sees in her a "passionate, discriminating, instantaneous sympathy for worthy people and beautiful things," a "basic opposition to lying and the forms of lying."[26] But if one sees Marianne not only as an aspect of her author (which she is, I think) but also as a representative of sensibility, then her outlook is not so unequiv-

[26] Mudrick, *Irony as Defense*, pp. 75, 74.

ocally to be affirmed nor her subsequent chastening wholly deplored. Rather than unconsciously destroying what is authentic in her nature, I would argue that Jane Austen is consciously rejecting a tendency, in herself as in her time, which she sees to be mistaken and, when taken to an extreme, immoral.

Marianne is the legatee of a philosophy of sentiment, which, wherever its roots are exactly to be located, was generally considered to have begun in the *Characteristics of Men, Manners, Opinions, Times* (1711) of the third Earl of Shaftesbury.[27] Happiness for the sentimental philosopher, in opposition to the Calvinist view of man's innate depravity and necessarily troubled life in this world, is possible for the individual who recognizes the promptings of virtue and exercises his innate benevolence. Morality is discoverable in the "heart" rather than the "head," in feelings rather than in conformity with received precepts. Shaftesbury's thought did not deny a rational access to truth, but his emphasis on an innate moral sense tended in later writers to become a full-fledged sentimentalism, and when his views were joined with the sensationalist epistemology of the empiricists, who were reducing the function of the mind to that of passive receptor of external impressions, ethical rationalism was frequently discredited. In Hume's moral philosophy, for example, morality is "more properly felt than judged of."[28] The tendency toward ethical sentimentalism did not go unchallenged; Bishop Butler, for example, opposed it, arguing that any theory of ethics must include judgment as a primary component;[29] but when the rapprochement of Shaftesburian rationalism and Humean empiricism was aided by Adam Smith's theory of sympathy and

[27] Ronald Crane, "Suggestions Toward a Genealogy of the 'Man of Feeling,'" *ELH*, 1 (Dec. 1934), 205–30, argues for an earlier expression of the sentimental outlook in the latitudinarian preachers of the late seventeenth and early eighteenth centuries. Other critical studies which consider the philosophy of sentiment and its development in the eighteenth century are: A. S. P. Woodhouse, "Romanticism and the History of Ideas," *English Studies Today* (Oxford: Oxford University Press, 1951), pp. 120–41, and Walter Jackson Bate, "The Premise of Feeling," in *Classic to Romantic*. Perhaps the best treatment of the idea in Jane Austen's novel is found in Ian Watt's introduction to *Sense and Sensibility*, ed. Ian Watt (New York: Harper & Row, 1961); reprinted in *Jane Austen: A Collection of Critical Essays*, ed. Ian Watt (Englewood Cliffs, N.J.: Prentice-Hall, 1963).

[28] *Treatise on Human Nature*, ed. T. H. Green and T. H. Grose (London: Longmans, Green, 1874), p. 235.

[29] *The Works of Joseph Butler*, ed. W. E. Gladstone (Oxford: The Clarendon Press, 1896), II, 14–15.

Rousseau's immense influence as a philosopher of "natural" goodness, not only was a rational access to moral truth frequently denied, but the validity of all external structures was called into question.

Jane Austen sets herself against these tendencies in *Sense and Sensibility*, insisting on the necessary aid of judgment in the process of moral decision, and requiring, as she will elsewhere in her fiction, that the individual respect and support his cultural heritage. The major limitations of Marianne's sensibility, adequately dramatized as we will see, are that it places excessive faith in the self's inner ability to reach moral decisions intuitively and rejects entirely the need for living within conventional limits.

The dangerous tendencies of Marianne's individualism only become apparent in her relationship with Willoughby, who is, like Anna Karenina's Vronsky, to a large degree an invention of the imaginative mind. This is not to deny that he is handsome and possessed of "ardour," "talents," and "spirit," which put Ferrars and Brandon in the shade, merely to note that from the moment he becomes her "preserver" (46), Willoughby is defined, and is willing to be defined, in terms of "the hero of a favourite story" (43). Hearing of his indefatigable dancing powers, Marianne cries: "That is what I like; that is what a young man ought to be. Whatever be his pursuits, his eagerness in them should know no moderation, and leave him no sense of fatigue" (45)—and his expressed passion for dancing on their first meeting is sufficient to earn him from Marianne "such a look of approbation" (46). Thereafter, the "general conformity of judgment" that is discovered between them is not a little due to her enthusiasm and his compliance. It is she who brings forward and rapturously describes her favorite authors, while Willoughby "acquiesced in all her decisions, caught all her enthusiasm" (47).

In company with Willoughby, Marianne is drawn into increasingly serious acts of impropriety. She accepts from Willoughby the gift of a horse, forgetting that the expense of keeping it will be a burden to the family's reduced income. Faced with the additional charge that it may be improper to accept a gift of this kind from a man so lately known to her, Marianne answers with spirit that "it is not time or opportunity that is to determine intimacy;—it is disposition alone" (59). Though Marianne is persuaded by Elinor to give up the horse, Willoughby is heard to promise that "when you leave Barton to form your own establishment in a more lasting home, Queen Mab shall receive you" (59), and this hint, together with his use of Marianne's Christian name, is sufficient to convince Elinor of their being engaged.

Such instances of their disregard of decorum culminate in their unchaperoned visit to Allenham, the home of Mrs. Smith, the elderly relative and benefactress of Willoughby. This trip is not only indecorous, it more seriously shows an entire lack of concern for the feelings of others. From the point of view of the present owner, the unannounced visit of her heir and a young female companion can only indicate barely concealed impatience for her death. In her Shaftesburian defense of her conduct on this occasion the weakness of Marianne's position is evident: "If there had been any real impropriety in what I did, I should have been sensible of it at the time, for we always know when we are acting wrong, and with such a conviction I could have had no pleasure" (68).

In keeping with the tenets of the tradition she represents, propriety and morality in Marianne's definition are innate qualities of the self and not conformity to any set of social rules. She has responded to her experience of seemingly universal selfishness by retiring into a subjective world into which she will allow only a few privileged and manifestly worthy people. When Willoughby comes dramatically into view, Marianne looks to him for the limits of her happiness, and, like Hester Prynne in *The Scarlet Letter*, argues that what she and her lover do together has "a consecration of its own." Like Hawthorne, however, Jane Austen refuses to sanction the spiritual autonomy of a relationship.

In rejecting the forms of this world in her passion for Willoughby, Marianne has substituted emotional laws for social laws: "I felt myself . . . to be as solemnly engaged to him, as if the strictest legal covenant had bound us to each other" (188). Willoughby, however, is unwilling to obey the unwritten laws of Marianne's private world, and instead prudently adheres to the propriety of society for his own selfish ends. Thus it is that in the climactic scene of their meeting in London, the sincerity of her sensibility is noticeable in her manner of speech and salutation, while the falsity of his sensibility (and its prudent content) is seen in the reserved manner of his response. Marianne, on sighting him across the room, started up, and pronouncing his name in a tone of affection, held out her hand to him. He approached, and addressing himself rather to Elinor than Marianne, as if wishing to avoid her eye, and determined not to observe her attitude, inquired in a hurried manner after Mrs. Dashwood, and asked how long they had been in town. Elinor was robbed of all presence of mind by such an address, and was unable to say a word. But the feelings of her sister were instantly expressed. Her face was crimsoned over, and she exclaimed in a voice of the greatest emotion, "Good God! Willoughby, what is the meaning of this? Have you not received my letters? Will you not shake hands with me?" (176)

Whereas at Barton the ancillary features of sensibility—extravagant language, the shaking of hands—had been found in both Willoughby and Marianne, in the London assembly Willoughby is aloof, "her touch seemed painful to him, and he held her hand only for a moment" (177).

Her relationship to Willoughby has been for Marianne the constitution of a society of two, and when this is lost through the defection of one of its members, Marianne has no rule for living, no motive for action, no "ground" on which to stand. Misery like hers, she admits, has no pride, and in keeping with the anti-stoical strain of the sentimental philosophy in which tears are considered the evidence of feeling, Marianne's subsequent behavior is an active soliciting of grief. Her illness at Cleveland is spiritual, and the death to which it might easily have led would have been suicide. We should not discount the solemnity of Marianne's retrospections on her recovery. Recognizing that, "Had I died,—it would have been self-destruction" (345), she wonders that she has been allowed to live, "to have time for atonement to my God" (346).

In Marianne's subjective attitudes Jane Austen has revealed how the self, unaided by the forms of culture and the administration of self-discipline, finds itself alienated from society and friends. By considering her internal inclinations sufficient arbiters of moral action, Marianne has denied external sources of obligation in family, society, and religion. The inevitably negative effects of her extreme, individualistic response are sufficiently clear, but even if they were not so, Elinor's contrasting behavior in regard to personal grief, no less than in regard to the maintenance of a decorous politeness even in the company of fools, would indicate her author's requirement for a positive and social response. When Elinor discovers that Edward is engaged to Lucy Steele, "she wept for him, more than for herself" (140), yet when she joins Mrs. Jennings and Marianne at dinner, "no one would have supposed . . . that Elinor was mourning in secret over obstacles which must divide her for ever from the object of her love" (141).

Elinor's characterization in *Sense and Sensibility* is more successful than has generally been recognized in critical discussion. She starts off with the disadvantage of being the single normative representative of "sense" in the novel. Other characters—the John Dashwoods, Lady Middleton, Mrs. Ferrars, Lucy Steele—exhibit "sense," as well as "prudence" and "reserve," only in debased and "economic" meanings. Added to this, the two possible male representatives of the term fail entirely to provide an effective counterbalance to the selfishness and expedient behavior everywhere evident. (In later novels, Darcy and Knightley will successfully provide such counterbalance.) Elinor's task of upholding the true moral conception of the word is, therefore, large—too large for her to achieve unaided. Yet Elinor is not quite the bloodless figure of sense she has been considered. It is clear, for example, that Marianne's vital and central position in the novel is in part accounted for by the fact that she is the object of Elinor's observation. If the first volume describes the rise of Marianne's hopes and their temporary disappointment on Willoughby's departure from Devonshire, the second volume her renewed hopes in London and their cruel destruction, and the third volume her near fatal illness and gradual recovery, they describe these events often through Elinor's consciousness. Consequently, while it is Marianne's acts that are described, they are frequently filtered through Elinor's subjective experience of them. Edmund Wilson was perhaps the first to understand the importance of this when he commented upon the scene in which Marianne meets Willoughby in London (the scene which for George Moore revealed the "burning human heart in English prose fiction for the first and alas the last time"). "Isn't it rather," Wilson asks, "the emotion of Elinor as she witnesses her sister's disaster than Marianne's emotion over Willoughby of which the poignancy is communicated to the reader?"[30]

---

[30] "A Long Talk About Jane Austen," *Classics and Commercials: A Literary Chronicle of the Forties* (New York: Farrer, Straus & Cudahy, 1950), p. 203.

In this partial internalization of the debate in Elinor's consciousness—as Marianne's actions and Elinor's perception of these actions merge—Jane Austen's technical advance over *Northanger
Abbey*, and her movement in the direction of *Pride and Prejudice*,
are evident. Elinor may seem to others to be reserved, rational, and
cold, but the reader is given access to her continued inner struggle,
not only with respect to her own love affair, but vicariously, as she
watches Marianne impetuously fall in love, and, her love slighted,
no less passionately give way to melancholy. Elinor, much more
than Catherine Morland, though less than Emma, has become a
center of consciousness. She is the only character (apart from Mrs.
Jennings on one occasion [III, iii] which must be judged a technical lapse) whose mind the reader is allowed to enter. Opaque to
the other characters, Elinor is transparent to the reader. By allowing us frequent access to Elinor's observing mind, the narrator
reveals that "sense" need not be cold, nor introspection selfish.

Elinor's sense is neither a Mandevillian self-interest nor an emo-
tionless calculation. In its affirmation of social principles it resembles, rather, the "early received and uniformly continued sense
of mankind" (*R*, 111), which Burke considered had not only built up
the "august fabric of states" but had continued to preserve it from
ruin. Like her lover Edward, Elinor accepts the validity of social
institutions and acts within received principles of ethical and social
conduct. Against the private instinct of her sister, as against the
selfish motivations of those around her, Elinor opposes a stoical
fidelity to traditional and basically Christian values. Her withdrawal
into a personal reserve is a committed withdrawal.

The theme of profession, so central to *Mansfield Park*, and found
in all the mature novels, is relevant here. In the moment of social
discontinuity, the responsible individual can only look conscienti-
ously to his duty and actively profess his role. Unlike Willoughby,
who is "of no profession at all" (61), or Mr. Palmer, who "idled
away the mornings at billiards, which ought to have been devoted to
business" (305), or John Dashwood, who is always "thinking about
writing a letter to his steward in the country" (259), but never does,
the responsible characters of the novel, Ferrars and Brandon, are
characterized by their commitment to their roles. Edward, indeed,
agrees with Mrs. Dashwood when she suggests that he would "be a

happier man if [he] had any profession" to engage his time (102). He admits, "It has been, and is, and probably will always be a heavy misfortune to me, that I have no necessary business to engage me, no profession to give me employment" (102). And, later, looking back on the foolish infatuation which caused him to engage himself to Lucy, he recognizes that his error sprang from his ignorance of the world, his "want of employment," and his lack of an "active profession" (362). Yet, having made the betrothal, Edward has proved himself willing to take responsibility for his actions, as Willoughby for all his superior appearance and talents has not.

The need for "employment," "duty," "responsibility," is sounded again and again in Jane Austen's novels, as her heroines all learn that the act of living itself is a profession. After Edward has left the Barton cottage, his melancholy over his commitment to Lucy having communicated itself to Elinor, her reaction may be taken as the positive response that is to be affirmed: she *"busily* employed herself the whole day" and addressed herself to the *"business* of self-command" (104; my italics). In comparison with this self-discipline, Marianne's "indulgence of feeling" and "nourishment of grief" (83) are hardly admirable.

Only when Marianne's recovery is assured by the attentions of Elinor and the much maligned Mrs. Jennings may Elinor's self-discipline be relaxed. At the end of the novel we are given explicit indications of Elinor's sensibility. First she feels for Marianne, who, "restored to life, health, friends . . . was an idea to fill her heart with sensations of exquisite comfort, and expand it in fervent gratitude" (315). Then she responds sympathetically to Willoughby's tempestuous arrival and self-pitying tale, and for a time, "Willoughby, 'poor Willoughby,' as she now allowed herself to call him, was constantly in her thoughts" (334). Finally with Edward's arrival the question becomes, "How are [Elinor's] feelings to be described?" (363), and on news of Edward's freedom from the duty of his engagement to Lucy, we are given the answer:

Elinor could sit it no longer. She almost ran out of the room, and as soon as the door was closed, burst into tears of joy, which at first she thought would never cease. Edward, who had till then looked any where, rather than at her, saw her hurry away, and perhaps saw—or even heard, her emotion. . . . (360)

Marianne's danger over, her morality now properly directed, Elinor may release the emotional tension thus far contained, and herself give way to a temporary display of feeling. By choosing sense as her point of view over sensibility, Jane Austen has made a statement about the priority of discipline to freedom, and of social principles to individual propensities; but, that statement made, she has also recognized in Elinor's emotion the necessary presence of feeling in the ethical constitution of the individual, if rationality is not to become cold and inhuman.

The novel ends with a union of terms similar to that which will be more successfully achieved in *Pride and Prejudice*. Marianne, like Elizabeth Bennet, comes to the recognition of the need for self-discipline. She promises that "[her] feelings shall be governed and [her] temper improved" (347), and instead of further indulging her grief, she exercises a "reasonable exertion" (342). Coming to a gradual awareness of Willoughby's false sensibility, his prudent core of self, she compares her conduct to "what it ought to have been" (345). Her language is characterized now by its ethical vocabulary, and while her sister may show that the individual emotion is a component part of the social response, Marianne determines that, though Willoughby can never be forgotten, his remembrance "shall be regulated, it shall be checked by religion, by reason, by constant employment" (347). Although her marriage to Colonel Brandon fails to convince, it at least demonstrates the imprudence of her previous arguments that wealth had nothing to do with happiness, for with Brandon's £2,000 a year Marianne gains for herself the "competence" which Elinor earlier had laughingly considered her own idea of "wealth" (91).

There is no doubt that the decision to portray two heroines, and the selection of the "sensible" sister as point of view, led Jane Austen into aesthetic difficulties from which she could not entirely escape. Given the vivacity of Marianne, Elinor's explicitly normative function can only seem didactic on occasions, though this is less often so than is sometimes charged. By looking through the eyes of one of the heroines, Jane Austen has escaped the narrative problem of *Northanger Abbey* without discovering the solutions of *Pride and Prejudice* and *Emma*. She has to some degree dramatized her standards in the psychology of Elinor (as she failed to do in either Henry Tilney or Catherine) and has thus escaped the problems that arise when judgments remain at the level of the presiding and anonymous narrative consciousness, but she has still left herself with a task of persuasion, of making art and morality coincident. The reader must be made to accept the priority of one sister's moral vision, and the task is complicated by the author's refusal in any way to limit the attractive individualism of the other sister. In *Pride and Prejudice* and *Emma* this problem is successfully avoided by making the individualistic heroines also the central intelligences of their novels, and by allowing these heroines to come to a gradual internal awareness of the insufficiency of their outlooks. Whereas in *Sense and Sensibility* there is a bifurcation of action and reflection, in the later novels the two modes are one in the actions and retrospective reflections of the heroine. In *Sense and Sensibility*, Marianne's moral growth can only be seen externally in her words and actions, frequently as they are observed through Elinor's consciousness of them. Elinor herself does not so much evince a moral growth as a constant internal moral struggle. In *Pride and Prejudice* and *Emma* (though in ways to be distinguished), the movement from an individualistic to a social morality is followed within the psyche of a single heroine.

CHAPTER 3

Pride and Prejudice:
THE RECONSTITUTION
OF SOCIETY

But in this, as in most questions of state, there is a middle. There is something else than the mere alternative of absolute destruction, or unreformed existence. . . . A disposition to preserve, and an ability to improve, taken together, would be my standard of a statesman. Every thing else is vulgar in the conception, perilous in the execution.

Edmund Burke, *Reflections on the Revolution in France*

MORE SUCCESSFULLY than *Sense and Sensibility, Pride and Prejudice* moves from an initial condition of potential social fragmentation to a resolution in which the grounds of society are reconstituted as the principal characters come together in marriage. As in the former novel, there is a recognition of widespread economic motivation in human conduct, but a more important bar, initially, to the continuity of a traditionally grounded society is the existence everywhere of separations—between classes in the context of society as a whole, between minds in the smaller context of the home.

The fragmentary nature of the novel's world is humorously evident from the beginning in the constitution of the Bennet family itself, as any number of scenes could illustrate. Consider, for example, the various reactions to Mr. Collins's letter announcing his intention to visit Longbourn:

"There is some sense in what he says about the girls however;" [said Mrs. Bennet] "and if he is disposed to make them any amends, I shall not be the person to discourage him."

"Though it is difficult," said Jane, "to guess in what way he can mean to make us the atonement he thinks our due, the wish is certainly to his credit."

Elizabeth was chiefly struck with his extraordinary deference for Lady Catherine, and his kind intention of christening, marrying, and burying his parishioners whenever it were required.

"He must be an oddity, I think," said she. "I cannot make him out.— There is something very pompous in his stile.—And what can he mean by apologizing for being next in the entail?—We cannot suppose he would help it, if he could.—Can he be a sensible man, sir?"

"No, my dear; I think not. I have great hopes of finding him quite the reverse. There is a mixture of servility and self-importance in his letter, which promises well. I am impatient to see him."

"In point of composition," said Mary, "his letter does not seem defective. The idea of the olive branch perhaps is not wholly new, yet I think it is well expressed."

To Catherine and Lydia, neither the letter nor its writer were in any degree interesting. It was next to impossible that their cousin should come in a scarlet coat. . . . (63–64)

Mr. Bennet's somewhat cynical irony, his wife's fixed concern to marry off her daughters, Jane's indiscriminate benevolence, Mary's pedantry, the youngest sisters' love of the military, are all evident, as, too, are Elizabeth's perceptiveness and special position (hers are the only thoughts reported). But beyond the humorous revelation of character the scene discloses an important concern of the novel. The meaning of any statement or action, such a method suggests, is not single, but multiple in ratio to the number of minds perceiving it. In such an individualistic—almost Shandean—world, meaning is in danger of becoming a function of private desire, and all that does not accord with the individual vision is in danger of being discredited. Only when self-interest encounters self-interest, seemingly, is communication, indeed conversation, possible. Mr. Collins and Mrs. Bennet understand each other perfectly in their "tête-à-tête" before breakfast at Longbourn (71). When coincidence of interest is absent, mind is closed to mind and conversation is in vain, as Mrs. Bennet interminably complains about the injustice of the entail, Sir William Lucas recalls his presentation at St. James's, Mr. Collins descants on the beauty of Rosings.

The distances of the drawing room, moreover, are the mirror of social distances outside. As a "gulf impassable" (311) seems to loom between Darcy and Elizabeth, so there are seemingly uncrossable distances between the aristocracy (Darcy and Lady Catherine), the gentry (the Bennets), and "trade" (the Phillipses and the Gardiners). Those who were "formerly in trade" (18)—the Lucases and the Bingleys—add mobility, but hardly continuity, to the social moment, as they seek landed security at their different levels.

How in this world of distances are people, and classes, to come together? This, the crucial question underlying *Pride and Prejudice,* is answered primarily through the education of the hero and heroine, whose union is not only to their mutual advantage, but brings together widely separate outlooks and social positions. As many critics have argued, it is in the mutuality of the concessions made by Elizabeth and Darcy that the novel's attraction lies. If Elizabeth's private vision is shown to be insufficient, then so, too, is

Darcy's arrogant assumption that status is value-laden. Only when Elizabeth recognizes that individualism must find its social limits, and Darcy concedes that tradition without individual energy is empty form, can the novel reach its eminently satisfactory conclusion.[1]

That Darcy's pride is convincingly humiliated needs little documentation, but it is more important, I think, to consider Elizabeth's education in the novel. Hers is the only mind to which we are granted continual access, and through her internal development from a private to a social outlook we discover again that for Jane Austen an individual's moral duty is necessarily to society, properly understood, and that any retreat into a subjective morality is misguided. While *Pride and Prejudice* quite clearly looks with a critical eye upon automatic social responses, it also validates inherited social principles as they are made relevant to the conditions of the moment and properly informed by individual commitment. To support this argument, it will be necessary, first, to demonstrate how carefully Jane Austen has qualified Elizabeth's largely admirable individualism.[2]

[1] That *Pride and Prejudice* achieves an ideal relation between the individual and society seems now to be generally agreed. Cf. Lionel Trilling's succinct summary of the novel's thesis: "a formal rhetoric, traditional and rigorous, must find a way to accommodate a female vivacity, which in turn must recognize the principled demands of the strict male syntax" (*The Opposing Self* [New York: Viking Press, 1955], p. 222). Samuel Kliger's brilliant article, "Jane Austen's *Pride and Prejudice* in the Eighteenth-Century Mode," *University of Toronto Quarterly*, 16 (July 1947), 357–70, sets the novel in the context of the history of ideas, by showing how the various relationships of the novel depend upon commonplace antitheses of ethical and aesthetic debate—art and nature, the rules and originality—the impulse of the whole being toward a reconciliation of extremes and the establishment of a normative mean. Noting the "Whig" resonance of the hero's name, Donald J. Greene, in "Jane Austen and the Peerage," *PMLA*, 68 (Dec. 1953), 1017–31, argues for a historical rapprochement, suggesting as a "unifying thesis" of the novel (and of Jane Austen's fiction) "the rise of the middle class, a process of which the middle class itself became acutely conscious when Pitt, in effect, overthrew the entrenched political power of the Whig aristocracy in 1784."

[2] Not everyone would agree that *Pride and Prejudice* is a novel of the heroine's education. Marvin Mudrick, for example, finds Elizabeth's attitudes admirable and normative: "Like Mary Crawford later, Elizabeth is a recognizable and striking aspect of her author" (*Jane Austen: Irony as Defense and Discovery* [Princeton: Princeton University Press, 1952], p. 120). There is, Mudrick argues, "no compulsion—personal, thematic, or moral—toward denying the heroine her own powers of judgment" (p. 107). But such a reading ignores the heroine's own gradual awareness of the excesses of her individualism.

For a long time the inadequacy of the heroine's outlook is concealed, as the narrative strategy emphasizes its undoubted virtues. Elizabeth's morality, when seen in action, is praiseworthy. On learning that her sister is ill at Netherfield, and discovering that the carriage is not to be had, she walks the three miles to Bingley's house, "jumping over stiles and springing over puddles with impatient activity, and finding herself at last within view of the house, with weary ancles, dirty stockings, and a face glowing with the warmth of exercise" (32). Clearly, the context of Elizabeth's morality is personal. What is important to her are friendship and love, the mutual reciprocation of kindness and concern by two people—sisters, lovers, or friends. This present, all is excusable; this absent, nothing is. But the very reduction of the area of her moral concern renders her outlook susceptible, for, if the other in a close relationship fails to reciprocate affection or trust, disappointment must ensue. A common theme in the eighteenth century novel treats the withdrawal of the idealist, disappointed in friendship or love, into misanthropy. (One thinks of the Man of the Hill in *Tom Jones,* the Hermit in *Rasselas,* the "misanthropist" in *The Man of Feeling.*) And at one point in the novel Elizabeth seems about to follow in this tradition: "The more I see of the world, the more am I dissatisfied with it; and every day confirms my belief of the inconsistency of all human characters, and of the little dependence that can be placed on the appearance of either merit or sense" (135). Like many eighteenth century figures, Elizabeth has been misled by "appearance": Bingley, who seemed about to propose to Jane, has left Netherfield for London without declaring himself; and Charlotte Lucas, who ought to have had more "sense," has accepted Collins's proposal of marriage. Justified as Elizabeth seems to be in her censure of "inconsistency" in these two cases, her outlook has nevertheless been shown incapable of distinguishing appearance from reality—and in a heroine whose most laudable characteristic has been considered her "discrimination," this is surely matter for comment.[3]

[3] Quite apart from her failure to see through Charlotte, is her angry response (135-36) as meritorious as it is usually considered? When she visits Charlotte at

Elizabeth's experience with Wickham, of course, reveals this inadequacy even more clearly. Like Willoughby, Wickham is at first view "most gentlemanlike" (72); "he had all the best part of beauty, a fine countenance, a good figure, and very pleasing address" (72). But these are external qualities only, and it is significant that we hear nothing of his "character," "understanding," "mind"—the inner qualities which Jane Austen invariably requires to inform the outward show. As Elizabeth herself will later realize, the "impropriety" of Wickham's communications (207) at a first meeting is blatant; but, already prejudiced against Darcy, she accepts Wickham's slanderous perspective, and in later refusing Darcy's proposal of marriage will adduce as a major reason his treatment of Wickham: "In what imaginary act of *friendship* can you here defend yourself?" (191; my italics).

Wickham, it seems to Elizabeth initially, like herself and Jane, holds brief for the holiness of the heart's affections. He discovers value, so it appears, in friendship or in the spontaneous action of the self, and not in a conformity to sterile social principles. In this way, he is the opposite of Darcy, who, in Elizabeth's eyes, allows "nothing for the influence of friendship and affection" (50). Thus, when Jane wishes to see both Wickham and Darcy as in some way right—"do but consider in what a disgraceful light it places Mr. Darcy" (85)—Elizabeth refuses to be persuaded that Wickham's view is just another perspective on Darcy's character. "There was truth in his looks," she says of Wickham, "one knows exactly what to think" (86). And at the Netherfield ball which follows, although it is Wickham and not Darcy who is absent—in spite of the former's assertion that he has "no reason for avoiding" Darcy (78)—it is against Darcy that Elizabeth's "feeling of displeasure" is directed (89).

Hunsford Elizabeth discovers that her friend has found ways of coexisting with the outrageous Collins and of modifying his obsequiousness to Lady Catherine. Elizabeth's belief that Charlotte could never be happy is contradicted when she sees the parsonage, in which "every thing was fitted up and arranged with a neatness and consistency of which Elizabeth gave Charlotte all the credit" (157). Elizabeth is not, of course, persuaded to accept Charlotte's antiromantic view that marriage is the "only honourable provision for well-educated young women of small fortune" (122). Still less is she persuaded that Charlotte's schemings are exemplary or that economic pressures should be permitted to determine an individual's future. But what the visit does suggest is that Charlotte's action is excusable, and, insofar as it allows her to adopt a useful social role, even positive.

In accepting Wickham at face value, Elizabeth repeats the folly of the naive protagonist in the eighteenth century novel. And she has yet to learn the lesson that "as for faces—you may look into them to know whether a man's nose be a long or a short one."[4] But beyond the inherited theme of appearance versus reality, there is in *Pride and Prejudice* an additional awareness of the difficulties involved in reaching a true interpretation of any character. Even without bias, different people will respond to a particular person in different ways—as the Bennet family variously react to Mr. Collins's letter. It may also be that no individual is the same from one day to the next. As Reuben Brower has shown, a sense of the relativity of interpretation and of the variability of character is central to *Pride and Prejudice*. But, as Brower further insists, Jane Austen's vision is, finally, "not one of Proustian relativity."[5] The possibility is presented and then withdrawn, and through Elizabeth's education in this matter we learn how relativity can be excluded from social relations and from a moral outlook.

The relativistic (or better, perspectivistic) aspects involved in knowing another person are touched upon at the Netherfield Ball, where a conversation between Elizabeth and Darcy reveals the extent to which initial interpretations of character are constructions, or sketches, based on available (and often inadequate) information. When Elizabeth accuses Darcy of "an unsocial, taciturn disposition" (91), he concedes that this may be a "faithful portrait" (91) in her eyes; and when Elizabeth later questions him about his "temper," she admits that her questions are intended to provide an "illustration" of his character (93). Darcy has earlier been made aware of her meeting with Wickham, a fact that has bearing on the following exchange:

She shook her head. "I do not get on at all. I hear such different accounts of you as puzzle me exceedingly."

"I can readily believe," answered he gravely, "that report may vary greatly with respect to me; and I could wish, Miss Bennet, that you were

---

4 The advice given to, but not of course taken by, Harley in Henry Mackenzie's *The Man of Feeling* (1771). Cf. too, Parson Adams's naive defense of physiognomy in *Joseph Andrews*, refuted by the innkeeper who was formerly a sea captain (in Bk. II, chap. 17).

5 "Light and Bright and Sparkling: Irony and Fiction in *Pride and Prejudice*," in *The Fields of Light: An Experiment in Critical Reading* (New York: Oxford University Press, 1951), p. 173.

not to sketch my character at the present moment, as there is reason to fear that the performance would reflect no credit on either."

"But if I do not take your likeness now, I may never have another opportunity." (93–94)

Darcy is here suggesting that Elizabeth should avoid basing her judgment of him on "report," whether the general report of Meryton or the particular report of Wickham. In either case the sketch she will draw will be partial, for its perspective will be limited. Darcy's true character is not to be immediately derived, as Wickham's character has been by Elizabeth, from external appearances. Unwilling to accede to Darcy's implied request that she postpone her judgment, however, Elizabeth takes his likeness now. Her decision angers Darcy, and they part, not to meet again until they come together at Hunsford.

There, in his letter to her following her rejection of his proposal, Elizabeth begins to see Darcy's character in a different "light" and to recognize how badly she has misjudged him from a too easy acceptance of Wickham's partial view and a too hasty response to externals —"every charm of air and address" (206). The perspectivist theme is more importantly continued in the second great recognition scene, Elizabeth's visit to Pemberley. At Darcy's estate Elizabeth comes to an awareness of Darcy's intrinsically worthy character and of the deficiencies of her own outlook. Taken with her response to his letter, her visit to Derbyshire marks a crucial change in the direction of her critical views, which now turn inward on herself and her family, at the same time as her ethical outlook broadens to take in other than personal and interpersonal factors. At first, Pemberley seems only to add contradictory perspectives on the man; but on larger view the visit refutes perspectivism as a bar to true moral discrimination, as it recognizes its inevitable existence in human relations.

Mrs. Reynolds, the Pemberley housekeeper, is the source of new views of both Darcy and Wickham. In his housekeeper's eyes, Darcy is nothing less than "the best landlord, and the best master . . . that ever lived" (249). Wickham's previous grudging concessions of Darcy's landed and familial pride take on different import in the "amiable light" of Mrs. Reynolds's representation (249). But Elizabeth's discovery of a portrait of Darcy in the picture gallery provides the most radical change of perspective. It is fitting that Elizabeth, the "natural" character, who knows "nothing of the art" (250), should come upon this artistic representation of Darcy. Pictured "with such a smile over the face" (250), Darcy appears differently from her own previous "illustration" of him as "unsocial" and "taciturn." Taken with the housekeeper's freely offered information that Darcy had been the "sweetest-tempered, most generous-hearted" of children (249), this "striking resemblance" can only provide food for "contemplation" (250): "as she stood before the canvas, on which he was represented, and fixed his eyes upon herself, she thought of his regard with a deeper sentiment of gratitude than it had ever raised before; she remembered its warmth, and softened its impropriety of expression" (251). Noticeably, she does not so much look at Darcy in the picture, as have him look at her; she "fixed his eyes upon herself." Now she tries to see herself from Darcy's vantage point, and it is therefore appropriate that, soon after, when Darcy unexpectedly comes upon her in the grounds, she should recognize "in what a disgraceful light" (252) *she* must now appear to him.

At Pemberley, Darcy is "so desirous to please, so free from self-consequence" (263) that had she and the Gardiners "drawn his character from their own feelings, and his servant's report, without any reference to any other account, the circle in Hertfordshire to which he was known, would not have recognised it for Mr. Darcy" (264).[6] In his home Darcy is exemplary, and the description of his estate, though general, is a natural analogue of his social and moral character.

Pemberley is a model estate, possessing those indications of value that Jane Austen everywhere provides in her descriptions of properly run estates—beautiful trees, well-disposed landscapes, a handsome house, and finely proportioned rooms. Its grounds, while aesthetically pleasing, are quite without pretension or evidence of extravagance. There is a kind of scenic *mediocritas* about the estate, a mean between the extremes of the improver's art and uncultivated nature:

6 Mrs. Reynolds is not, however, without "family prejudice," and Jane Austen is careful to provide more than one view of Darcy even at Pemberley. The Lambton community view has "nothing to accuse him of but pride" (265); but they also acknowledge his liberality and charity.

It was a large, handsome, stone building, standing well on rising ground, and backed by a ridge of high woody hills;—and in front, a stream of some natural importance was swelled into greater, but without any artificial appearance. Its banks were neither formal, nor falsely adorned. Elizabeth was delighted. She had never seen a place for which nature had done more, or where natural beauty had been so little counteracted by an awkward taste. (245)

Darcy has evidently given his estate the kind of "modern dress" Edmund Bertram calls for at Sotherton. There is perhaps something here, too, of a Shaftesburian recognition that excellent aesthetic taste denotes an excellence of moral character.[7] Thus, when Elizabeth comes to exclaim to herself that "to be mistress of Pemberley might be something" (245), she has, we might conjecture, come to recognize not merely the money and the status of Pemberley, but its value as the setting of a traditional social and ethical orientation, its possibilities—seemingly now only hypothetical—as a context for her responsible social activity.

Following Elizabeth's journey through the park the perspectivist theme is interestingly continued as she accompanies the housekeeper into the dining parlor:

It was a large, well-proportioned room, handsomely fitted up. Elizabeth, after slightly surveying it, went to a window to enjoy its prospect. The hill, crowned with wood, from which they had descended, receiving increased abruptness from the distance, was a beautiful object. Every disposition of the ground was good; and she looked on the whole scene, the river, the trees scattered on its banks, and the winding of the valley, as far as she could trace it, with delight. As they passed into other rooms, these objects were taking different positions; but from every window there were beauties to be seen. (246)

By looking through the dining parlor window, Elizabeth sees the "whole scene" from one point of view and "as far as she could trace it." She recognizes the harmony of the scene with delight. As she moves from room to room, however, the "objects were taking dif-

---

[7] A point made by Walton Litz in *Jane Austen: A Study of Her Artistic Development* (London: Chatto & Windus, 1965), pp. 103–4. Cf. also Martin Price's remarks in "The Picturesque Moment," in *From Sensibility to Romanticism*, ed. Frederick W. Hilles and Harold Bloom (Oxford: Oxford University Press, 1965), p. 268.

ferent positions." Nevertheless, it is still the same landscape that she views. Her position, not the disposition of the ground, is what has altered. By traveling first through the park, then by looking back over it, Elizabeth is made aware of the permanence of the estate and yet of the necessarily partial and angled view of the individual. She sees that no overall view is possible to the single vision, but that an approximation to such a view is possible provided the individual is both retrospective and circumspect. More than this, it is not only the angle of the view but the distance from the object which renders the individual sight fallible. An abrupt hill may have its steepness emphasized, just as Darcy's personal abruptness may be exaggerated, by the distance from which it is viewed.

Elizabeth's journey through the park, from its boundary to the house, is a spatial recapitulation of her association with Darcy from her first prejudiced impressions of his external appearance, through a recognition of other (and seemingly contradictory) views, to a final arrival at the central core of his character. As the reader follows Elizabeth's journey, he learns that although relativism and perspectivism are facts of existence—different people will see life from different windows, and movement through time and space inevitably provides different angles of view—variability is a function of human perception and not a characteristic of truth itself. That which is good and true in life resists the perversions of the individual viewpoint, as Pemberley is a beautiful scene from wherever it is viewed by Elizabeth.

Something of this Elizabeth had learned even before her visit to Darcy's estate; earlier, in a second discussion with Jane about Darcy's character, she had shown an awareness of the variability of the human viewpoint. Comparing Darcy to Wickham, she had once again refused to accede to Jane's indiscriminate benevolence, and had insisted (and here rightly) on a choice between the men: "There is but such a quantity of merit between them; just enough to make one good sort of man; and of late it has been shifting about pretty much. For my part, I am inclined to believe it all Mr. Darcy's but you shall do as you chuse" (225). As Elizabeth's ironical tone implies, it is not the "merit" that has been shifting about, but the angle of view from which the two men have been judged. The merit is "all Mr. Darcy's," or as she later puts it, "One has got all the goodness, and the other all the appearance of it" (225).

From the visit to Hunsford onward Elizabeth's vocabulary and the vocabulary of her reported thoughts take on something of Darcy's seriousness. If she had never entirely lacked judgment, her expressions now are studded with judicial phrases. As she "studie[s]" his letter, the "justice" (209) of Darcy's charges becomes evident, and the "folly and indecorum of her own family" (213) are brought home to her. Now, in a pivotal change of psychic direction, "her anger [is] turned against herself" (212). Henceforth, her criticisms are frequently self-criticisms, or are directed inward on her family. She calls upon her father to "judge differently" (231) in the affair of Lydia and the Brighton trip:

"It is not of peculiar, but of general evils, which I am now complaining. Our importance, our respectability in the world, must be affected by the wild volatility, the assurance and disdain of all restraint which mark Lydia's character. Excuse me—for I must speak plainly. If you, my dear father, will not take the trouble of ... teaching her that her present pursuits are not to be the business of her life, she will soon be beyond the reach of amendment. . . ." (231)

Her vocabulary adopts a Johnsonian tone as she argues for general principles. She has moved from a personalist toward a social morality, and long before she is obliged to convince her father of her sincere love for Darcy, she has come to a recognition that "indeed he has no improper pride" (376).

As WE SEE Elizabeth's prejudice modified, so we see Darcy's pride humbled.[8] But we have also learned, with Elizabeth, that Darcy possesses a "proper pride"—whose definition Mary Bennet, characteristically, has already supplied (20)—and that much (if not all) of what had seemed "so high and so conceited" (13) in

---

[8] For an interesting reading of Darcy as a deflated version of the "patrician hero" figure in eighteenth century fiction, and of Elizabeth as an "anti-Evelina," refusing to take the sycophantic role of the typical Richardson-Burney heroine, see Kenneth L. Moler's chapter in *Jane Austen's Art of Allusion* (Lincoln: University of Nebraska Press, 1968). Though Moler goes on to show that Jane Austen "does not allow her anti-Evelina to rout her patrician hero completely," he is clearly not concerned to stress—as I am—the education of the heroine in the novel.

his early behavior is open, retrospectively, to a more favorable interpretation.[9] Darcy's "proper pride" is not merely a stereotyped literary attitude but a well-established commitment to propriety in a time of collapsing standards—the pride of a responsible landlord who recognizes with some apprehension "in such days as these" (38) that the norms by which men have lived for generations are in danger of neglect or destruction. Averse to anything that is or tends to be subversive of social standards, Darcy adopts a mask when away from the harmony of Pemberley and becomes, to borrow a distinction from Dorothy Emmet, a person, in the sense of *persona*, and not an individual.[10] Opposed to easy familiarity, quick friendships, immediate agreements, he is not at ease in public places. Refusing to become pliant, he appears as the arrogant figure which Meryton —with a good deal of excuse—considers him. Only those, like Elizabeth, who have seen the face without the mask (and this is surely one significance of the portrait at Pemberley) can know that his public appearance belies his inner character.

It is appropriate to use a dramatic metaphor in describing Darcy, provided one keeps in mind the theme of profession that pervades Jane Austen's fiction. Darcy sees his role in life as a permanent one which will fix the nature of the self. "Disguise of every sort" is his abhorrence (192). His role-behavior is not to be considered an act of *mauvaise foi*, though the Sartrean accusation permits an instructive comparison. Like the "Presiding Judge" and "Chief Treasurer" for whom Sartre has so much distaste, Darcy—as Jane Austen describes him—identifies himself with his role.[11] There is nothing pejorative for Jane Austen in the belief that pride in function is a safeguard against contingency. Whereas for Sartre the acceptance of a role is the evasion of personal freedom, the refusal to see that we can act roles other than the one we now act, for Jane Austen freedom is only authentic when given a proper social context. This is not to say that social position for Jane Austen inevitably confers personal worth—the absurd pretensions of Lady Catherine and Mr. Collins,

---

9 Reuben Brower, "Irony and Fiction in *Pride and Prejudice*," points out how "the simultaneity of tonal layers" in the early conversations of the novel permits a favorable interpretation of many of Darcy's apparently rude utterances.

10 *Rules, Roles and Relations* (New York: St. Martin's Press, 1966), esp. chap. 8, "Persons and Personae."

11 *Being and Nothingness*, trans. Hazel Barnes (New York: Philosophical Library, 1956), p. 485.

based as they are solely on position, are satirically exposed. It is to argue that Jane Austen affirms a positive interpretation of social role. Charlotte's marriage to Collins is not the total loss of integrity that Elizabeth considers it, for it shows her willingness to become part of society, to play a social part. Mr. Bennet, on the other hand, so much more witty and attractive than Charlotte, is a less than responsible character in his refusal to play a part. Always the spectator who watches others play their roles, quick to observe discrepancies or ridiculous mannerisms in a performance, Mr. Bennet himself refuses to adopt the role of father and landowner. His chosen freedom from social commitment and his withdrawal from the proper stage of his behavior are serious faults in his character.

A contemporary context may be given to Darcy's attitudes if one turns to Burke, whose advice Jane Austen might have followed in her portrayal of Darcy. "High and worthy notions of . . . function and destination" (*R*, 111), to introduce a phrase from the *Reflections*, explain Darcy's stiff posture and uncompromising demands. Like Burke's responsible official, Darcy does not "look to the paltry pelf of the moment, nor to the temporary and transient praise of the vulgar, but to a solid, permanent existence, in the permanent part of [his] nature" (*R*, 111). Again, it might be argued that it is his manifest desire to save traditional customs and usages from "prophanation and ruin" (*R*, 111) which accounts for the acerbity of some of his remarks to Bingley, a man who has not yet chosen his permanent role, who has not yet discovered his stage of action. Moreover, though Darcy is constantly and appropriately associated with judgment and justice (his favorite uncle was a judge), there is in his outlook something of the Burkean "prejudice," which "renders a man's virtue his habit and not a series of unconnected acts. Through just prejudice, his duty becomes part of his nature" (*R*, 106).[12]

12 The title terms are, of course, interchangeably applicable to both hero and heroine. That Elizabeth has her own "proper" pride as well as prejudice is best shown when, in conversation with Lady Catherine, she insists that she is a gentleman's daughter. But the possibility of a favorable interpretation of prejudice, especially when the word is applied to Darcy, seems not to have been considered. Yet the word had a favorable meaning in the eighteenth century. The quotation from Burke, for example, is part of a long section in the *Reflections on the Revolution in France* (ed. William B. Todd [New York: Rinehart & Co., 1959], pp. 105–6), in which he defends "our old prejudices" on the grounds

That Darcy has a Burkean regard for the wisdom of his ancestors is shown on several occasions in the novel. We recall the long picture gallery at Pemberley, where there "were many family portraits" (250), and we remember his attitude toward libraries. In an interesting conversation at Netherfield, the subject of reading, introduced by Miss Bingley in order to disparage Elizabeth, takes on symbolic dimensions as Elizabeth, accused of being a "great reader" (37), denies the charge, but nevertheless walks over to a table on which some books are lying. Bingley immediately offers to fetch other books from his library, admitting at the same time that his collection is small and that he—"an idle fellow" (38)—is unlikely to augment it. This admission by her brother leads Miss Bingley to express her astonishment that "my father should have left so small a collection of books" (38), and she then turns to Darcy to congratulate him on his library at Pemberley.

> "It ought to be good," he replied, "it has been the work of many generations."
> "And then you have added so much to it yourself, you are always buying books."
> "I cannot comprehend the neglect of a family library in such days as these." (38)

Darcy's pride in his library is the proper pride of the responsible owner of a large house who is conscious of his responsibilities as trustee and who is aware (in Burkean terms) that he is not the "entire master" but only the "life-renter" of Pemberley. In "the modes of holding property [and] exercising function" (*R*, 116) Darcy is an instructive contrast not only to the idle and negligent Bingley but to Mr. Bennet himself, whose library can provide no emblem of trusteeship, but is instead a refuge from responsibility, a sub-

---

that they constitute "a general bank and capital" greater than the individual's "private stock of reason." It may be added that Burke joins a long list of authors who preceded Jane Austen in the use of both title words, though in his instance the words are not used phrasally. In his speech, "A Plan for the Better Security of the Civil and Other Establishments" (1780), Burke, speaking of the nobility's relation to the crown, argues that "it is rather an useful prejudice that gives them a pride in such a servitude." Both words clearly appear in favorable meanings.

jective retreat which he is "anxious to . . . have . . . to himself"
(71).[13]

Given his prejudice in favor of society, Darcy's disagreement with
Bingley on other apparently inconsequential matters is understandable. Chapter ten introduces the subject of letter-writing, and just
as Miss Bingley will later choose the second volume of the book that
Darcy is reading, so here she shows her matrimonial intentions by
offering to mend his pen (47). Darcy, however, refuses the offer, only
to become involved in a debate with Bingley over their respective
styles of writing. The debate is introduced by Bingley's explanation
of his sister's charge that "Charles writes in the most careless way
imaginable": "My ideas flow so rapidly that I have not time to
express them—by which means my letters sometimes convey no
ideas at all to my correspondents" (48). Though Elizabeth praises
him warmly for the humility of his excuse, Darcy accuses Bingley
of an "indirect boast." His "rapidity of thought and carelessness of
execution" (48) constitute an "imperfection of the performance"
(49), and, as Howard Babb has shown well, "performance" is a key
word, extending in sense "from a mere display of skill to a deed
expressive of one's whole being."[14] Bingley's rapid and careless writing becomes, therefore, another manifestation of his "precipitance"
—which, as Darcy suggests, can be a serious matter in "the very
necessary business" (49) of running an estate.

Here again, it is not only Bingley whose performance receives
comment. Letters are perhaps Jane Austen's most consistent pointer
to personal responsibility, and it is therefore appropriate, if unfortunate, that Mr. Bennet should be a "most negligent and dilatory correspondent" (294). Especially during his stay in London, as he searches
for Wickham and Lydia, is Mr. Bennet's irresponsibility evident, for
he makes no effort to inform his family of his progress, leaving this
duty to Mr. Gardiner. Lydia too is a poor letter writer. Before leaving
for Brighton she had "promised to write very often and very minutely
to her mother and Kitty; but her letters were always long expected,

[13] A library motif runs through the novel. In addition to the libraries of
Bingley, Darcy, and Mr. Bennet, there are the libraries of the lending sort that
provide Kitty and Lydia with the opportunity for meeting officers. As for Mary,
her response to Lydia's sexuality—"I should infinitely prefer a book" (223)—
indicates the consolatory role that libraries play in her existence.

[14] *Jane Austen's Novels: The Fabric of Dialogue* (Columbus: Ohio State University Press, 1962), p. 125.

and always very short" (238), and after her marriage she claims that "married women have never much time for writing" (330). When these members of the Bennet family do take it into their heads to write, their letters are not of the kind to merit praise. Mr. Bennet is pleased enough to write to Collins, but his motive is his own amusement, and Lydia's letters are invariably concerned with her own selfish affairs.

A retrospective realization of Darcy's social responsibility allows a more favorable interpretation of his attitudes in the early conversations. Himself a great reader, as a letter writer "he does *not* write with ease" (48). In both instances his performance is an index to his judicious and gravely taken sense of responsibility. A letter to his sister is, for Darcy, a matter of "business," and this word, important in *Sense and Sensibility*, is crucial to *Pride and Prejudice*. The professional theme, so basic to *Mansfield Park*, appears in the character of Darcy, who is, like Knightley and Wentworth in their different ways, pre-eminently a man of "business."

If we keep this in mind, the meeting of Darcy and Mr. Gardiner at Pemberley, which results in Darcy's inviting the London businessman to fish in the Pemberley pond, exemplifies more than an act of *noblesse oblige*. Darcy recognizes that he and Gardiner are of a kind in their commitment to role and in their strict attention to the "business" aspects of their lives. It is significant that their visit, apparently so fortuitous, is thematically inevitable: Mr. Gardiner had been "prevented by *business*" (238) from taking a longer trip to the less accessible Lake District, and Darcy's return to Pemberley is a day earlier than expected on account of "*business* with his steward" (256). It is further significant, of course, that it is these two men of responsibility who together clear up the Lydia-Wickham mess. Mr. Bennet's "philosophic composure" (299) is revealed for the negative attitude it is in his total inability to deal with this affair. In contrast, Mr. Gardiner's actions, his letters to Longbourn, are a positive index to his character. When Elizabeth calls upon her father to bring Lydia to an awareness of the proper "*business* of her life" (231), she shows that she too has become, like Darcy and Gardiner, a person of responsibility. When her advice is ignored, and the news of Lydia's elopement is received by Elizabeth in Derbyshire, she is described as having her "share of *business*"; "there were notes to be written to all their friends in Lambton"

(281). Later, when Mr. Gardiner's letter announcing the discovery of the eloped pair is received in Longbourn, she calls on her father to "write immediately. Consider how important every moment is, in such a case" (303).

It is no accident that Elizabeth and Darcy should remain "on the most intimate terms" (388) with the Gardiners after their marriage. Elizabeth's journey to self-knowledge, which is also a knowledge of her social responsibility, permits the rapprochement prevented earlier by her prejudice. In effecting Elizabeth's marriage to Darcy, and in approving the friendship of Elizabeth and Darcy with the Gardiners, Jane Austen brings together what had been initially disparate. The three classes of her fictional world—nobility, gentry, and trade—come together finally in the park at Pemberley.

IN TRACING Elizabeth's acquisition of a social morality grounded in traditional ideas of conduct, and in pointing to the Burkean content of Darcy's "proper pride," I do not mean to suggest any passive or mechanical acceptance on Jane Austen's part of the given rightness of the social *status quo*. As I have already argued concerning *Mansfield Park*, society for Jane Austen is not absolutely constituted in accordance with some notion of the Natural Law (whatever Lady Catherine might avow), nor, in spite of the respect that is granted throughout her fiction to traditional usages, is it wholly sanctioned through an appeal to historically prescribed modes of thought and behavior. A properly constituted society, Jane Austen insists, emerges only from the interaction of cultural discipline and individual commitment, and only when inherited forms receive the support of individual energy do they carry value. Conversely, however (and this is where Elizabeth's education is important), individual energy must be generated within social contexts, for, lacking social direction and control, it turns too easily to withdrawal from society, or to irresponsibility and anarchy.

Several of the novel's recurring motifs might be examined to support these points, but none seems more appropriate to this "light and bright and sparkling" novel than the motif of laughter, an examination of which will serve the additional function of qualifying any suggestion that Darcy's social philosophy goes uncriticized in the novel.

Beginning with Darcy's opinion, expressed early in the novel, that Miss Bennet "smiled too much" (16), attitudes toward laughter divide the characters, as they provide a dialectic illustrative of the theme. Most obviously, Darcy, all "grave propriety" (26), is opposed to Elizabeth, who has a "lively, playful disposition, which delighted in any thing ridiculous" (12). We tend, perhaps, to consider Elizabeth's position normative, for modern theories of humor—Meredith's, Bergson's—have stressed the deflationary function of the laugh. One laughs at hypocrisy, vanity, pretension, the gap between statement and action, between theory and practice, and there are innumerable examples of this in the novel. Jane Austen is by no means averse to using the comic spirit as the sword of common sense. Yet in the eighteenth century, as she must have been aware, laughter was the subject of widespread debate. If on the one hand laughter was associated with the freedom which Englishmen had gained with the Glorious Revolution, on the other it was considered to be a sign of disharmony, of lack of restraint, and of chaos. When the third Earl of Shaftesbury in his "Essay on the Freedom of Wit and Humor" (1709) argued (or was credited with arguing) that "ridicule" was a test of truth, there were many who responded that certain matters (and especially, religion) should not be put to such a test.[15]

Clearly aware of this background, Jane Austen has Darcy take a conservative attitude toward laughter. His taciturn disposition and unwillingness to be the butt of mirth are clearly described. He tells those assembled in the Netherfield drawing room that "it has been the study of [his] life to avoid those weaknesses which often expose a strong understanding to ridicule" (57), and his attitude toward laughter places him in the company of, for example, Lord Chesterfield, who considered that "frequent and loud laughter is the charac-

[15] For an excellent survey of eighteenth century attitudes toward laughter, with particular application to Fielding, see Ronald Paulson, *Satire and the Novel in Eighteenth-Century England* (New Haven: Yale University Press, 1967), pp. 52–72. In "Shaftesbury and the Test of Truth," *PMLA*, 60 (March 1945), 129–56, A. O. Aldridge conclusively argues that not only did the Third Earl of Shaftesbury *not* use the phrase "ridicule as the test of truth" in the *Characteristics of Men, Manners, Opinions, Times*, but that the sense of his theory of laughter is contrary to such an interpretation: "Shaftesbury is not urging that ridicule be brought to bear against religion or anything else, but merely that there be freedom to use it." The quotations I later use from Shaftesbury suggest that he was aware of the possibly subversive nature of ridicule.

teristic of folly and ill manners," and who, in another letter to his son, advised: "Loud laughter is the mirth of the mob, who are only pleased with silly things; for true wit of good sense never excited a laugh, since the creation of the world. A man of parts and fashion is therefore only seen to smile, but never heard to laugh."[16] Darcy's aversion to laughter is more than a wish to appear as a man of parts, however. Like the man of zeal whom Shaftesbury views with some irony, Darcy seems to feel that "all Professions must fall to the ground, all Establishments come to ruin, and nothing orderly or decent be left standing in the world" if "Matters of Importance [are] treated with this frankness of Humour."[17] For him laughter is the disparagement of the good and the subversion of the established. He opposes any theory of laughter as corrective.

The deficiencies of this view, evident enough in Darcy's own demeanor, are revealed in the parodies of it which appear in the novel. Everywhere in *Pride and Prejudice*, pompous gravity is laughed out of existence. By absorbing didacticism into the absurdly formal utterances of a Mary Bennet or a Mr. Collins (neither of whom is ever known to laugh), Jane Austen demonstrates that the uncritical acceptance of precept and the literalistic observance of sanctioned moral attitudes may have effects the reverse of what the situation demands. We cannot forget Mr. Collins' vicious parody of the parable of the prodigal son in his letter of "consolation" to Mr. Bennet on news of Lydia's elopement: "Let me advise you . . . to console yourself as much as possible, to throw off your unworthy child from your affection for ever, and leave her to reap the fruits of her own heinous offence" (297). Nor can we be unaware of the total lack of feeling in Mary's formulaic response to the same event:

[16] Quotations from Chesterfield are, respectively, from *Letters to his Son*, Bath, 9 March O.S. 1748, and 19 October O.S. 1748; both quoted by Frank W. Bradbrook, *Jane Austen and Her Predecessors* (Cambridge: Cambridge University Press, 1966), p. 31. Bradbrook also notes the resemblance between Chesterfield's attitudes and those of Darcy.

[17] "Essay on the Freedom of Wit and Humour," in *Characteristics of Men, Manners, Opinions, Times*, 4th ed. (Dublin, 1743), pp. 74–75. All subsequent references will be to this edition and will be included parenthetically in the text. In using Shaftesbury as a gloss on Jane Austen's motif, I am not arguing for direct influence. As already stated, distrust of laughter and of wit is a common eighteenth century attitude; a more contemporary expression of this distrust is to be found, for example, in Thomas Gisborne's *An Enquiry into the Duties of the Female Sex* (London, 1797), pp. 108–10.

"we must stem the tide of malice, and pour into the wounded bosoms of each other, the balm of sisterly consolation" (289). The humor of these characters lies in their lack of humor, their failure in their unawareness of the claims of spontaneity in certain situations. They can produce, as if by rote, a prior "institutional" response, but they have no conception that circumstances sometimes alter cases. Mr. Collins admits to Mr. Bennet that he arranges beforehand "such little elegant compliments as may be adapted to ordinary occasions" (68), and it is clear that for him "ordinary occasions" are to be defined by the same kind of ceremonial ritual as a church service, or an introduction to the redoubtable Lady Catherine.[18]

Elizabeth's attitude toward experience is very different, as an early conversation (I, xi) makes sufficiently plain. She and Miss Bingley have formed a temporary alliance to poke fun at Darcy. He has shown his awareness of Miss Bingley's design in walking round the room—she is showing off her figure to the best advantage—and she in reply, asks Elizabeth, "How shall we punish him for such a speech?" Elizabeth suggests that they should "Teaze him—laugh at him" (57), but Miss Bingley, ever anxious to please Darcy, demurs:

"Teaze calmness of temper and presence of mind! No, no—I feel he may defy us there. And as to laughter, we will not expose ourselves, if you please, by attempting to laugh without a subject...."

"Mr. Darcy is not to be laughed at!" cried Elizabeth. "That is an uncommon advantage, and uncommon I hope it will continue, for it would be a great loss to *me* to have many such acquaintance. I dearly love a laugh." (57)

Elizabeth, like Lord Shaftesbury, is a defender of raillery as a means of proving the worth of a person or idea. "Truth 'tis suppos'd," says Shaftesbury, "may bear *all* Lights: and *one* of those principal Lights or natural Mediums, by which Things are to be view'd, in order to a thorow Recognition, is *Ridicule* it-self, or that Manner of Proof by which we discern whatever is liable to just Raillery in any Subject" (61). And when Darcy defends himself by pointing out that "the wisest and the best of men, nay, the wisest and best of their

---

[18] Mary Bennet and Collins are both described by Addison's definition of "pedant" (*Spectator* No. 105): one "that does not know how to think out of his profession, and particular way of life"; quoted by Paulson, *Satire and the Novel*, p. 62.

actions, may be rendered ridiculous by a person whose first object in life is a joke" (57), Elizabeth disassociates herself from the accusation: "Certainly," replied Elizabeth,—"there are such people, but I hope I am not one of *them*. I hope I never ridicule what is wise or good. Follies and nonsense, whims and inconsistencies *do* divert me, I own, and I laugh at them whenever I can" (57). Elizabeth would agree with the third earl that there is "a great difference between seeking how to raise a Laugh from every thing; and seeking, in every thing, what justly may be laugh'd at" (*Characteristics*, 128). She might indeed be echoing Shaftesbury's assertion that, "as I am earnest in defending Raillery, so I can be sober too in the Use of it" (*Characteristics*, 128), and she clearly seems to win this particular exchange. When Darcy somewhat pontifically distinguishes between pride and vanity, "Elizabeth turned away to hide a smile" (57). As Bergson knew, humor is the great deflator of men who act like machines.

Yet the motif is not confined to this scene, and in other appearances Elizabeth's point of view does not come off so well, as laughter becomes on occasions everything that the grave Darcy suggests it to be. Mr. Bennet, for example, employs his wit as a barely concealed misanthropy, as an assertion of superiority required by his sense of defeat: "For what do we live, but to make sport for our neighbours, and laugh at them in our turn?" (364) No less subversive is Lydia's laughter, however different her loud buffoonery is from her father's cool satire. Like Lord Chesterfield's "mirth of the mob," Lydia's laughter is excessive and silly, but beyond this, her immoderate mirth, like her lexical hyperboles ("Aye," "Lord"), her grammatical failures ("Kitty and me were to spend the day there" [221]), and her constant inattention to the decorum required of the occasion (as when she interrupts Mr. Collins in his reading of Fordyce), indicates a vulgarity and a selfishness which bid fair to subvert established forms.

A good gloss for Jane Austen's treatment of Lydia is discoverable in *The Covent-Garden Journal*, Nos. 55 and 56, where Fielding, taking a conservative position toward humor, disputes the view, argued by Congreve specifically, that the abundance of "Characters of Humour" in England is to be attributed to the "Liberty" that this country enjoys. Only if "Liberty" includes within its meaning "an Exemption from all Restraint of municipal Laws, but likewise from all Restraint of those Rules of Behaviour which are expressed in the general Term of good Breeding," Fielding argues, may it properly be associated with humor. And he goes on, in No. 56, to provide two reasons of his own for the abundance of humorous characters in England: "The first is that Method so general in this Kingdom of giving no Education to the Youth of both Sexes"; and the "second general Reason . . . seems to me to arise from the great Number of People, who are daily raised by Trade to the Rank of Gentry, without having had any Education at all."[19] In this context, Lydia's "wild volatility" (231) is attributable to both her parents: to her father, who has failed to educate her in the "Rules of Behaviour" (Elizabeth sees that he has not taken the "trouble of checking her exuberant spirits" [231]); and to her mother, who has become through her marriage a member of the gentry, but who again and again—to Elizabeth's mortification—shows she lacks entirely the "breeding" required by her new position.

Lydia's "exemption from all Restraint," in Fielding's phrase, becomes a focus of attention when she accompanies Elizabeth and Jane in the coach returning to Longbourn. As she informs Mary Bennet on arrival, "we were so merry all the way home! we talked and laughed so loud, that any body might have heard us ten miles off" (222). Further evidence of her indecorous conduct during the absence of her older sisters is revealed in her description of a "piece of fun" recently enjoyed at Colonel Forster's:

"We dressed up Chamberlayne in woman's clothes, on purpose to pass for a lady,—only think what fun! Not a soul knew of it, but Col. and Mrs. Forster, and Kitty and me, except my aunt, for we were forced to borrow one of her gowns; and you cannot imagine how well he looked! When Denny, and Wickham, and Pratt, and two or three more of the men came in, they did not know him in the least. Lord! how I laughed! and so did Mrs. Forster. I thought I should have died. And *that* made the men suspect something, and then they soon found out what was the matter." (221)

As Lydia takes evident delight in turning normal relations upside down, there is here, perhaps, an anticipation of the theatricality that is so suspect in *Mansfield Park.*

19 *The Covent-Garden Journal,* ed. Gerard E. Jensen (New Haven: Yale University Press, 1915) II, 59–69.

The disequilibrium that Lydia introduces into previously ordered structures is evident in her speech and manners long before she runs off with Wickham. But it is this assertion of her "liberty" that calls unfettered individualism into question and reveals Jane Austen taking a more conservative view of humor. In the letter that Lydia writes to Harriet Forster following her elopement, the laughter motif finds its culmination, as Lydia's determination to see everything without exception as hilarious gives every reason for viewing laughter with suspicion:

"You will laugh when you know where I am gone, and I cannot help laughing myself at your surprise tomorrow morning, as soon as I am missed. I am going to Gretna Green, and if you cannot guess with who, I shall think you a simpleton, for there is but one man in the world I love, and he is an angel. I should never be happy without him, so think it no harm to be off. You need not send them word at Longbourn of my going, if you do not like it, for it will make the surprise the greater, when I write to them, and sign my name Lydia Wickham. What a good joke it will be! I can hardly write for laughing. Pray make my excuses to Pratt, for not keeping my engagement. . . . I wish you would tell Sally to mend a great slit in my worked muslin gown, before they are packed up." (291–92)

The moral chaos of Lydia's character is here revealed in her choice of correspondent (not her family but her friend), in her motive for writing (not to dispel alarm, but to inspire admiration), and in the transparent inconsistency of her avowals (within a breath of her declared intention to love "but one man in the world," she expresses an interest in another). Linguistically, as usual, all is disorder, as grammatical errors and lexical hyperboles silently comment upon the enormity of Lydia's "scheme of infamy" (292). The Popean, if not Freudian, skill of the "great slit in my worked muslin gown" is obvious. Serious as her action is, however, Lydia has no sense of guilt. When she returns to Longbourn with Wickham, she is "Lydia still; untamed, unabashed, wild, noisy, and fearless" (315), and from the moment her "voice [is] heard in the vestibule . . . and she [runs] into the room," Elizabeth is disgusted by her attitude.[20]

---

[20] That Lydia is described as running into the room is also significant. Like laughter, running may be indecorous; young ladies do not, in general, run. Here, as elsewhere, Elizabeth can break the rule and get away with it, as when she rushes off to Netherfield in response to the news of her sister's illness. Neverthe-

But Lydia can only observe "with a laugh, that it was a great while since she had been there," and "Wickham was not at all more distressed than herself" (315).

It is clear that the basically worthy orientations of Darcy and Elizabeth, like those of Elinor and Marianne Dashwood, receive comment in the perverse parodies of them that the novel provides. Almost all the characters are illuminated by the laughter theme, which embraces a whole series of discriminations of humor—joke, piece of fun, playfulness, good humor, smile, wit, laughter, and so on—serving to distinguish decorous from indecorous action, moral from immoral motivations. In these descriptions, traditional—fundamentally classical—principles are operative; rules, including the due observation of the subject under discussion, the character of the speaker, the character of the audience, and the situation of the utterance, guide the reader to the degree of humor permissible in a given instance. Like Fielding, Jane Austen believes in "Rules of Good Breeding" (and especially in the "golden rule") and knows that when laughter or humor exceeds these rules it is to be censured.

In granting to Elizabeth an access to the significance of humor, Jane Austen reveals that her heroine has learned to make ethical discriminations separately from subjective desires, to distinguish between what is spontaneously permissible and what is immorally subversive. Her intrinsic accessibility to such a recognition is shown early, when she "checked her laugh" (51) on seeing that Darcy is really offended by Bingley's portrait of him as an "aweful object" (50) at Pemberley, and in a later conversation with Jane she shows that she has learned to view "wit" with some suspicion:

"And yet I meant to be uncommonly clever in taking so decided a dislike to him, without any reason. It is such a spur to one's genius, such an opening for wit to have a dislike of that kind. One may be continually abusive without saying any thing just; but one cannot be always laughing at a man without now and then stumbling on something witty." (225–26)

---

less, Lydia serves as a comment on the possible dangers of Elizabeth's impetuosity. The connection between running and impetuosity is humorously made when Collins gives his proposal "in form" to Elizabeth: "Before I am *run* away with by my feelings on this subject, perhaps it will be advisable for me to state my reasons for marrying" (105)—sentiments suspiciously close to Darcy's first proposal: "My feelings will not be repressed. You must allow me to tell you how ardently I admire and love you" (189).

She has come round practically to repeating Darcy's own view on the subject of wit. And when she is married to Darcy, she comes to regulate her laughter somewhat: "She remembered that he had yet to learn to be laught at" (371). Of course, Elizabeth does not subdue her playfulness entirely, nor is it thematically necessary that she should. She will continue to shock Darcy's passive and obedient sister by the "lively, sportive, manner" (387–88) in which she addresses Darcy, and she will distinguish herself from Jane in a letter to her aunt by writing, "she only smiles, I laugh" (383). And this is appropriate, for culture without life, like discipline without humor, is empty form. As Elizabeth brings judgment to her laughter, Darcy must learn to be laughed at, for Truth may indeed bear all lights.

THE LAUGHTER motif is a good example of how effortlessly Jane Austen is able to integrate her serious concern over the proper relation of the individual to society into a delicate fabric of description and dialogue. Humorless formality, on the social side, and both cynical withdrawal and excessive amusement, on the individual side, are extremes whose deleterious effects are made evident in the widening of separations between minds and between social groups. Jane Austen has advanced in this novel beyond the negative definitions of *Northanger Abbey* and beyond the inescapable didacticism of *Sense and Sensibility* in which wayward action and responsible reflection were largely divided between two heroines. Though certain critics have seen the novel as the celebration of the individual spirit, this is at best only half the story. The individual vision is inevitably partial, prone to relativistic impressionism, and in need of a social context. The special attraction of the novel is that it allows a vital personality herself to learn through retrospection the limitations of a private view. Elizabeth's final location within the park of Pemberley is also the self's limitation of its power to define its own essence, the heroine's recognition of moral and social limits within which she must live.

As Elizabeth enters the park, so what had been an enclosure opens to receive an infusion of individual energy. Though an admirable model of society, Pemberley, unlike Mansfield Park, is not a central focus, but a peripheral ideal to which Elizabeth moves. When Darcy leaves his ideal center and moves into the center of less perfect worlds—the assemblies of Meryton or the drawing rooms of Long-bourn—his deficiencies become apparent. If Elizabeth's movement is from personality to character, Darcy's movement is from *persona* to person. His strict attention to his station and its duties, admirable as it is, must yet allow access to the claims of spontaneity and relaxation, whilst remaining vigilantly opposed to the social and ethical subversion of both unbridled freedom and passive indolence. If Elizabeth—to put it in the scenic terms of the novel—is out of place with muddy petticoats in the Netherfield drawing room, Darcy is equally "out of his element in a Ball-room."[21] When he wishes to introduce responsibility and tradition there by asking Elizabeth what she thinks of books, he is to be told, "I cannot talk of books in a ball-room" (93). There are still spaces for spontaneity in the world of *Pride and Prejudice.*

Just as Elizabeth's admirable individualism is reflected in the less admirable attitudes of a number of other characters, so Darcy's pride, however proper it is, is parodied in other versions and per-versions of the characteristic. The improper social pride exempli-fied by Lady Catherine, Mr. Collins, Miss Bingley; the pedantic pride in erudition displayed by Mary Bennet; the "courteous" in-anity of Sir William Lucas—all these unreflectingly consider prece-dent automatically to confer value, and if they are mainly significant for the ways in which they are distinct from Darcy's attitudes, they nevertheless provide a warning of what might happen if Darcy were to move in the direction of their extreme interpretations of social imperatives. Though the possibility of Darcy and Elizabeth becom-ing their genetic extremes (Lady Catherine and either Mr. Bennet or Lydia) seems remote, the novel provides certain plausible matri-monial solutions which would effect such a possibility. Were Darcy to marry either Miss Bingley or the sickly daughter of Lady Cather-ine, Pemberley would become an enclosed world of social and finan-cial privilege. On the other hand, were Elizabeth to marry Wickham or Colonel Fitzwilliam (Mr. Collins, given Elizabeth's character, is never a possibility), then constant change and movement, in the

21 This quotation actually describes Lord Osborne in *The Watsons* (*MW*, 329), a character in some respects like Darcy.

absence of money and place, must ensue. (As it is, Wickham and Lydia are "always moving from place to place in quest of a cheap situation" [387].)

The novel is structurally balanced between the basic orientations of the two principals. The central chapters of Darcy's proposal and letter reveal that Elizabeth's objections to him are dual: he has ruined the happiness of her sister by his influence over Bingley, and he has been unjust to Wickham. If, as we have seen, Elizabeth's acceptance of Wickham's charges seriously called into question her personalist ethic, her first accusation is more valid. Darcy's prudent and social point of departure has led him to be blind to the real love that exists between Bingley and Jane. The best solution, clearly, is neither society alone, nor self alone, but self-in-society, the vitalized reconstitution of a social totality, the dynamic compromise between past and present, the simultaneous reception of what is valuable in an inheritance and the liberation of the originality, energy and spontaneity in the living moment. *Pride and Prejudice* is no contradiction of the meaning of *Mansfield Park*. Elizabeth is no Mary Crawford at the end, though she may have resembled her at the beginning. She has moved from individualism to a sense of social identity (as Mary Crawford never does), and though Pemberley is "improved" by Elizabeth's marriage to Darcy, the alteration cannot be radical, for the "disposition of its ground" is already good.

Recognizing (in "A Letter to William Elliot, Esq." [1795]) that authority needs "other support than the poise of its own gravity," Burke might be describing the characteristic limitation of Fitzwilliam Darcy. In calling "the impulses of individuals at once to the aid and control of authority," he might be describing Elizabeth's movement in the novel.[22] And in a passage from the *Reflections* that I have used as an epigraph, we may discover the thesis and antithesis of *Pride and Prejudice*. Burke requires as qualities of his ideal statesman a "disposition to preserve and an ability to improve" (*R*, 193–94), and it is exactly these requirements which are united in the marriage of Darcy and Elizabeth. Darcy's is the disposition to preserve, Elizabeth's the ability to improve, and taken together they achieve a synthesis which is not only (as Elizabeth recognizes) a "union ... to the advantage of both" (312) but a guarantee of a broader union

---

[22] *The Works of Edmund Burke* (London: George Bell, 1906), V, 77, 79–80.

in the fictional world of the novel. By crossing the "gulf impassable" (311), Elizabeth and Darcy provide a fixed moral and social center around which the other marriages group themselves. The Collinses —all prudence—and the Bingleys—all benevolence—will remain; ruling passions will continue to prevail in the Longbourn drawing room and at Lucas Lodge; the Wickhams will continue to move from place to place; relativism and perspectivism will not miraculously vanish from the Meryton community. All these faults, however, are but the surface discontinuities of a ground that is, by the marriage of Elizabeth and Darcy, substantial and well disposed.

CHAPTER 4

Emma
AND THE DANGERS
OF INDIVIDUALISM

The sense of isolation, followed by the sense of menace and of fear, is bound to arise as the feeling of oneness and community with our fellow men declines, and the feeling of individualism and personality, which is existence in isolation, increases. The so-called "cultured" classes are the first to develop "personality" and individualism, and the first to fall into this state of unconscious menace and fear.

D. H. Lawrence, *A Propos of "Lady Chatterley's Lover"*

Nothing can more clearly follow than the manifest Repugnancy between Humour and good Breeding. The latter being the Art of conducting yourself by certain common and general Rules, by which Means, if they were universally observed, the whole World would appear (as all Courtiers actually do) to be, in their external Behaviour at least, but one and the same Person.

Henry Fielding, *The Covent-Garden Journal*, No. 55

CERTAIN CRITICS have called into question the social and moral significance of *Emma*. Arnold Kettle, while granting to the novel the power of extending "human sympathy and understanding," has asked us to consider whether Jane Austen's vision is not limited by her "unquestioning acceptance of class society"; and Graham Hough has not only stressed the importance of certain extra-moral elements in the novel but has also, somewhat gratuitously, deprecated the quality of Jane Austen's moral vision. Against this tendency one may set the opinions of other readers who conceive of *Emma*, not necessarily as a "Christian-existentialist introduction to the devout life" (the phrase is Hough's), but as a novel treating the most serious of themes. Lionel Trilling, for example, has considered Emma's snobbery to be of "nothing less than national import"; and in the essay which inspired Hough's polemic response, Malcolm Bradbury has argued that, after reading *Emma,* "we have been persuaded . . . to see the full human being as . . . fine, morally serious, totally responsible, entirely involved, and to consider every human action as a crucial, committing act of self-definition."[1]

[1] Quotations in the first paragraph are from Arnold Kettle, *An Introduction to the English Novel* (rev. ed., 1967; rpt. New York: Harper and Row, 1968), pp. 90, 93; Graham Hough, *The Dream and the Task* (New York: W. W. Norton, 1964), p. 45; Lionel Trilling, *Beyond Culture* (New York: Viking Press, 1968), p. 40; Malcolm Bradbury, "Jane Austen's *Emma,*" *Critical Quarterly*, 4 (Winter 1962), 345–46. Hough's interpretation, entitled "Morality and the Novel," was first published in *The Listener*, 69 (1963), 747–48; Trilling's essay, entitled "*Emma* and the Legend of Jane Austen," was first written as the introduction to the Riverside edition of *Emma* (Boston: Houghton Mifflin, 1957). Kettle's view of *Emma* will be discussed later in this chapter. Hough's reading, to the extent that it brings into prominence the "dense atmosphere of the contingent, the small-scale, and the ludicrous" (p. 46) in *Emma*, has had perhaps a salutary effect: critics may well have been so concerned, in his words, to "distil the pure moral elixir" from the "particularized texture" (pp. 46–47) of the novel that they have missed an important—though, I think, still secondary—dimension of the work. But when Hough goes on to characterize Jane Austen's ethic as an "English middle-class version of Christian morals—Christian morals with all the heroism, all the asceticism, all the *contemptus mundi* left out" (p. 47), he is arguing for effect. Cf., at any rate, his different recognition of a "firm and extensive culture" lying behind Jane Austen's novels, in his review of Frank Bradbrook's *Jane Austen and Her Predecessors* (*The Listener*, 76 [1966], 27).

As my choice of epigraphs may suggest, I am on the side of those who consider *Emma* as a novel of high seriousness. Following closely on the heels of *Mansfield Park* (*Emma* was published in December, 1815), the novel is not the "throwing off of chains" it has been considered.[2] Indeed, it may be argued that *Emma* does not so much describe a different moral world from *Mansfield Park* as mix the same basic ingredients in different proportions in order to test further fictional possibilities. In some respects, for example, Emma bears resemblance to the vivacious Mary Crawford; she is a Mary made central and stationary, and to whose mind, significantly, we are granted access. As for the socially deprived female we have been accustomed to encounter in the previous fiction, she is not absent from *Emma*, merely displaced and dispersed among four secondary candidates: Jane Fairfax, Miss Bates, Harriet Smith, and (before her marriage) Mrs. Weston. But the most telling comparison between the two novels, we will see, is thematic, the central opposition between "house" and "theatre" in *Mansfield Park* reappearing as an opposition between "culture" and "games" in *Emma*.

In *Mansfield Park* Jane Austen had first broken free from the thematic dualisms inherited from eighteenth century fiction. No longer pushed toward effecting some mode of reconciliation between opposed terms—sense and sensibility, society and the self—she had chosen for special focus in this novel the social structure itself as this was symbolically represented in the estate. She had described the imperative need for preserving and, where necessary, improving a cultural inheritance, and had set the subdued but morally determined character of Fanny Price against the superficial and destructive vitality of the Crawfords. Against this background *Emma*'s special focus is clear. If *Mansfield Park* addresses itself to the subject of a culture endangered by excessive individualism, *Emma* focuses on the individual self as it becomes a conceivable threat to culture, the titles of the two novels thus being accurate predictions of their thematic directions. Given the prominence of her social position, as well as her greater powers of imagination, Emma is a greater social danger than Elizabeth Bennet, with whom she shares certain characteristics. For this reason, the novel, like

[2] See Marvin Mudrick, *Jane Austen: Irony as Defense and Discovery* (Princeton: Princeton University Press, 1952), p. 181.

Mansfield Park, is not dialectical, if by this we require equal and mutual concessions from hero and heroine. In spite of recent criticism, and apart from occasional jealousy, Knightley remains the normative and exemplary figure he has traditionally been considered, while Emma, with all her attractive qualities of wit and vitality, is the character whose education we observe. As in *Mansfield Park,* however, the most serious threat to the social world of *Emma* comes from outside, the place of Henry Crawford, the actor and improver, being taken by Frank Churchill. From Churchill's arrival until the end of the novel Emma is faced with the choice of two directions, Churchill and Knightley, and the choice she comes to from the depths of her true self is as crucial as that made by Edmund Bertram in *Mansfield Park* when faced with the matrimonial possibilities of Mary Crawford and Fanny Price. Like Edmund, Emma in the end chooses society rather than self, an inherited order rather than a spontaneous and improvised existence.

As many critics have noted, the setting of *Emma* is carefully chosen. Like Henry James, Jane Austen is interested in the problem of human freedom. What consequences will ensue, she asks, if, instead of describing a heroine in a position of insecurity as to her social place, I postulate an heiress as my central figure and give her complete freedom of action? Like Isabel Archer in *The Portrait of a Lady* after Ralph Touchett's legacy of £70,000, Emma is condemned to be free, as if by fictional fiat. "Handsome, clever, and rich" (5)—her inheritance of £30,000 makes her a *bona fide* heiress in Jane Austen's financial scale—she differs from all previous Austen heroines in having no sense of insecurity, social or otherwise. At the center of a world apparently unendangered by any possibility of discontinuity, Emma's boundaries are where she wishes to place them.

The origins of Emma's subjectivism are therefore not so much Quixotic as familial.[3] Her father is a senescent valetudinarian whose debility carries to an extreme the parental ineffectiveness that may be traced through the complacency of the Morland parents, the cynicism of Mr. Bennet, and the educational misconceptions of Sir Thomas Bertram. By his abrogation of all parental function—

---

[3] For a reading of *Emma* placing it in the tradition of the "female Quixote" novels of Eaton Stannard Barrett and Charlotte Lennox, see Kenneth L. Moler's chapter in *Jane Austen's Art of Allusion* (Lincoln: University of Nebraska Press, 1968).

indeed by his lack of any evidence of masculinity—he has re-
linquished effective power over Hartfield to Emma. His stipulation
against taking his position "at the bottom of the table" (291) at the
Hartfield dinner party for the Eltons is an index of his withdrawal
from social and domestic responsibility. His only assertions are
negatives: he wishes people would not marry, would not go out in
the rain, would not overindulge in their eating; and his remedies
are that everyone should stay single, remain beside their home fire-
sides, and follow his own weak diet of thin gruel. Certainly, as
Trilling has warned, it would be wrong to read Mr. Woodhouse's
character too harshly. At least as important as his old-maidishness is
his function as the recipient of Emma's piety.[4] That she consistently
honors her father is a major reason for our never losing faith in her
fundamental goodness. Nevertheless her father's weakness is what
permits Emma to assume unusual domestic power, so that when the
"shadow" of Miss Taylor's authority leaves Hartfield, Emma's situation is one in which the "power of having rather too much her own
way, and a disposition to think a little too well of herself" constitute, as the narrator explicitly says, "real evils" (5).

The evils of Emma's imagination resemble, but go beyond, those
of Catherine Morland at Northanger. Like the "Gothic" heroine,
Emma's intuitions are never wholly wrong. Indeed her snobbish
dismissal of Mrs. Elton before she even sees her turns out to be a
remarkably accurate prediction of her character, and Jane Fairfax
does after all have a secret motive for coming to Highbury. As in
Catherine's case, however, there is a difference between the sympathetic intuition of a truth and its exact intellectual formulation.
Undisciplined by the rational faculty, the imagination may quickly
distort the real nature of a situation. Emma's "genius for foretelling
and guessing" (38) may occasionally be a "poet's demand" that life
be made more colorful than it is, but this faculty leads her into
increasingly more serious misconceptions, as in each of the three
movements of the novel she attempts not only to judge but to
define her world from a center of self.[5] First she attempts to match
Harriet Smith with Mr. Elton, only to find the Highbury vicar

4 Trilling, *"Emma,"* in *Beyond Culture*, p. 48.
5 The quoted phrase is Trilling's, *ibid.,* p. 45. For a reading of "the significance and the consequences . . . of Emma's endeavor to force an aesthetic ideal
upon her world," see David Lee Minter, "Aesthetic Vision and the World of
Emma," Nineteenth-Century Fiction, 21 (June 1966), 49–59.

proposing to her instead. Then she considers Frank Churchill as a husband for Harriet, only to discover that he is secretly engaged to Jane Fairfax. Finally she discovers to her horror that she has been unwittingly promoting a match between her friend and the man she herself wishes to marry.[6]

In these increasingly serious "errors of the imagination" (343), Emma does more than endanger her own happiness and that of her circle of friends. Beyond the personal, her imaginative errors have social and even epistemological implications; initially humorous, they become, especially after the arrival of Churchill and his games, "total violations of a whole worthwhile universe."[7]

EMMA'S POSITION as "first in consequence" (7) in Highbury entails a certain social responsibility, and it is in her social arrogance that she most nearly merits the dislike that Jane Austen expected her to elicit from her readers. Though she is described as fulfilling her charitable obligations to the poor (I, x), there is a suspicion that this task is done without a sincere sense of obligation. Certainly, when she is not able to patronize her inferiors, as in the case of the Martins, she exhibits an unlikable snobbery:

"The yeomanry are precisely the order of people with whom I feel I can have nothing to do. A degree or two lower, and a creditable appearance might interest me; I might hope to be useful to their families in some way or other. But a farmer can need none of my help, and is therefore in one sense as much above my notice as in every other he is below it." (29)

Part of her animus here is occasioned by her wish to turn Harriet's thoughts from Robert Martin to Mr. Elton, but even after the Highbury vicar spoils her scheme by having "the arrogance to raise his eyes to her" (135) rather than to Harriet, Emma's snobbery is not cured, however much she seems to learn about the errors of the imagination. Toward the end of the first volume she realizes that

---

6 Perhaps the best structural analyses of *Emma* are Edgar F. Shannon's "*Emma*: Character and Construction," *PMLA*, 71 (Sept. 1956), 637–50, and Joseph M. Duffy's "*Emma*: The Awakening from Innocence," *ELH*, 21 (March 1954), 39–53.

7 Bradbury, "Jane Austen's *Emma*," p. 345.

she has "taken up the idea . . . and made every thing bend to it" (134), that she has been "adventuring too far" (137), and she comes to a resolution of "repressing imagination all the rest of her life" (142). Significantly, however, she feels no contrition over her decision to dissuade Harriet from accepting Robert Martin: "There I was quite right. That was well done of me" (137).

As Trilling has argued, Emma's dismissal of Robert Martin has important implications. The industrious tenant farmer is as significant a figure in *Emma* as Mr. Gardiner is in *Pride and Prejudice*. Status alone, as her father most clearly shows, is not enough. Social position must be informed by personal worth, and as Emma expresses her unwillingness to have anything to do with the Martins, whom she considers on one occasion "another set of beings" (27), she aligns herself with those other characters in Jane Austen's novels —Lady Catherine, General Tilney, Mrs. Ferrars, the Bertram sisters, and others—who wish to retain rank as privilege, money as an assertion of exclusiveness. *Emma* is filled with descriptions of social separations, of "first sets" and "second sets" (I, iii), of "the second rate and third rate" (II, i), of those families who move in the "first circle" and those who do not (II, xvii), but it would be to repeat D. H. Lawrence's error if one were to consider that Jane Austen condoned these separations.[8] Such a vocabulary of separation is mediated through the words or thoughts of Emma, or through that parody of Emma, Mrs. Elton, for whose unwelcome entrance into the Highbury scene Emma must herself take a large part of the blame. The snobbery, that is, belongs to the character and not to the author, whose concern in *Emma* is to heal through her art the social gaps described and to reconstitute a sense of community.[9]

D. H. Lawrence's remarks in *A Propos of "Lady Chatterley's*

[8] Lawrence's attack on Jane Austen, shortly to be quoted, occurs in *A Propos of "Lady Chatterley's Lover,"* in *Sex, Literature, and Censorship,* ed. Harry T. Moore (New York: Viking Press, 1959), p. 109. It should be added that Lawrence was not always so severe with Jane Austen. In the chapter titled "A Chair" in *Women in Love,* Rupert Birkin grants Ursula's charge that Jane Austen's England was materialistic but goes on to insist that it "had the power to be something other." Just prior to this, Birkin claims that Jane Austen's England "had living thoughts to unfold . . . and pure happiness in unfolding them."

[9] Cf. Edgar F. Shannon: "In the other major novels, Jane Austen has portrayed her heroines as victims of snobbery. In *Emma,* she has undertaken the much more difficult task of incorporating and correcting snobbery within the character of the heroine herself" ("Character and Construction," p. 644).

Lover" have always seemed to me, in this context, to be curiously misapplied. Take away his terminology of "blood connection" and "phallic consciousness" and his concern is not distant from Jane Austen's own, as the Lawrentian epigraph to this chapter may suggest. There Lawrence laments the loss of "togetherness" and the rise of individualism in modern English society; but shortly after this passage he goes on to write one of the most vicious attacks on Jane Austen in existence:

> This . . . is the tragedy of social life today. In the old England, the curious blood-connection held the classes together. The squires might be arrogant, violent, bullying, and unjust, yet in some ways they were *at one* with the people, part of the same blood-stream. We feel it in Defoe or Fielding. And then, in the mean Jane Austen, it is gone. Already this old maid typifies "personality" instead of character, the sharp knowing in apartness instead of knowing in togetherness, and she is, to my feeling, thoroughly unpleasant, English in the bad, mean, snobbish sense of the word. . . .

Yet with how little change can these remarks be made properly applicable to *Emma*. Lawrence has confused authorial identity with dramatic presentation. Had he argued that Jane Austen dramatically represents "personality" and "the sharp knowing in apartness"—had he accused the character Mrs. Elton of being "English in the bad, mean, snobbish sense of the word"—then, surely, we could have agreed with him. Certainly, as I shall argue later, Lawrence's description of social fragmentation seems precisely to describe the state of affairs at Box Hill, where we do indeed encounter "hostile groupings . . . for the sake of opposition, strife." But this is a social condition, possible certainly, which Jane Austen deplores.[10]

It is, of course, difficult to prove precisely when such an elusive concept as "class consciousness" came into being, but if with Lawrence and Raymond Williams one accepts the beginning of the nineteenth century as roughly the date, it is perfectly feasible to cite Jane Austen's fiction as supporting evidence.[11] *Emma* is "about" the relatively new phenomenon of class consciousness, as Emma's description of the Martins, quoted above, and Mrs. Elton's comments

[10] Lawrence, *Sex, Literature and Censorship*, p. 109.
[11] See Williams, *Culture and Society: 1780–1950* (London: Chatto & Windus, 1958), esp. the introduction, for a consideration of such terms as "class," "class prejudice," and "class consciousness."

passim, would indicate. But it needs to be repeated that Jane Austen shares Lawrence's concern over the rise of "personality" and snobbery, dramatizing these traits in Mrs. Elton and for a time in Emma, no less effectively than Lawrence represents the inhumanity of capitalism in Gerald Crich.

Contrary to Arnold Kettle's contention, therefore, Jane Austen did "notice the existence of the problem of class division," though one has still to face the charge he raises that her "standards" are "inseparably linked with a particular form of social organization."[12] Kettle's argument is not easy to answer, since his chapter, despite its reservations, is a genuine appreciation of the novel, and he has taken care to anticipate opposition. One can take exception to some of the readings of particular scenes with which he supports his thesis (of Emma's view of property qualifications,[13] for example, or of the inadequacy of her charity[14]), and one can object to a certain looseness of sociological terminology,[15] but the main charge merits a more direct answer. One has, I think, to question whether his critical requirements are reasonable. When he writes, for example, that "the true elegance which Emma so values could not exist in Hartfield without the condemnation to servility and poverty of hundreds of unnamed (though not necessarily unpitied) human

---

[12] Kettle, *English Novel,* p. 94. Future page references will be made in the text of the chapter.

[13] Kettle often seems to miss the wood for the trees. Thus, though we may accept that Emma has "an attitude to marriage typical of the ruling class" and "sees human relationships in terms of property qualifications," it is surely weak support of these statements to argue that "her chief concern about Mr. Knightley is that his estate should be preserved for little Henry" (*ibid.,* p. 90). Her chief concern—did she but know herself—is that Donwell Abbey be preserved for herself! Moreover, when she comes, under Knightley's influence, to a "more critical and more fully human view," is she not being educated to a more *social* view also? Knightley represents Jane Austen's ideal social responses throughout the novel.

[14] Here again I differ from Kettle. Emma's too quick transition from pious concern for the Highbury poor to renewed interest in the Harriet-Elton scheme on the latter's sudden appearance on the scene (I, x) is not a shelving of the "essential moral issue" (*ibid.,* p. 97); rather it is another indication of Emma's lack of consistency and real sense of obligation. In trying to shift from Emma's psychology to a consideration of the social inequities of Highbury, Kettle is forcing his thesis.

[15] As Avrom Fleishman has done in *A Reading of "Mansfield Park": An Essay in Critical Synthesis* (Minneapolis: University of Minnesota Press, 1967), pp. 14–15.

beings" (p. 95), the Marxist assumption is surely prescriptive. One need not be among those "who think aristocracy today a morally defensible form of society" (p. 94) to accept as authentic Jane Austen's affirmation of traditional social values. Nor need one exhibit a narrow historicism if one entertains doubts as to Jane Austen's capability—given her social environment and predilections —of ever espousing the socialist ethic Kettle seems to require. The logic of his argument, indeed, has curious repercussions if one carries it backwards to authors who exist in even more indubitably hierarchical societies than Jane Austen: is one to consider Chaucer's "Knight's Tale" inadequate because its moral values are inseparably linked with an outdated cosmological scheme and view of divine providence? Is Pope's "Epistle to Bathurst" vitiated because it embodies the untenable doctrine of *concordia discors*? Or is it only in post-French Revolutionary literature, where other, perhaps Godwinian, possibilities are available to an author that one is to question his social and moral outlook?

Kettle would perhaps argue the latter case, for what he particularly values, it seems, are those parts of the novel which suggest that all is not well in the social world of Jane Austen's England: "[*Emma*] gives us glimpses of something Mr. Woodhouse never dreamed of—the world outside the Highbury world and yet inseparably bound up with it: the world Jane Fairfax saw in her vision of offices and into which Harriet in spite of (no, *because of*) Emma's patronage, was so nearly plunged: the world for which Jane Austen had no answer" (p. 98). The question here is one of emphasis: are we to pay more attention to what Kettle calls "the dark side of the moon" in *Emma*—to Jane Fairfax's dependent situation and the hypothetical horrors outside of Highbury—than to Emma's own problems? I think not, though Kettle's point about Jane Austen's concern for the fate of women in her society is better taken than his criticism of her "unquestioning acceptance of class society." As I have argued in previous chapters, the predicament of the unsupported woman was never far from Jane Austen's thoughts. The "degradation" of the Dashwoods in *Sense and Sensibility*, Fanny Price's stay at Portsmouth, Jane Fairfax's dependent situation, all exist on the periphery of Jane Austen's vision as they exist in the backgrounds of her novels as problems to be solved. They are not the *subject* of these novels, and it would be wrong to suggest that Jane Austen was evading the problem or somehow failing to write of a world for which she had no answer. At the end of her life, in *Persuasion*, she describes a "world outside the Highbury world," and reaches an answer. It is an answer which might not satisfy Kettle, since it puts faith in a Christian stoicism in face of adversity, but it is, as I shall argue in the next chapter, an honestly arrived at and estimable answer.

While *Emma* takes into account the predicament of the socially reduced self—"ours is rather a dark staircase" (239), says Miss Bates, as usual telling us more than she knows—it is more centrally concerned with the social obligations of those in positions of authority. This is why the tensest moment of the novel, the perigee of Emma's moral journey, occurs when Emma insults Miss Bates on Box Hill. Without a sense of social responsibility on the part of the privileged, there is a very real danger of society becoming what Lawrence describes; properly informed by individual commitment, however, society for Jane Austen in *Emma* is a structure to be quite uncomplacently affirmed.

The point is clear even as Emma's snobbery bids fair to obscure it, for against her attitudes the exemplary conduct of Knightley is set. As Emma's undisciplined imagination permits her to confer on Harriet an illusory parentage and fictional status, Knightley's "thorough regard" for Robert Martin and his family (59) evidences his respect, as it predicts the rise of the tenant farmer. Knightley and Martin together, indeed, offer instructive contrast to Emma and Harriet. Whereas Martin reads the Agricultural Reports, Harriet has only read "the Romance of the Forest" and "the Children of the Abbey" (29). Whereas he writes a letter which Emma is forced to admit "as a composition . . . would not have disgraced a gentleman" (51), Harriet's education—or lack of it—is revealed in her ugly grammar, even as she denies that "Mr. Martin would ever marry any body but what had had some education" (31). Emma's intelligence and education of course far exceed Harriet's, but, as with Elizabeth Bennet's piano playing, application is lacking. Unlike Knightley, who, when at home "is either reading to himself or settling his accounts" (312), Emma is not to be expected to pursue a "course of steady reading" (37).

Knightley is another of Jane Austen's "professionals," and the most convincing of them. Like Robert Martin, he is always at work, "busy" around the estate or in Highbury. Fully aware of the responsibilities which his position entails, "with his farm, and his sheep, and his library, and all the parish to manage" (225), Knightley has little time for leisure. What Darcy may reliably be imagined to do, Knightley is constantly described as doing. Darcy retains much of the air of an eighteenth century landowner, and when he speaks most feelingly of his landed responsibility it is to his library that he naturally refers. Knightley, too, has a library, but he also has a farm, and we can imagine him as an heir of Coke and Townsend more easily than we can Darcy. Aware, like Darcy, that his is an office of trust, Knightley is given more opportunity in this novel to demonstrate his social responsibility in words and actions. Thus, when his brother comes on a Christmas visit, the conversation is sure to be of a "business" nature:

> As a magistrate, he had generally some point of law to consult John about, or, at least, some curious anecdote to give; and as a farmer, as keeping in hand the home-farm at Donwell, he had to tell what every field was to bear next year.... The plan of a drain, the change of a fence, the felling of a tree, and the destination of every acre for wheat, turnips, or spring corn, was entered into with as much equality of interest by John.... (100)

Later, at the Coles's, and doubtless initiated by Knightley, the after-dinner talk is "over parish business" (221).

Knightley's name is well and intentionally chosen, for not only does he continually bring into the daily life of Highbury the spirit of chivalry—providing his coach as transport for Miss Bates whenever she needs it, and not, as the Eltons do on the occasion of the ball at the Crown, promising to provide it and then forgetting—but more importantly he exemplifies the kind of behavior Jane Austen considers necessary for the maintenance of a morally founded society. Until Emma comes to realize the values and importance of such behavior, she will remain a danger to the social community in which she plays such a prominent part.

IF THE social evils of Emma's individualism are in primary evidence, the novel goes more than a little way toward suggesting that part of Emma's problem is epistemological, that she is a victim of subjective idealism. Her relations with others typically reveal an egoism that goes beyond a social or moral selfishness to suggest a consciousness unaware of the real existence of others. Like a later novel heroine, Emma fails to grant to the other in a relationship "an equivalent centre of self."[16] This aspect of the novel merits attention, for Emma's subjectivism compounds the potential evil of her social attitudes and, with the arrival of Churchill on the scene, finds insidious company.

At the end of the novel Emma will herself come to formulate the error of her mode of relating to others; she has, she sees, "with unpardonable arrogance proposed to arrange everybody's destiny" (413); she has attempted nothing less than a god role. This role is already latent in her early relationship with Harriet. Though she is "not struck by any thing remarkably clever in Miss Smith's conversation" (23), Emma finds her "altogether very engaging": "not inconveniently shy, not unwilling to talk—and yet so far from pushing, shewing so proper and becoming a deference, seeming so pleasantly grateful for being admitted to Hartfield, and so artlessly impressed by the appearance of every thing in so superior a style to what she had been used to, that she must have good sense and deserve encouragement" (23). But the "good sense" which Harriet exhibits is not so much the property of Harriet as of Emma's perception of Harriet, and even in this first description of Mrs. Goddard's boarder, it is her deficiencies rather than her qualities of which we are made aware.

Emma's view of Harriet is comparable to the subjective speculation of Henry Crawford, who, imaginatively planning to improve Thornton Lacey, "saw how it might all be" (*MP*, 242). As Crawford wishes to improve an estate (or the delivery of a sermon), so Emma wishes to improve Harriet. "*She* would notice her; she would improve her; she would detach her from her bad acquaintance, and introduce her into good society; she would form her opinions and her manners. It would be an interesting, and certainly a very kind undertaking; highly becoming her own situation in life, her leisure, and powers" (23–24). Harriet is to become a mode of Emma's activity, a psychic extension of Emma's self.[17]

Only with the entrance of Mrs. Elton in the second volume are the evils of Emma's patronage fully realized. As wife of the High-

16 George Eliot's phrase, describing the egoism of Dorothea in her relationship with Casaubon in *Middlemarch*, chap. 21 (end).

17 The most perceptive and incisive account of Emma's "will-to-power" is contained in Marvin Mudrick, *Jane Austen: Irony as Defense and Discovery*, pp. 181–206.

bury vicar, she takes precedence over Emma though she has only
£10,000 and, in Emma's words, brings "no name, no blood, no alliance" (183) into Highbury. At the ball at the Crown, "Emma must
submit to stand second to Mrs. Elton. . . . It was almost enough to
make her think of marrying" (325). With her *nouveau riche* snobbery, Mrs. E. (as her husband doubtless came to call her) is a more
subtle form of the parody of the heroine first illustrated in *Sense
and Sensibility* and *Pride and Prejudice.* Jane Austen's intention is
clearly to repeat certain of Emma's characteristics in a manifestly
inferior personality and thus to expose them. As Emma in the
first volume had patronized Harriet Smith, so for much of the rest
of the novel Mrs. Elton patronizes Jane Fairfax. She does not, as
Emma did, try to find a husband for her protégée, but her attempt
to force on Jane a "situation" with some of her "respectable" friends
is no less noxious, and in spite of Emma's hint that "those who have
known her longer than yourself" (283) are the ones who should help
Jane, Mrs. Elton, with magnificent imperiousness, pre-empts the
office. Her vulgarity and lack of breeding are as obvious to us as
they are to Emma, of course, and when her patronage of "Knightley" (as she immediately begins to call him) sends Emma into an
ecstasy of indignation, we feel as Emma does (279). Still, the point is
made to the reader, if not to Emma, that patronage may all too
easily become an egoistical praise of the self rather than the selfless
act it purports to be.[18]

Not surprisingly in view of her wish to improve reality, Emma is
an artist. She considers Harriet, with "all the natural grace of
sweetness of temper and artlessness" (42), as a kind of unimproved
nature in need of the hand of the designer. She only needs "drawing
out" (42), and when Mr. Elton seconds her wish to make a "likeness" (43) of Harriet, Emma is all too pleased to concur:

There was no want of likeness, she had been fortunate in the attitude,
and as she meant to throw in a little improvement to the figure, to give a
little more height, and considerably more elegance, she had great confidence of its being in every way a pretty drawing at last, and of its filling
its destined place with credit to them both—a standing memorial of the

[18] In my remarks concerning Mrs. Elton's function as a parody of Emma, I am
indebted to Mudrick. As he sees, Mrs. Elton is "Emma's true companion in
motive." *Ibid.*, p. 194.

beauty of one, the skill of the other, and the friendship of both; with as many other agreeable associations as Mr. Elton's very promising attachment was likely to add. (47)

Reminiscent of Crawford's plans for Thornton Lacey as this scene is, it also objectifies one of several triangular relationships set up by Emma in the novel. In these groupings, Emma is able (as she thinks) not only to bring together two people in a little world of her own creation, but also to participate vicariously in the relationship she has created. Here, her "skill" will "improve" Harriet's beauty so that Mr. Elton's "very promising attachment" may be consummated. But Emma's triangles have a way of coming out differently from what she expects. Sitting at the apical point, she is soon to be surprised when one of the bases of her construction, instead of closing the gap to the other base, turns his eyes in her direction, and makes out of what had been a vicarious experience an actuality: returning in the carriage from the Christmas party at Randalls, "she found . . . her hand seized—her attention demanded, and Mr. Elton actually making violent love to her" (129).

Emma has of course no excuse for her impercipience. Even before she had sketched Harriet's picture, Elton's "perception of the striking improvement of Harriet's manner" (42) had been praise of the improver and not of the material. "Skilful has been the hand," he tells Emma (43). Additionally, she has been told by Mr. Knightley that Elton is not "at all likely to make an imprudent match" (66), and by his sagacious, professional brother that she herself is "Mr. Elton's object" (112). But Emma (like Catherine Morland) refuses to include a sense of the probable in her outlook, and even amuses herself, when John Knightley warns her, "in the consideration of the blunders which often arise from a partial knowledge of circumstances, of the mistakes which people of high pretensions to judgment are for ever falling into" (112).

Emma's inability to make objective assessments of actuality is best revealed in her finished portrait of Harriet. At the same time the portrait becomes a means of exposing the characteristic deficiencies of several other figures and an important indication that an objective reality exists against which the unbiased observer may measure the truth of a subjective construction. For the hopeful lover, Mr. Elton, the portrait "appears . . . a most perfect resem-

blance in every feature. I never saw such a likeness in my life" (48).
Mrs. Weston is more perceptive but still unwilling to criticize her
former pupil. She sees that it is not a true likeness—"Miss Smith
has not those eye-brows and eye-lashes"—but she cannot find it in
herself to blame Emma: "It is the fault of [Miss Smith's] face that
she has them not" (48). Emma's father mixes indiscriminate praise
—"So prettily done! Just as your drawings always are, my dear"—
with his inevitable hypochondria: "The only thing I do not
thoroughly like is, that she seems to be sitting out of doors, with
only a little shawl over her shoulders—and it makes one think she
must catch cold" (48). Only Mr. Knightley is able to free his judgment from a desire to please, on the one hand, and a subjective
response, on the other: "You have made her too tall, Emma" (48).
Though Emma knows he is right, she will not admit it. From this
point on, *pace* J. F. Burrows, Knightley remains the reader's objective point of reference within the novel.[19]

As Wayne Booth has shown, the narrator of the novel is herself an
important measure against which to set the heroine's subjective
aberrations.[20] Nevertheless, it is well to stress that the problem of
subjectivity is at the heart of the book. Late in the novel, in a
crucial scene, Knightley will remind himself of Cowper's line, "Myself creating what I saw," before allowing rein to his imaginative
intuition; and throughout the novel there are indications of Jane
Austen's concern with the nature and origin of mental knowledge.
The narrative presentation itself comes nearer to suggesting the processes of subjectivity than any of the earlier works. Not only are
we for much of the time within the consciousness of the heroine
(in a way that, as several critics have noted, anticipates the Jamesian
third person limited point of view) but Jane Austen has also indicated the prominence of subjectivity in experience by including in
Emma a large number of characters who exist only as references
in another character's speech or thoughts. I am not only thinking
here of Mr. and Mrs. Churchill of Enscombe, or of the Campbells

19 Much of the argument of Burrows's carefully detailed monograph (*Jane
Austen's "Emma"* [Sydney: Sydney University Press, 1968]) is aimed at discredit-
ing Knightley's claim to be a normative figure in the novel (see esp. his introduction).

20 "Control of Distance in Jane Austen's *Emma*," in *The Rhetoric of Fiction*
(Chicago: University of Chicago Press, 1961).

and Mr. and Mrs. Dixon who are in Ireland during the course of
the novel, but of certain characters much nearer at hand. Robert
Martin, for example, so important in connection with the social
theme, is hardly ever encountered, as it were in person, by the
reader. We hear frequent good accounts of him from Mr. Knightley; he is the object of one of Emma's snobbish attacks; Harriet
gives a breathless description of her accidental meeting with him in
Ford's. But apart from a brief glance (I, iv), this is as near as we get
to him. William Larkins, Mr. Knightley's responsible steward, is
another character who has existence only in other characters' speech.
Then there are the Highbury and London medical authorities, Mr.
Perry and Mr. Wingfield. Did Mr. Perry really say, as Mr. Woodhouse
claims, that "colds have been very general, but not so heavy as he has
very often known them in November" (102)? Did Wingfield really
consider "the vicinity of Brunswick Square decidedly the most favourable as to air" (103), as Isabella Knightley avers? Or are these figures
merely the embodiments of subjective opinions? In Mrs. Elton's conversations, at any rate, the use of characters as reference is suspect; she
introduces a whole setting—Selina, Maple Grove, and the barouche-
landau—to support whatever position she is for the moment defending.

Amusing as many of these references are, they testify to a concern
over the problem of subjectivity which, from Sterne onward, has
occupied many novelists. *Emma*, one might suggest, exists in a tradition begun by *Tristram Shandy* and only finding its culmination
in such novels as *Mrs. Dalloway* and *To the Lighthouse*, in which
no objective reality outside of the consciousness of the various
characters can be inferred. For Jane Austen, though not for Virginia
Woolf, an objective reality outside of consciousness does exist, yet
W. J. Harvey is right to qualify Wayne Booth's reading of *Emma*
by pointing to the importance of what he terms the "shadow-novel-
within-the-novel" which results from the narrator's choice of keeping us, as well as Emma, in the dark about the Jane Fairfax–Frank
Churchill engagement.[21] The opacity of the plot is quite deliberate,
as a late comment of the narrator suggests: "Seldom, very seldom,
does complete truth belong to any human disclosure" (431). The
remark leaps out of its immediate context, the proposal scene, to

21 "The Plot of *Emma*," *Essays in Criticism*, 17 (Jan. 1967), 48–64.

define a central concern of the novel, the essentially limited nature of individual human perception. In limiting her point of view largely to the horizon of her heroine's vision, the narrator also limits the point of view of the reader. Of course we know much more than Emma does; the narrator has permitted us again and again to measure the heroine's aberrations against norms that are present in the *oratio obliqua* of the narrative discourse. But for a long time, as Harvey points out, we are left in the dark about many truths.

Thus Jane Austen has allowed the plot of the novel itself to demonstrate the frequently "closed" nature of interpersonal relations which is part of its subject. As readers we are teased by the possibility of that complete subjective imprisonment, which haunts so many later writers of the nineteenth and twentieth centuries, of that enclosed world in which "my experience falls within my own circle, a circle closed on the outside; and, with all its elements alike, every sphere is opaque to the others which surround it."[22] Even after many readings of the novel, Jane Fairfax's character remains impenetrable to us, not because Jane Austen has failed to draw a "round" character but precisely because she has wished to suggest the limitations of an individual's ability to know another in a problematic world.

WHEN *Emma*'s comedy of errors becomes, with the arrival of Jane Fairfax and Frank Churchill in volume two, a comedy of intrigue, both the social and epistemological implications of Emma's subjectivism are compounded.[23] If, as we have seen, Mrs. Elton usurps Emma's social position, then Jane Fairfax pre-empts her intellectual prominence (she is "the really accomplished young woman, which Emma wanted to be thought herself" [166]), and Churchill takes over her powers of managing and directing. Though in one amusing scene she goes so far as to imagine Churchill in

[22] T. S. Eliot is here quoting from F. H. Bradley's *Appearance and Reality*. The quotation, of which I have given part, is found in his note to line 411 of "The Waste Land."

[23] For a discussion of *Emma*'s movement from a "comedy of errors" to a "comedy of intrigue," see Burrows, *Jane Austen's "Emma,"* pp. 34–35.

love with her, making his declaration, and being tenderly refused, all such dreaming is without possibility of enactment. For, with Churchill's entrance, Emma is no longer the puppet-mistress of Highbury but instead becomes a marionette in Churchill's more subtle show.

A dramaturgical vocabulary is inevitable with Churchill, for if he reminds us of any other character in Jane Austen's fiction it is the histrionic Henry Crawford. Like that actor, Churchill is an impresario of some ability. When, on his initial walk through the town, he sights the Crown Inn, "its character as a ball-room caught him; and instead of passing on, he stopt for several minutes . . . to look in and contemplate its capabilities" (197–98). The last word, of course, alerts us to Churchill's desire to "improve." Like Crawford at Mansfield or Sotherton, Churchill wishes to introduce movement and flexibility into a landscape of peace and stability.

It is not sufficient to argue that his schemes are forced on him by the restraints of his dependent social position and the enforced secrecy of his engagement to Jane Fairfax. The secret engagement is important to the novel, but it is not the only, or even the major, reason for Churchill's "manœuvring and finessing" (146). He delights to play-act. He will, of course, use the secret engagement as his excuse in his late letter of apology: "you must consider me as having a secret which was to be kept at all hazards" (437). And in his personal apology to Emma, he will say: "I had always a part to act.— It was a life of deceit!" (459) But there can be little doubt that Jane Austen intended us to see him taking a positive delight in "disguise, equivocation, mystery" (475). There is something gratuitous about his secrecy. No less than Henry Crawford looking back with pleasure on the play period, Churchill recalls with gratification his Highbury career. At the end of the novel, his claims of honorable expediency merely reveal another pose.

There are no actual theatricals in *Emma*, but the theme is continued in minor key in the preparations for the ball and in the children's games which are a curious feature of the novel. Both aspects of *Emma* invite somewhat detailed attention.

When Emma takes up Churchill's enthusiasm for the ball, plans are immediately made. Randalls is their first choice of location, and they are soon engaged, with the help of Mrs. Weston, in the "interesting employment . . . of reckoning up exactly who there would be, and portioning out the indispensable division of space to every couple" (248). It is at once evident that the number of couples is greater than the room can comfortably hold. In what follows we are reminded of the preparations for the play at Mansfield, as the communal desire of a group of people bent on pleasure is sufficient to overcome material objections to their "scheme." Furthermore, something of the ontological subversiveness suggested by the mistreatment of the Mansfield house is here repeated as more and more of the house is appropriated for the ball: "The doors of the two rooms were just opposite each other. 'Might not they use both rooms, and dance across the passage?' It seemed the best scheme; and yet it was not so good but that many of them wanted a better" (248). As the disagreements of the participants in the scheme recall the bickering of the would-be actors in *Mansfield Park*, so the increasing list of couples to be invited reminds us of the plans to invite more and more of the neighborhood to take part in the play at Mansfield. Finally, when Mr. Woodhouse's hypochondriacal objections to the use of more than one room force them to return to the "first scheme," we are shown how subjective desire may ignore objective facts in the pursuit of its goal. Through Churchill's persuasion, "the space which a quarter of an hour before had been deemed barely sufficient for five couple, was now endeavoured to be made out quite enough for ten" (249).

Churchill's pre-eminence in the preparations for the ball—his revised plan for holding it at the Crown—reveal how far he has already usurped Emma's powers of directing and organizing. But Churchill's real power over Emma, and the nature of his threat in the novel, are more evident in his love of games. Games are not, of course, introduced by Churchill—the amusing episode of the misunderstood charade announces the motif in the first volume (chapter ix); but it is Churchill who initiates the word game at Hartfield (III, v) and the games on Box Hill (III, vii). Moreover, it is Churchill who makes a running game out of his conversations with Emma on the subject of the mysterious piano—at Mrs. Cole's (II, viii), for example, and in Miss Bates's parlor (II, x).

Such games need have no meaning in individual instances beyond revealing the characteristic deficiencies of the players. In the episode of the charade, for instance, Harriet's immaturity is evident: "the only mental provision she was making for the evening of life, was the collecting and transcribing all the riddles of every sort that she could meet with" (69); and her irresponsibility is indicated when she prefers the flowery sentiments of Elton's verse to the "good sense in a common way" of Martin's letters (76). Beyond this, Elton's charade, "To Miss _____," reveals the characteristic deficiency of Emma's imagination, her preference for believing what she wants to happen rather than what her sense of the probable would indicate. Obviously addressed to her (who but a deluded Emma could imagine "ready wit" as a description of Harriet?), the charade exists, like the blank of the title, as an empty space to be filled by the imagination. When Emma, thinking further to promote the match between Harriet and Elton, transcribes the verse into Harriet's book, we have a repetition of the sketch episode: each of the three participants misapprehends the real situation, but Emma is responsible for the confusion. Mr. Elton is hardly to be blamed if he thinks his suit is progressing well when he hears Emma admire the hidden meaning of his poem (court-ship).

Taken cumulatively, however, games carry crucial meaning in *Emma*; they are Jane Austen's means of conveying her apprehension over the continuity of a public and "open" syntax of morals and of manners. Whatever Huizinga might argue, games for Jane Austen—at least as she explores the motif in *Emma*—are antisocial, and the "ludic" personality as exemplified by Churchill is a threat to the structures of society and morality that she affirms.[24] Both play and player are suspect, play because it sets up a world of freedom from the ordinary patterns of existence ("it is . . . a stepping out of 'real' life into a temporary sphere of activity with a disposition all of its own"[25]), the player because while playing—for Jane Austen

[24] J. Huizinga, *Homo Ludens: A Study of the Play-Element in Culture* (Boston: Beacon Press, 1955), esp. chap. 1. Huizinga, in support of his view that "civilization arises and unfolds in and as play" (p. ix), insists upon the ethical neutrality of play—"It lies outside of the antithesis of wisdom and folly" (p. 6). And from Huizinga's point of view, no doubt, even Knightley is a player, if of a different kind from Churchill. But Jane Austen sets culture against play in *Emma* (as, in *Mansfield Park*, she sets the estate against theatricality), and invests her games with negative social and moral value. It may be as well to add that I am aware that Jane Austen delighted in domestic games, as in her youth she is said to have delighted in private theatricals. Interested readers are referred to *Charades Etc. Written a hundred years ago By Jane Austen and Her Family* (London: Spottiswoode, 1895).

[25] Huizinga, *Homo Ludens*, p. 8.

—he is absolved from the rules and requirements of ordinary social discourse.

Even before Churchill's entry upon the Highbury scene, the episode of the charade, in exemplifying the concealment and opacity of a game world, had foreshadowed Churchill's behavior. With his entry a whole vocabulary of concealment begins: nouns like riddle, enigma, conundrum, mystery, equivocation, puzzle, espionage, double-dealing; verbs such as guess, conceal, blind; adjectives such as hypocritical, insidious, suspicious. There is "doubt in the case" (120) even of his arrival, and Churchill takes care to maintain a doubt as to his motivations and character, not merely because he is secretly engaged to Jane (a transgression of some magnitude in contemporary terms), but also in order to retain his sense of superior manipulation and secret power. His unpredictability is particularly disliked by Mr. Knightley, who considers surprises to be "foolish things" (228).

In requiring predictability of her exemplary characters Jane Austen reveals an attitude toward behavior that will be found in many later English novelists of manners, from Trollope and James to Ford and Waugh. Predictability is pre-eminently the mark of the gentleman; further, it points to the existence of a structured society with a large body of shared assumptions, to a world where few situations lack appropriate and public response and where individuals can communicate by means of a common vocabulary of words and gestures. In such a world dramatic tension is to be expected when a character thought to be a gentleman fails to act predictably. In Trollope's *The Last Chronicle of Barset*, the drama of the novel centers on the horrifying possibility that the curate of Hogglestock may have stolen a check entrusted to him. In *A Portrait of a Lady*, Madame Merle's claims to the status of lady, and Gilbert Osmond's to that of gentleman, are suddenly put into question when Isabel sees her standing while he sits. In Ford's *The Good Soldier*, the narrator, Dowell, speaks of the "modern English habit . . . of taking everyone for granted," and much of the irony of the novel stems from the fact that the good soldier, Ashburnham, is incapable of acting like the gentleman he is considered to be.[26] In

---

[26] The title of the first volume of *Parade's End*, "Some Do Not . . . ," is of further interest here. Although it has numerous applications in the volume, one implication is that there are certain things that gentlemen do not do.

Evelyn Waugh's fiction, of course, the gentleman, from Tony Last to Guy Crouchback, is doomed to be duped by persons who do not act as they might once have been expected to act.

Given the residual faith in, or nostalgia for, behavioral predictability which these and other novelists exhibit, we may understand more forcibly the importance of the issue in *Emma*. Someone like Frank Churchill, who suddenly goes "off to London, merely to have his hair cut" (205), poses a threat to the trust and confidence of an ordered world; he drops a "blot" (205) on the transparency that should characterize his behavior. This is why Knightley is justified in suspecting Churchill even before he sees him. The point in question is quite clear. Frank's father has married again, and it is his son's duty to call on his stepmother. Though Emma argues that it is "unfair to judge of any body's conduct, without an intimate knowledge of their situation," Knightley points out: "There is one thing, Emma, which a man can always do, if he chuses, and that is, his duty; not by manœuvring and finessing, but by vigour and resolution. It is Frank Churchill's duty to pay this attention to his father" (146). And later (after Emma has excused Frank by citing his obligations to his adoptive parents) Knightley adds: "Respect for right conduct is felt by every body. If he would act in this sort of manner, on principle, consistently, regularly, their little minds would bend to his" (147). Knightley introduces into *Emma* the serious tone and social commitment that are characteristic of *Mansfield Park*. His call for duty, for the observance of certain prior moral and social imperatives, for consistent and predictable action—these mark Knightley as an exemplary gentleman.[27]

The contrast with Churchill is consistently drawn, often in terms that remind us of Fielding's distinction, quoted as an epigraph to this chapter, between "Humour" and "good Breeding." While Churchill sees life as a game, Knightley sees it as a serious responsibility; while Churchill is typically described as amiable (or "aimable") and gallant, Knightley is described as courteous and humane;

---

[27] Clearly I do not agree with J. F. Burrows's reading of the debate between Emma and Knightley over Churchill's delay in visiting Randalls (*Jane Austen's "Emma,"* pp. 55–56). Knightley will himself admit to Emma later in the novel that he was "not quite impartial in [his] judgment," but he will add that even if Emma had not been "in the case" he would still have distrusted Churchill (445).

while Churchill promotes his schemes of secrecy, "Mr. Knightley does nothing mysteriously" (226).[28] Churchill, the "closed" personality, is a creature of interiors; he prefers the company of women. Knightley, who loves an "open manner" (260), is a man of the outside, a man's man. At the Coles's, while Mr. Knightley stays behind to discuss "parish business" with the other gentlemen, Churchill is the "very first of the early" gentlemen to rejoin the ladies (220). And on that later occasion at Miss Bates's, while Churchill plays his double game with Emma and Jane (and before an audience of no less than six ladies), Mr. Knightley rides by outside, on an errand of duty, as a reminder of the values of an "outside" existence. Moreover, when he hears that Churchill is inside, he refuses to come in at Miss Bates's invitation. His refusal is in its implications a refusal to leave an "open" world of consistency and regularity for the interior existence of variability and process which Churchill stage-manages.

Churchill's game-playing is not to be dismissed as venial. It is symptomatic of a world in which once given certitudes of conduct are giving way to shifting standards and subjective orderings. Churchill rejects an inherited body of morals and manners for a little world he himself creates. He is at home in a world of opacity and of separation, preferring it, indeed, to the older world where communication existed by way of public assumptions, for that world required responsibility and consistency, qualities conspicuous by their absence in his character.

We may now be in a position to understand why all the fuss is made about the "entirely unexpected" (215) gift of the piano to Jane Fairfax. All the doubt and speculation that occupy the minds

[28] Knightley himself sets the contrast in terms of English versus French behavior: "No, Emma, your amiable young man can be amiable only in French, not in English. He may be very 'aimable,' have very good manners, and be very agreeable; but he can have no English delicacy towards the feelings of other people: nothing really amiable about him" (149). For a discussion of Jane Austen's conception of a "specifically English ideal of life," see Trilling, *"Emma,"* in *Beyond Culture*, pp. 40–41. For an interesting argument setting the Churchill-Knightley contrast in terms of "the contrast between Lord Chesterfield's and Dr. Johnson's social and ethical points of view," see Frank W. Bradbrook, *Jane Austen and Her Predecessors* (Cambridge: Cambridge University Press, 1966), pp. 32–33. In condemning Churchill, Bradbrook suggests, Knightley "condemns by implication, the point of view of Lord Chesterfield."

of the characters are intentionally introduced by Frank Churchill, when he deposits his gift anonymously in Miss Bates's drawing room. (The piano was of course his real reason for going to London.) The object of the game is known; it is addressed to Miss Fairfax. And there is no secrecy as to what it is: it is a "very elegant looking instrument—not a grand, but a large-sized square pianoforté" (214–15). Only its sender is unknown, as if—like another charade—it were "From _____."

Again it can be argued that Churchill's gift stems from no other wish than to provide his beloved Jane with an instrument for her musical talents. Churchill's schemes, however, are never this simple. In addition to providing a topic for surmise in Highbury, Churchill soon finds that he is able to play a game with Emma. In one of her flights of fancy, "an ingenious and animating suspicion" (160) enters Emma's brain concerning a possibly illicit relationship between Jane Fairfax and Mr. Dixon, the husband of Jane's friend. Thus when Miss Bates and Mrs. Cole assume that the pianoforte "of course . . . must be from Col. Campbell" (215), Emma refuses to agree, but instead conveys her suspicions of the "real" identity of the giver to Churchill. At first pretending to think she means Mrs. Dixon, he quickly accedes to Emma's real suspicion of Mr. Dixon, and convinces her that he is her secret accomplice in knowledge. Churchill is now in his favored position of superior awareness and power—and not only with respect to Emma. Jane is almost as powerless as Emma. Though Emma is vulnerable, since she is being laughed at behind her back, she is invulnerable in that she cannot know until near the end that she is being duped. Jane, on the other hand, presumably discovers from Churchill the nature of Emma's suspicions, but this cannot give her much satisfaction when she sees Churchill taking obvious delight in Emma's company, or when, on Box Hill, he and Emma conduct themselves in a way that "no English word but flirtation could very well describe" (368).

The Emma-Churchill-Jane triangle provides the structural setting of many of the scenes in the second half of the novel, scenes in which, though Emma remains the center of attention, the reader increasingly suspects that it is Churchill who is pulling the strings. At the Coles's, for example, the triangular relationship appears as first Emma plays, and is surprised when Churchill accompanies her singing, and then Jane plays, and Churchill sings again (II, viii). Later, at Miss Bates's (II, x), Churchill is again able to play his double game with great enjoyment. Jane and Frank have been left alone with the sleeping Mrs. Bates while Miss Bates has gone to invite Emma, Mrs. Weston, and Harriet into her house for a brief visit. The chapter opens with the entrance of the ladies at a point just after one of the few moments of intimacy that Frank and Jane have been able to enjoy. The visitors see Mrs. Bates slumbering by the fire, "Frank Churchill, at a table near her, most deedily occupied about her spectacles, and Jane Fairfax, standing with her back to them, intent on her pianoforté" (240). They have no inkling (nor, surely, does the average reader on first reading) that the lovers have just sprung apart. The rest of the chapter is a subtle description of Churchill's expert ability to play a double game with consummate skill. Consider, for example, how in the following passage, as he addresses first Emma and then Jane, he is able to poke fun at both girls while delighting both. (He is speaking of the piano which he himself has introduced into the house):

"Whoever Col. Campbell might employ," said Frank Churchill, with a smile at Emma, "the person has not chosen ill. I heard a good deal of Col. Campbell's taste at Weymouth; and the softness of the upper notes I am sure is exactly what he and *all that party* would particularly prize. I dare say, Miss Fairfax, that he either gave his friend very minute directions, or wrote to Broadwood himself. Do not you think so?" (241)

By mentioning Col. Campbell, Churchill seems to be entering into complicity with Emma, to whom at this point he turns "with a smile." This impression can only be reinforced when he seems (to Emma) to make a clandestine reference to Mr. Dixon with the phrase, *"all that party."* And when he next addresses "Miss Fairfax" by referring to the "friend" who is supposed to have undertaken the purchase of the piano, Emma still believes that he is teasing Jane about Mr. Dixon. She even feels that he is going too far. "It is not fair," says Emma in a whisper, "mine was a random guess. Do not distress her" (241). On a first reading, such an interpretation would be reasonable. But if we now consider how the scene appears to Jane, a very different meaning is evident: to her Churchill's remarks can only appear as an amusing ridicule of Emma, and as a series of embarrassing but touchingly nostalgic remembrances of their shared experiences.[29]

Churchill's games are not always as successful as this. At the ball at the Crown, Emma senses that "Frank Churchill thought less of her than he had done" (326), and the reason is that his genuine love for Jane, and his frustration at the distance that separates them, lead him to lower his mask of amiability to Emma. If we consider the "shadow-novel-within-the-novel" of which W. J. Harvey speaks, however, we can infer other reasons for Churchill's diminishing success as player. The time draws near when Jane must decide whether or not to accept the position as governess so officiously arranged for her by Mrs. Elton—to place herself in what she regards as slavery; and still Churchill has not committed himself. In this light it is not to be wondered at that Jane should find his continued game-playing repugnant. Certainly in the last two games played in the novel—at Hartfield and on Box Hill—Churchill's attempts to communicate with Jane by the indirect means of a game will be rebuffed.

THE TWO episodes are excellent examples of Jane Austen's ability to carry major themes on apparently trivial vehicles. In the first instance, an insidious note is present from the first sentence of the chapter (III, v): "In this state of schemes, and hopes, and connivance, June opened upon Hartfield" (343). Soon after, we are witness to Churchill's famous "blunder," when he asks those assembled "accidentally" outside Hartfield, "what became of Mr. Perry's plan of setting up his carriage?" (344) This information—it becomes clear from one of Miss Bates's rambling speeches—must have

---

[29] The question arises as to how far Churchill thinks he is keeping Emma in the dark. Soon after this scene (in II, xii), Churchill, before leaving for London, calls on Emma and almost reveals to her the secret of his engagement. She thinks, however, that he is about to propose to her. At the end, in his letter of apology to Mrs. Weston, Churchill will say: "I have no doubt of her having since detected me, at least in some degree.—She may not have surmised the whole, but her quickness must have penetrated a part" (438). Whether Churchill was really mystifying Emma or merely conniving with her remains, therefore, in some doubt, but the cruelty to Jane remains, whatever one decides, as does his use of Emma as foil.

come from his secret correspondence with Jane, and not, as he had thought, from his legitimate correspondance with Mrs. Weston. (Whether all readers gather this the first time round is an interesting question; certainly clues as to the secret correspondence have previously been deposited, as in the argument between Mrs. Elton and Jane over whether or not she should be permitted to go to the post office in the rain [II, xvi].) Since, as in *Sense and Sensibility*, a correspondence constitutes evidence of engagement, Churchill is anxious to cover up his blunder, and he says that he must have dreamed it. Nevertheless—and here surely we have conclusive evidence for the gratuitous nature of his game-playing—when they enter Hartfield, Churchill invites Emma to join him in a children's game of letters.

The scene is carefully set around the "large modern circular table which Emma had introduced at Hartfield:"³⁰ "Frank was next to Emma, Jane opposite to them—and Mr. Knightley so placed as to see them all" (347). Knightley's position is especially important, for in this chapter, in the one major shift of point of view in the novel—indeed in Jane Austen's fiction—Knightley is granted knowledge given to no other character.³¹ Prior to the game we have been informed of Knightley's growing dislike of Churchill, and of his suspicion—started by a "look" he had seen Churchill give Jane at the Eltons'—of "some double dealing" (343). Now, as he stands apart from the game, he sees Churchill pass an anagram to Jane, and she "with a faint smile" push it way. At this point, Harriet

---

³⁰ A nice touch this, when one recalls the dubious significance that is attached both to Marianne Dashwood's wish to give Allenham new furniture in *Sense and Sensibility* and to Mary Crawford's wish to make Thornton Lacey a "modern" residence in *Mansfield Park*. Why a round table should merit comment is perhaps best indicated in *Barchester Towers* where Archdeacon Grantly says: "A round dinner-table . . . is the most abominable article of furniture that ever was invented" (chap. 21). For Grantly there is "something peculiarly unorthodox" in the idea of a round table, "something democratic and parvenue."

³¹ Jane Austen on only one other occasion, and there unsuccessfully, changes her point of view in this radical way. I refer to the curious scene in *Sense and Sensibility* (III, iii) where we are given a conversation between Elinor and Colonel Brandon on the subject of the Delaford living through the misconceiving eyes of Mrs. Jennings. She thinks that she is witnessing the Colonel's proposal to Elinor, whereas in fact they are really discussing the timing of his gift to Edward Ferrars. Having demonstrated Mrs. Jennings's misconception, Jane Austen then repeats the conversation as it really occurred, a narrative device she never repeated.

steps in to retrieve the word. She is too stupid to solve the anagram, but Mr. Knightley, to whom she turns for help, sees that the word is *"blunder"* (348). His thoughts are reported:

Mr. Knightley connected it with the dream; but how it could all be, was beyond his comprehension.... He feared there must be some decided involvement. Disingenuousness and double-dealing seemed to meet him at every turn. These letters were but the vehicle for gallantry and trick. It was a child's play, chosen to conceal a deeper game on Frank Churchill's part. (348)

When Churchill continues his "double-dealing" by now pushing the anagram for *Dixon* to Emma "with a look sly and demure" (348), Knightley sees that Emma, though she judges it "proper to appear to censure" it, is in spite of herself seduced by Churchill's cunning and charm. "Nonsense! for shame!" she answers, as she opposes "with eager laughing and warmth" (348) his suggestion for now giving the word to Jane. Jane, for her part, is "evidently displeased," and on seeing Knightley watching her, she says with some anger, "I did not know that proper names were allowed" (349).

The anagram game repeats Churchill's previous game in Miss Bates's parlor and anticipates the climactic scene on Box Hill. Inside Miss Bates's house, and with Knightley absent, Churchill had been able to satisfy the vanity and trust of both girls, without betraying either. Knightley could only there serve as a passing reminder of responsible conduct. Here, inside the Hartfield house, and with Knightley present, Churchill's maneuvering is not only a quite voluntary danger to Jane's reputation, but is also a cause of justifiable jealousy, as she sees Frank and Emma indulging in a kind of "courtship" game.

The scene reveals more. By allowing us access to Knightley's rational consciousness, we are granted an awareness of the permissible use of the imagination. Careful to avoid the errors of the undisciplined imagination (even as he speculates, Knightley reminds himself of Cowper's line, "Myself creating what I saw"), he is able to intuit a "something of private liking, of private understanding . . . between Frank Churchill and Jane" (344), and the word game confirms and gives substance to his well-grounded suspicions. Secrecy and concealment, the scene allows us to see, are not invulnerable to the intelligent and responsible mind.

But precisely here Emma reveals how far her participation with Churchill has taken her, for when Knightley asks her if she perfectly understands "the degree of acquaintance" (350) between Churchill and Jane, her confident reply—"I will answer for the gentleman's indifference" (351)—leads him to assume a much closer relationship between Emma and Churchill than he had ever considered possible, and he "walk[s] home to the coolness and solitude of Donwell Abbey" (351). In spite of Knightley's judicious assessment of probabilities, that is, Emma's collusion with Churchill has caused further concealment. Because of this, the novel at this point reaches toward solemn possibilities; through the next two chapters, at Donwell and on Box Hill, a satisfactory resolution seems remote. Frank's rash actions have alienated his already nervous confidante, so that she will cut him short on their meeting in Donwell Lane; the vacuous Harriet is lost in her impossible, Emma-inspired dreams of Knightley; and Emma has unwittingly damaged her own best prospects.

It is important to stress that the combined actions of Emma and Churchill have done more than endanger three relationships; whether one calls it a culture, an ethos, or a social disposition, what has been threatened is an entire way of life, and in face of the symbolic resonance of the scenes which follow, it is quite insufficient to argue that "we do not get from *Emma* a condensed and refined sense of a larger entity."[32] Consider, for example, the implications of the walk taken by most of the major characters in the pleasure grounds of Donwell (one is reminded of the walk in the wilderness at Sotherton in *Mansfield Park*):

It was hot; and after walking some time over the gardens in a scattered, dispersed way, scarcely any three together, they insensibly followed one another to the delicious shade of a broad short avenue of limes, which . . . seemed the finish of the pleasure grounds.—It led to nothing. . . . (360)

The suggestion, even in this brief extract, of a group without sense of community or feeling ("insensibly" carries due force) is strongly made, as is the implication that the selfish pursuit of pleasure may, indeed, lead to nothing. The possibility of social disintegration is very real at this juncture. But, having made her point, Jane Austen

---

[32] Kettle, *English Novel*, p. 93.

now posits an alternative hope in her description of the view from Donwell of the Abbey-Mill Farm, as if to underscore the contrast between the present fragmentation of the party and the enduring possibilities of an organic society (360). Emma, who has yet to commit her grossest act of selfishness, is here provided with her true "grounds" of moral and social action, though full awareness is still some way off. A little earlier, like Elizabeth at Pemberley, she had reached some awareness of the value of Knightley's estate, noticing

... the respectable size and style of the building, its suitable, becoming, characteristic situation, low and sheltered—its ample gardens ... of which the Abbey, with all the old neglect of prospect, had scarcely a sight—and its abundance of timber in rows and avenues, which neither fashion nor extravagance had rooted up.... [The house] was just what it ought to be, and it looked what it was.... (358)

The distrust of fashionable improvements here expressed not only reminds us of the theme in *Mansfield Park*, but comments, too, on the recent actions and intentions of the visitors to Donwell—especially, perhaps, on Mrs. Elton's attempt to redefine what is "natural" by coercing Knightley into giving an alfresco "gipsy-party," complete with donkey and "caro sposo" (355–56).[33]

Emma not only views Donwell with "honest pride" (358); her view will soon include, as Trilling notes, what she has previously excluded from her outlook: "at half a mile distant was a bank of considerable abruptness and grandeur, well clothed with wood;—and at the bottom of this bank, favourably placed and sheltered, rose the Abbey-Mill Farm, with meadows in front, and the river making a close and handsome curve around it" (360). The Martins' farm is indeed "favourably situated," and Emma's visit to Donwell is followed not only by her discovery of her hidden love for Mr. Knightley (and her consequent acceptance of the values which he upholds), but by her admission that now "it would be a great pleasure to know Robert Martin" (475). As Elizabeth and Darcy

---

33 Knightley, of course, will have nothing to do with Mrs. Elton's absurd "scheme." As opposed to her plan for gathering strawberries, Knightley's "idea of the simple and the natural will be to have the table spread in the dining-room" (355).

"were always on the most intimate terms" (*PP*, 388) with the Gardiners, so Emma and Knightley will remain the friends of the Martins. And in *Emma*, no less than in *Pride and Prejudice* and *Mansfield Park*, the social gaps which individual actions threatened to widen, will be closed around the marriage of the central figures.

Richard Poirier has most clearly understood the importance that such scenes have in promoting Jane Austen's "positive vision of social experience," and in illustrating her capacity, as contrasted with American writers of the nineteenth century, "to imagine society as including the threat of conformity and artificiality and as offering, nevertheless, beneficial opportunities for self-discovery."[34] In a brilliant comparison of the episode on Box Hill and Huck's treatment of Jim in chapter fifteen of *Huckleberry Finn*, he comes to the conclusion that "the stakes for Jane Austen and her heroine are very high indeed—to prevent society from *becoming* what it is condemned for *being* in *Huckleberry Finn*," and one well appreciates the point. For it is in this famous episode that the novel— and, with it, the games motif—reaches a fitting climax, and here too that the specter of social fragmentation comes closest to actualization.

On Box Hill, where, as one eighteenth century description has it, the mazes make it "very easy for amorous couples to lose and divert themselves unseen,"[35] a "principle of separation" (367) divides the company into separate groups. There is a "want of union" (367) which the indiscriminately benevolent Mr. Weston is quite incapable of harmonizing: "The Eltons walked together; Mr. Knightley took charge of Miss Bates and Jane; and Emma and Harriet belonged to Frank Churchill" (367). Here is Lawrence's "sharp knowing in apartness," but how greatly is the separation to be deplored, and how appropriately does Jane Austen distinguish between the selfishness of the Eltons, the social stewardship of Knightley—he at least is concerned about the fate of single women in society—and the continued and misguided collusion of Emma and Churchill, with Harriet, as usual, in tow. What follows on the hill is an em-

---

[34] Richard Poirier, "Transatlantic Configurations: Mark Twain and Jane Austen," in *A World Elsewhere* (New York: Oxford University Press, 1966), pp. 144–207.

[35] Quoted in G. E. Mingay, *English Landed Society in the Eighteenth Century* (London: Routledge and Kegan Paul, 1963), p. 154.

blem of a vitiated society where selfishness is uncurbed and no publicly accepted rules of behavior permit free and "open" communication.

In Poirier's terms, what Emma does when she so flagrantly insults Miss Bates is to violate a social contract; spurred on by Churchill, she forgets her social obligation (or proper role) and adopts the role of an ironic and theatrical wit.[36] After the insult, and a short-lived attempt to play a conundrum game (the last game of the novel), the group erupts into barely concealed hostility (between Mrs. Elton and Emma, between Elton and Churchill, between Churchill and Jane), and were it not for Knightley's fidelity to his social duty and Emma's ability soon after to realize the "evil" of her words and wit and truly to repent of them, the ultimate social vision of the novel would be bleak. Something of the seriousness of the issue involved is apparent in Knightley's rebuke to Emma: "How could you be so unfeeling to Miss Bates? How could you be so insolent in your wit to a woman of her character, age, and situation?—Emma, I had not thought it possible" (374). Only in the degree that Emma comes to an awareness of her fault and to an acceptance of the principles by which Knightley lives is a positive social alternative to the game world convincingly affirmed.

Emma's repentance is genuine, and the novel succeeds in achieving, in the end, a positive vision of society. But something of the seriousness of the issues treated is revealed in Jane Austen's careful choice of a religious vocabulary in the closing chapters: we hear, for example, of Emma's "contrition" and "penitence" (377). Given the degree of her transgression, moreover, her absolution cannot be immediate; Miss Bates and Jane Fairfax for a long time resist her penitential overtures. But henceforth her sorrow and guilt, unlike her previous temporary resolutions to suppress her imaginative tendencies, are real. Now her eyes are "towards Donwell" (378), the proper home of her values, and, like Elizabeth before Darcy's portrait at Pemberley, all her actions are now considered in the light of Knightley's imagined regard: "could Mr. Knightley have been privy to all her attempts of assisting Jane Fairfax, could he even have seen into her heart, he would not . . . have found any thing to reprove" (391).

[36] Poirier, *World Elsewhere*, p. 176. My argument in this paragraph is much indebted to Poirier's reading.

Emma must still come to a recognition of the personal evils of her subjective schemes when Harriet reveals to Emma's momentary horror that Knightley is the unnamed superior she hopes to marry. And she must become aware of the degree to which she has been sucked into the vortex of Churchill's play-acting: "What has it been but a system of hypocrisy and deceit,—espionage, and treachery?— To come among us with professions of openness and simplicity; and such a league in secret to judge us all!—Here we have been, the whole winter and spring, completely duped . . ." (399). But she will soon agree with Knightley's views on the desirability and "the beauty of truth and sincerity in all our dealings with each other" (446), and with her marriage to Knightley, Harriet's to Martin, and Jane's to Churchill, society is finally reconstituted as the plot is resolved.

Let it be admitted, however, that the Churchill marriage leaves some "doubt in the case" even at the end. Had the domineering Mrs. Churchill not fortuitously died, would Frank still have married Jane and saved her at the eleventh hour from a life of "slavery"? It will be said that the question is not legitimate, yet the novel's presentation of Churchill's menace has tended to arouse expectations of a less rewarding fate for Jane. Perhaps we should be satisfied with the circumscriptions of his power which are provided. Churchill's epistolary *apologia pro vita sua* in chapter fourteen of the third volume is followed by Knightley's searching explication of the text in chapter fifteen, and as throughout the novel he has stood as a model of excellence against which the reader may judge Churchill, so now Knightley points out to Emma where in Churchill's excuses the unthinking act becomes immoral, where undisciplined behavior becomes antisocial.

Yet Jane's character and role remain in the memory after the novel ends, and if it is true that another novel "shadows" the novel we read, it is also true that other possible outcomes shadow the resolution we have. It may be that Jane Austen sensed this herself.[37] At any rate, in *Persuasion* she wrote a novel about a heroine whose predicament is closer to that of Jane Fairfax, and in so doing, defined a new outlook in her fiction.

[37] According to family tradition, Jane Austen divulged that Jane Fairfax survived her marriage to Frank only nine or ten years.

CHAPTER 5

Persuasion:
THE ESTATE ABANDONED

[Anne's astonishment] was soon lost in the pleasanter feelings which sprang from the sight of all the ingenious contrivances and nice arrangements of Captain Harville, to turn the actual space to the best possible account, to supply the deficiencies of lodging-house furniture, and defend the windows and doors against the winter storms to be expected.

How was the truth to reach him?

✦✦✦ Written soon after *Emma* (between 8 August 1815 and 6 August 1816), *Persuasion* addresses itself to the predicament of the isolated self responding to social deprivation. In curious ways its heroine is the mirror-image of Emma Woodhouse, the very different protagonist of the previous novel. We are granted as much access to Anne's inner life as we are to Emma's, but Anne is never a conceivably destructive principle to the society in which she lives; she exemplifies rather, in Burke's phrase, a "disposition to preserve" her inherited culture. If *Emma* asks what will result if an entirely free spirit without external restraint is allowed to define her existence in a basically structured world, then *Persuasion* explores the existence of a heroine who, recognizing the importance of moral and social conventions, is deprived of the structured world she once enjoyed. *Emma*, that is, examines self as danger to order; *Persuasion* examines self as it responds to a world without external manifestation of design. Yet, whereas in *Emma* the dangerous aspects of individualism are corrected and the social community finally reinstated, in *Persuasion*, for all the socially positive attitudes of the heroine, society never really recovers from the disintegration evident at the beginning.

Persuasion describes explicitly what had always been a latent possibility in the other novels, the total alienation of the individual from society, friendship, and love. Its typical experience is one of loss. Anne Elliot's mother died when she was fourteen; at nineteen she loses her lover, and at twenty-seven her home. Mrs. Musgrove's son died while serving in the navy. Captain Benwick's fiancée succumbed while he was at sea. And Mrs. Smith's husband's death left her with "difficulties of every sort" (152). All these tragedies surround the central sense of loss of the heroine, commenting upon her own feelings of "perpetual estrangement" (64) and conveying the apprehension that society may not always provide a secure place, even for its worthy members. In this connection, it can be argued that the final marriage of the novel is not a "social" marriage in the way that previous marriages are in Jane Austen; Anne's union with Wentworth fails to guarantee a broader union of themes and attitudes in *Persuasion* as say, Elizabeth's union with Darcy does in *Pride and Prejudice*. Nor, uniquely among Austen heroines, does Anne return to the stable and rooted existence of the land; she has "no Upper-cross-hall before her, no landed estate, no headship of a family" (250). Instead she becomes a sailor's wife, "glorying" in this role, but also—if Mrs. Croft is any indication—committing herself to an itinerant existence in which she must pay "the tax of quick alarm" (252).

In other ways, *Persuasion* signals shifting emphases on Jane Austen's part. For example, the novel gives a sense of temporal uncertainty that is largely absent from her previous fiction: "What might not eight years do? Events of every description, changes, alienations, removals,—all, all must be comprised in it; and oblivion of the past—how natural, how certain too! It included nearly a third part of her own life" (60). Here, seemingly, there can be no trust that the morrow will rectify the sorrows of the present day. Not a providential ordering, but rather an existence in which luck and fortuitous circumstance play a predominant part, defines the world of *Persuasion*.[1]

Most noticeably, perhaps, Jane Austen seems in her last novel to have lost faith in manners, that mode of public conduct which ideally exists as the outward and visible sign of an inward moral condition. Thus the "vigour of form" (48) and frank behavior of the naval characters are preferred not only to the vanity and arrogance of Sir Walter Elliot and his eldest daughter but also to the "exceedingly good manners" (104) of the smooth Mr. Elliot. Social decorum had always, of course, been available to the hypocrite as a mask for selfish ends, but the mask was usually visible in the earlier novels. In *Persuasion* the mask is often indistinguishable from the face. One passage is particularly troubling, for although it seems to bring together in one catalogue most of the characteristics of social and moral excellence that were elsewhere desiderata—suggesting a normative union of sense and sensibility, of reason and feeling—it de-

[1] See Paul N. Zietlow, "Luck and Fortuitous Circumstance in *Persuasion*: Two Interpretations," *ELH*, 32 (June 1965), 179–95.

scribes Mr. Elliot, the heir in tail to the Kellynch estate, and as insidious a character as is to be seen in Jane Austen's gallery:

> Every thing united in him; good understanding, correct opinions, knowledge of the world, and a warm heart. He had strong feelings of family-attachment and family-honour, without pride or weakness; he lived with the liberality of a man of fortune, without display; he judged for himself in every thing essential, without defying public opinion in any point of worldly decorum. He was steady, observant, moderate, candid; never run away with by spirits or by selfishness, which fancied itself strong feeling; and yet, with a sensibility to what was amiable and lovely, and a value for all the felicities of domestic life, which characters of fancied enthusiasm and violent agitation seldom really possess. (146–47)[2]

Given the novel's pervasive sense of loss and of temporal uncertainty, and given, too, the apparent inability of manners to incorporate moral intentions, one understands why many critics have seen Jane Austen's last novel as marking new directions in her thought.[3] Especially in the rapprochement between Anne and

---

[2] Even when the qualification is made that the description is seen through the consciousness of Lady Russell, who has a certain "prejudice" in favor of rank which blinds her judgment, the passage remains disturbing. An earlier phrase of Lady Russell's adds to our uneasiness. Prejudiced against Mr. Elliot by reports of his rudeness to the Kellynch family, Lady Russell finds him better on acquaintance than on report: "His manners were an immediate recommendation; and on conversing with him she found *the solid so fully supporting the superficial*, that she was at first, as she told Anne, almost ready to exclaim, 'Can this be Mr. Elliot?' " (146, my italics). The solid in the case of Mr. Elliot is the superficial, for there are no moral grounds to his social behavior, and it is in such passages that we catch intimations of Jane Austen's apprehension in this "autumnal" novel that traditional grounds of conduct are vanishing, and that the solid base of her inherited world has seriously weakened.

[3] Walton Litz, in *Jane Austen: A Study of Her Artistic Development* (London: Chatto & Windus, 1965), pp. 150–53, considers *Persuasion* a "new landscape," and notices that whereas Jane Austen's earlier fiction is set against a man-made landscape, her last novel employs a symbolic use of natural setting. Marvin Mudrick entitles his chapter on the novel, "The Liberation of Feeling" (*Jane Austen: Irony as Defense and Discovery* [Princeton: Princeton University Press, 1952]). Virginia Woolf in a brilliant essay on Jane Austen in *The Common Reader* (1925; rpt. New York: Harcourt, Brace & World, 1953), p. 147, not only notices "a new sensibility to nature" but suggests that in *Persuasion* Jane Austen "is beginning to discover that the world is larger, more mysterious, and more romantic than she had supposed." Howard Babb considers that *Persuasion* "vindicates . . . a mode of apprehension that is essentially emotional and intensely subjective (*Jane Austen's Novels: The Fabric of Dialogue* [Columbus: Ohio State University Press,

Wentworth in the second volume, Jane Austen's departure from the fictional norms of her former novels is evident. If Anne's period of isolation resembles those of previous heroines, the nature of her relationship and final union with Wentworth is something quite different, the union coming about not, as before, through the rational enlargement of the hero or the heroine or of both, but through an emotional rapport that goes beyond rational processes. When one asks what sanctions the heroine's final happiness in this novel, on what "grounds" she is "blessed with a second spring of youth and beauty" (124), one closest to defining the new elements in Jane Austen's *Persuasion.*

On the other hand, one should be careful not to overemphasize the modernity of *Persuasion.* It would be quite wrong, for example, to argue that Jane Austen is in her last novel rejecting an inherited social morality and embracing, near her death, a moral subjectivism. Even as Anne Elliot, in ways that look back to Elinor Dashwood and Fanny Price, is forced into a spiritual solitude—as a consequence of her early broken engagement and her present loss of home —her responses remain selfless and social, a point that becomes clear as one examines the course of Anne's journey from Kellynch to Uppercross, then to Lyme, and finally to that dubious locality of *Northanger Abbey,* Bath. What is no longer present as a substantial "estate" remains present in Anne's inner thoughts and social actions. Unlike Mansfield Park, Kellynch Hall is in effect abandoned—Anne cannot preserve, much less "improve" her estate—but Anne does not reject with the loss of her home a whole moral inheritance.

A close examination of Anne's response to her deprived existence in the first volume will give the ethically conservative impulse of *Persuasion* its proper force. Anne's response has retrospective significance, for it brings into central focus the situation briefly or obliquely suggested in other novels—in Fanny's stay at Portsmouth, for example, in Jane Fairfax's dependent existence in Highbury.

1962], p. 203); W. A. Craik has noted that it describes a moral growth within the self rather than within society (*Jane Austen: The Six Novels* [London: Methuen & Co., 1965], p. 200); and a general critical view is summed up in Joseph M. Duffy's statement that in *Persuasion* "history is subversive to tradition without always providing an alternative to traditional ideals" ("Structure and Idea in Jane Austen's *Persuasion,*" *Nineteenth-Century Fiction,* 8 [March 1954], 274).

Persuasion, I believe, provides that answer to existence outside of the Highbury "idyll" denied by Kettle and others, though it may not be quite the extreme answer desiderated.[4] For all its apparent movement into the spiritual atmosphere of the later nineteenth century, the novel, like its heroine, retains to an extent that should not be underestimated an allegiance to inherited moral and social structures.

IF ANNE's sense of personal loss derives from her broken engagement, her sense of social deprivation comes, of course, from the loss of Kellynch. Given the importance I have ascribed to the estate in Jane Austen's fiction, the renting of Kellynch may be made a matter of immediate attention and the occasion of a brief review. In *Pride and Prejudice*, *Mansfield Park*, and *Emma*, in ways that have been described, the properly run estate exists as an exemplary social model, an objective paradigm of order. Central to *Mansfield Park*, present in *Pride and Prejudice* and *Emma* as that social space their heroines will come to respect, the estate has thus far existed as a physical emblem of a cultural heritage. And even in *Northanger Abbey* and *Sense and Sensibility*, where the traditions embodied in the Northanger and Norland estates are vitiated by the characters of their owners, the ideals of a socially corporate existence prevail. The heroines invariably become mistresses of estates or parsonages—Woodston, Delaford, Pemberley, Mansfield, Donwell —but only after they have learned, if they do not innately possess, qualities of social responsibility. "Right conduct" and "active principles" are discovered to be the "proper business" of all the heroines whom we have so far considered. Their journeys toward a social destination—often reversing an initial movement away from society —have stabilized the world of their novels, as their marriages have guaranteed the continuity of the community.

It is not so in *Persuasion*, for here the estate is not endangered but abandoned, and much as Anne would wish to maintain and properly improve her inherited home, she is helpless to act or to in-

4 See Arnold Kettle, "Jane Austen: *Emma*," in *An Introduction to the English Novel* (rev. ed. 1967; rpt. New York: Harper and Row, 1968), and my argument in the previous chapter.

fluence actions to this effect. Her fate is to watch with sorrow a "beloved home made over to others; all the precious rooms and furniture, groves, and prospects, beginning to own other eyes and other limbs" (47–48). And when she moves on the first of her journeys in search of spiritual stability, she discovers that Uppercross, a neighboring estate, is in a "state of alteration, perhaps of improvement" (40). Whereas the "father and mother were in the old English style," Anne recognizes that "their children had more modern minds and manners" (40).[5] There is an "air of confusion" in the Great House, a confusion which is tolerated and not extirpated as in *Mansfield Park* on Sir Thomas's return from Antigua. Anne's reaction to what she sees is nostalgic and resigned; the possibility of a return to order seems remote:

Oh! could the originals of the portraits against the wainscot, could the gentlemen in brown velvet and the ladies in blue satin have seen what was going on, have been conscious of such an overthrow of all order and neatness! The portraits themselves seemed to be staring in astonishment. (40)

In *Persuasion* the estate is defeated where in *Mansfield Park* it triumphed. Sir Walter Elliot is a later and more outrageous version of Rushworth—vain, extravagant, and with no awareness of the "duties and dignity of the resident land-holder" (138). His home is so full of looking glasses that, as Admiral Croft says, there is "no getting away from oneself" (128). Indeed, Sir Walter has no desire to get away from himself. His favorite and only reading is the Baronetage:

[T]here he found occupation for an idle hour, and consolation in a distressed one; there his faculties were roused into admiration and respect, by contemplating the limited remnant of the earliest patents; there any unwelcome sensations, arising from domestic affairs, changed naturally into pity and contempt, as he turned over the almost endless creations of the last century—and there, if every other leaf were powerless, he could read

---

[5] One may note, too, that "Uppercross Cottage, with its viranda, French windows, and other prettinesses, was quite as likely to catch the traveller's eye, as the more consistent and considerable aspect and premises of the Great House, about a quarter of a mile farther on" (36). Like the improvements of Rushworth in *Mansfield Park*, those of the younger Musgroves have concentrated on eye-catching appearance rather than on "use." Furthermore, the contrast between the houses suggests a society in the process of change.

his own history with an interest which never failed—this was the page at which the favourite volume always opened:

"ELLIOT OF KELLYNCH-HALL." (3)

Vanity is "the beginning and the end of Sir Walter Elliot's character; vanity of person and of situation" (4). It is the vanity against which Burke inveighed in his *Letter to a Member of the National Assembly* (1791), the vanity which is opposed to "true humility, the basis of the Christian system . . . the low, but deep and firm foundation of all real virtue." "In a small degree," Burke continues, "and conversant in little things, vanity is of little moment. When full-grown, it is the worst of vices, and the occasional mimic of them all. It makes the whole man false."

Thus it is not surprising that at Kellynch Hall the Baronetage is the "book of books" (7), for the Elliots have substituted a vanity of status for a pride in function, and have (with the exception of Anne) entirely neglected the religious dimension of their trust. When through the father's extravagance the estate falls into debt, and retrenchment of some kind is inevitable, Sir Walter is pleased to consider his eldest daughter's proposals for economy: "to cut off some unnecessary charities, and to refrain from new-furnishing the drawing-room" (9–10). And when even these revealing retrenchments are insufficient, it takes no great powers of persuasion on Mr. Shepherd's part to convince him that the renting of the house is the only solution to the problem.

The renting of Kellynch and the removal of the Elliots to Bath are not to be considered insignificant actions. The extravagance which has led to the necessity of such actions, open as it is to the charges of "waste" and "ostentation" that were traditionally brought against the irresponsible trustee, finds an appropriate contemporary censure in Thomas Gisborne's *An Enquiry into the Duties of Men in the Higher and Middle Classes of Society* (London, 1794). Gisborne might be speaking of Sir Walter Elliot when he states that "justice and every moral principle concur in reprobating that pride and false shame, which sometimes impels men to persist in a mode of life far more expensive than they can afford . . . rather than submit to lessen the parade and retrench the extravagance of their household." And though he goes on to admit that "when considerable retrenchments are to be made," it may be "prudent" for the

family "to remove to some distant quarter," he adds that "the rectitude of principle is more manifest, and the example more profitable,
when the change is made in the sight of those who had witnessed
the conduct which rendered it necessary; and with that genuine
strength of mind, which is neither ashamed of confessing an error,
nor of openly amending it."[6]

We need not, however, go to a contemporary conduct book to
illustrate Sir Walter's irresponsibility. In terms of Jane Austen's
own previous attitudes to the estate, Sir Walter's agreement to rent
Kellynch is tantamount to his rejecting an entire cultural heritage,
for though his house under his trusteeship can hardly have been a
center of traditional order, the intrinsic value of his inheritance is
indicated in its "valuable pictures" (18) and its "precious rooms and
furniture" (47). Something of the enormity of the baronet's action
is suggested by the reported thoughts of Lady Russell, as she looks
with pain on the "deserted grounds" (36) of Kellynch, and more is
conveyed later when Anne, on first seeing her family's home in Bath,
regrets that her father should "feel no degradation in his change"
(138), and that her elder sister, Elizabeth, once mistress of Kellynch,
should boast of the "space" of their reduced accommodations.

Anne is the only Elliot to show any respect for the traditions of
the estate. In a way that Gisborne would approve, she proposes
emendations "on the side of honesty against importance" in the
plan for retrenching: she advocates "more vigorous measures, a more
complete reformation, a quicker release from debt, a much higher
tone of indifference for every thing but justice and equity" (12).
And, significantly, when her proposals are rejected and removal is
imminent, one of her last acts before departure is to make "a dupli-
cate of the catalogue" of her father's books and pictures (38). Wherever she goes after leaving Kellynch, she carries with her a
"catalogue" of social principles for individual action.

Such a catalogue is soon found to be necessary, for at Uppercross,
her first location, she learns that "a removal from one set of people
to another, though at a distance of only three miles, will often include a total change of conversation, opinion, and idea" (42). At
first, recognizing that "every little social commonwealth should
dictate its own matters of discourse," she tries to become a "not

[6] Gisborne, *An Enquiry* (2nd ed.; London 1795), II, 461–62.

unworthy member;" she feels it "incumbent on her to clothe her imagination, her memory, and all her ideas in as much of Upper-cross as possible" (43). But this attempt to fit her character to the configuration of the Uppercross commonwealth cannot work, for Uppercross is far from being an exemplary society. Mary (a splendid portrait of extreme emotional covetousness) is selfish, incapable of disciplining her children, absurdly vain of her ancestry, and forever seeking "precedence" in personal as well as social areas. Her hus-band, like Sir John Middleton in *Sense and Sensibility*, is only interested in sport (this fact a comment on the displacement of his moral responsibility). And Anne finds she must resist the values, or the perversions of values, which here prevail; she must withdraw into herself, while still maintaining subjectively an adherence to received standards of behavior.

Yet, though Anne passively withdraws from the selfish modes of the Uppercross cottage, it is important to recognize that she does not repudiate her relationship with Mary and her family, or retire from any attempt at improving her temporary environment. As far as her limited opportunities permit, she acts positively and usefully. At Kellynch, only she had possessed the responsible attitudes to the estate that were properly her father's; here, as Mary and Charles neglect their parental responsibilities, Anne plays the role of a vicarious parent. When one of the Musgrove boys dislocates a collar bone, it is Anne who takes charge: "It was an afternoon of distress, and Anne had every thing to do at once—the apothecary to send for—the father to have pursued and informed—the mother to support and keep from hysterics—the servants to control—the youngest child to banish, and the poor suffering one to attend and soothe . . ." (53).

Anticipating the climactic scene of Louisa's accident on the Cobb at Lyme, where once more Anne will have "every thing to do at once," this episode at Uppercross is important in that it emphasizes the selflessness and "utility" of Anne's response. It suggests that the self, even when deprived of its social inheritance, may still respond affirmatively and in traditionally sanctioned ways, that deprivation need not lead to despair or to disaffection. The nature and quality of Anne's response at Uppercross, moreover, are not substantially altered by her subsequent experiences, even though these will soon include the unexpected arrival, in all the confidence of his naval achievement, of Captain Wentworth.

With Wentworth's arrival Anne's situation is especially trying, for it is quickly evident to her that he is on the lookout for a wife. As he dances and converses with Henrietta and Louisa, and his attentions become more and more directed to the latter, Anne's position resembles that of Fanny Price in *Mansfield Park*, who must attend, a suffering third, while the object of her love shows interest in another. In the scenes at Uppercross, and especially during the walk to Winthrop, Anne's spirits are understandably depressed, and it is not surprising that she should here attempt to find in the natural setting a comfort which her companions cannot give her. During the walk to Winthrop Anne's object is to keep out of everyone's way, a task that is easily achieved, for the "narrow paths across the fields made many separations necessary" (84). Her solitary reflections here have been taken to indicate a "romantic" attempt to discover value in nature rather than in society:

Her *pleasure* in the walk must arise from the exercise and the day, from the view of the last smiles of the year upon the tawny leaves and withered hedges, and from repeating to herself some few of the thousand poetical descriptions extant of autumn, that season of peculiar and inexhaustible influence on the mind of taste and tenderness, that season which has drawn from every poet, worthy of being read, some attempt at description, or some lines of feeling. She occupied her mind as much as possible in such like musings and quotations. . . . (84)

A little later, when Anne overhears Wentworth's enthusiastic response to Louisa's claim of lifelong constancy, these attempts to revive an affective memory fail—"unless some tender sonnet, fraught with the apt analogy of the declining year, with declining happiness, and the images of youth and hope, and spring, all gone together, blessed her memory" (85). Such passages are new in Jane Austen, and it cannot be denied that Anne is here made (without irony) to rely on subjective associations to restore her depressed spirits.[7] What is to be denied, however, is a view of the novel which takes such a passage in itself to demonstrate that *Persuasion* postulates the need for a subjective order. In later episodes, and in comparison with other responses she later encounters, Anne's behavior will appear

[7] For a careful analysis of these scenes, see Litz's chapter in *Artistic Development*, esp. pp. 151–53. Litz emphasizes the fact that the walk to Winthrop focuses not on the external scene but on Anne's consciousness of it.

less subjective and will retain the qualities of selflessness and "utility" first exemplified at Uppercross.

Three responses to misfortune are particularly important in *Persuasion*, for not only do they define, in both negative and positive ways, the choices open to the deprived individual, but they also comment interestingly on Anne's own moral conduct. Worthy of notice in each of these instances is the relation of character to environment. As Anne loses Kellynch, so each of these figures has been deprived of a previous home. Their present "accommodations" become metaphors for their spiritual conditions and indications of the quality of their endurance.

Captain Benwick at Lyme is the first character Anne meets whose position is in certain ways similar to her own. In mourning for the death of his fiancée, who died just when he made his fortune and gained promotion, Benwick lives with the Harvilles in their small house by the sea, his sorrowing mood attuned to the "grandeur" of the country and the "retirement" of the town. Wentworth believes it "impossible for man to be more attached to woman than poor Benwick had been to Fanny Harville" (96–97), and Benwick's sorrow excites general good will and sympathy—except from Anne, who is curiously unsympathetic:

"And yet," said Anne to herself, . . . "he has not, perhaps, a more sorrowing heart than I have. I cannot believe his prospects so blighted for ever. He is younger than I am; younger in feeling, if not in fact; younger as a man. He will rally again, and be happy with another." (97)

This is an important passage and not only for its prescience (Benwick will indeed rally again and be happy with Louisa Musgrove rather sooner than is socially respectable). What strikes us most is Anne's tough-minded attitude toward Benwick's grief. As in the notorious case of Mrs. Musgrove's "large fat sighings" over the loss of her son, Benwick's grief—as Anne, but not Wentworth, realizes—strikes a false note. Self has intruded into his sorrow, as Benwick, like Marianne Dashwood, pursues an "indulgence of feeling," a "nourishment of grief" (*SS*, 83). An emotional parasite who feeds on the sympathy of others, Benwick acts in character when, in spite of every "appearance of being oppressed by the presence of so many strangers" (99), he accompanies Captain Harville in a visit to the Uppercross group in their hotel. During the evening he fastens on Anne:

[H]aving talked of poetry, the richness of the present age, and gone through a brief comparison of opinion as to the first-rate poets, trying to ascertain whether *Marmion* or *The Lady of the Lake* were to be preferred, and how ranked the *Giaour* and *The Bride of Abydos* . . . he shewed himself so intimately acquainted with all the tenderest songs of the one poet, and all the impassioned descriptions of hopeless agony of the other . . . that she ventured to hope he did not always read only poetry; and to say, that she thought it was the misfortune of poetry, to be seldom safely enjoyed by those who enjoyed it completely; and that the strong feelings which alone could estimate it truly, were the very feelings which ought to taste it but sparingly. (100–101)

Revealing the mediated nature of Benwick's grief, this episode also importantly qualifies Anne's own previous efforts to discover a measure of consolation in poetry. When she goes on to recommend to Benwick the "works of our best moralists" and "memoirs of characters of worth and suffering" as proper examples of "moral and religious endurances" (101), the advice may not be as effective as Jane Austen intended it to be, but it nevertheless discloses a sincere belief in the need for fortitude in the face of adversity, for endurance founded in Christian principles.

If Benwick lacks these Christian virtues, a second character, Mrs. Smith, seems to possess them.[8] When Anne meets her old school friend in Bath, it seems that Mrs. Smith's attitude to the reduction of her personal and social horizons following her husband's death is exemplary. A "widow, and poor" (152), physically ill with crippling rheumatism, she is confined to lodgings, to "a noisy parlour, and a dark bed-room behind" (154). Anne can "scarcely imagine a more cheerless situation" (153), and she is led to admire Mrs. Smith's response to her "sick and reduced" life (158–59):

Anne had reason to believe that she had moments only of languor and depression, to hours of occupation and enjoyment. How could it be?—She

---

[8] Mrs. Smith's admittedly unsatisfactory function as a device in the Mr. Elliot plot—the concern of most critics who discuss her role in *Persuasion*—has apparently obscured her significance as the most socially "reduced" figure in Jane Austen's fiction. Under this aspect I discuss Mrs. Smith briefly in the introduction, pp. 2–3, 25.

watched—observed—reflected—and finally determined that this was not a case of fortitude or of resignation only . . . ; here was that elasticity of mind, that disposition to be comforted, that power of turning readily from evil to good, and of finding employment which carried her out of herself, which was from Nature alone. (154)

Yet Anne is to discover that Mrs. Smith's apparently exemplary attitudes mask a cynical view of society, that her charity is largely false. In association with her nurse, who sells Mrs. Smith's products among her rich patients, Mrs. Smith is able to obtain (almost to extort) enough money to survive. Nurse Rooke is a "shrewd, intelligent, sensible woman" (155), who knows the exact psychological moment to apply for money. As Mrs. Smith tells Anne: "Every body's heart is open, you know, when they have recently escaped from severe pain, or are recovering the blessing of health" (155).

As Mrs. Smith speaks of "the entertaining and profitable" information that her nurse-accomplice brings to her from her sick visits —she clearly takes a misanthropic pleasure in "the newest modes of being trifling and silly" (155)—Anne, mistaking her tone, agrees that Nurse Rooke must have many opportunities of observing heroism and fortitude: "A sick chamber may often furnish the worth of volumes" (156). But as Anne speaks like a Christian stoic, Mrs. Smith responds with observations that are Mandevillian in their cynicism: "it is selfishness and impatience rather than generosity and fortitude, that one hears of" (156). Disaffected with society, Mrs. Smith's response is not what it seems; society has become for her an alien structure in which all means are fair.

A third response to suffering is shown by Captain Harville, the wounded veteran. When the Uppercross group visits his house in Lyme it is to discover that its rooms are "so small as none but those who invite from the heart could think capable of accommodating so many" (98). But the smallness of these rooms, though indicating the diminution of his prospects, does not exemplify a narrowness of concern. Significantly, Anne has no unfavorable attitude toward this house. Any astonishment she feels at his inviting so many people into a space manifestly too small to accommodate them is "soon lost in the pleasanter feelings which sprang from the sight of all the ingenious contrivances and nice arrangements of Captain Harville, to turn the actual space to the best possible account, to supply the deficiencies of lodging-house furniture, and defend the windows and doors against the winter storms to be expected" (98).

No better symbolic indication of Jane Austen's required response to a world without prospects could have been provided than this description. Captain Harville's courageous refusal to be defeated comments unfavorably on those characters who have permitted circumstances to limit their responses. Sir Walter Elliot and Elizabeth abandon their home, with its spacious rooms, its beautiful paintings and fine furniture, and voluntarily choose to reduce the extent of their commitment to society by living among the "littlenesses" (138) of Bath. Mary Musgrove, having married beneath her (as she thinks), attempts to impose upon the space of a cottage the more gracious conduct of a great house. Captain Benwick's world, reduced by the death of his wife-to-be, becomes the home of another family in which he may find support and sustenance. And Mrs. Smith's "dark bed-room" is a secret conclave within the city from where she sends out Nurse Rooke as a scout for gossip and "profitable" information.

Unlike all these characters, Captain Harville turns his "actual space to the best account," and the phrase is striking enough to be taken as one epigraph for the novel. Harville demonstrates that, however reduced or deprived the self may be, response may still be affirmative. Whatever evils the future may threaten, inner resources can supply the deficiencies of external equipment, just as one can "defend the windows and doors against the winter storms to be expected." By the arrangement of valuable objects collected in his past travels, Harville is able to invest his drab, rented rooms with lustre and individuality. Though "no reader," he has generously "contrived excellent accommodations, and fashioned very pretty shelves, for a tolerable collection of well-bound volumes, the property of Captain Benwick" (99). And though physically restricted by his wound, he is constantly employed: "He drew, he varnished, he carpentered, he glued; he made toys for the children, he fashioned new netting-needles and pins with improvements; and if every thing else was done, sat down to his large fishing-net at one corner of the room" (99). Harville exemplifies what Mrs. Smith only seems to exemplify, the ability to find employment that will carry the mind out of itself. And of all responses in the novel, his is closest to Anne's and, Anne's excluded, his is the response nearest to Jane Austen's heart.

"PICTURES of perfection," Jane Austen wrote not long before her death in a letter to her niece Caroline, "make me sick & wicked," and she went on to admit that the heroine of her last novel was "almost too good" for her (*L*, 486–87). But in insisting on the essentially Christian virtue of Anne Elliot, one is not so much opposing her author's retrospective opinion of her creation (Jane Austen is, after all, speaking for effect) as going against a rather common critical view of *Persuasion*'s heroine. Most would agree that, of all the heroines, Anne is intended to come nearest to perfection and is treated with the least irony; but for not a few readers her character is impaired by her lack of a "light and bright and sparkling" quality and, especially, by what is considered her early failure of nerve in the breaking of her engagement to Wentworth. Though her refusal precedes the novel proper, its continuing consequences saturate the emotional atmosphere of the book and the memory of the act lingers in the consciousness of the two central characters. Young, motherless, and without benefit of paternal approval, Anne had at the age of nineteen acceded to the "persuasion" of her only real friend, Lady Russell, not to continue what the latter considered to be an imprudent engagement. For some critics she erred badly. D. W. Harding may be taken to summarize a fairly general opinion, when he writes of Anne's "lapse from her own standard, in letting worldly prudence outweigh love and true esteem for personal qualities."[9] Anne nearly throws away her chance of happiness, and the novel traces the gradual stages whereby she wins back Wentworth's love and becomes aware of her initial error.

The trouble with such a reading is that it misreads Anne's spiritual progress in the novel (she undergoes no radical change of

[9] See Harding's introduction to his edition of *Persuasion* (Baltimore: Penguin Books, 1965), p. 9. Remaining faithful to his celebrated essay, "Regulated Hatred: An Aspect of the Work of Jane Austen," *Scrutiny*, 8 (March, 1940), Harding considers that Jane Austen in *Persuasion* reveals a dislike for "the society in which she seemed comfortably embedded," and that the "conflict" in the novel is "between elderly prudence and the romantic love of two young people." *Per contra*, I shall argue that Anne's initial decision is not so unequivocally misguided as Harding considers it to be, and that the love of two people is not for Jane Austen a complete or sufficient substitute for a socially grounded existence.

mind) and it exaggerates Wentworth's normative function. At the end, reconciled with Wentworth, Anne will insist that she was right to act as she did (even though Lady Russell may have erred in *her* advice). She does not admit that her early obedience was an error. Further, for all the qualities Wentworth possesses, it is he who undergoes the major process of education.

Two episodes are of particular importance in supporting these points. Both have to do with the question of "fortitude;" both comment upon Anne's early refusal of Wentworth. The first episode occurs during the walk to Winthrop, when Wentworth adduces his analogy of the nut:

"Here is a nut," said he, catching one down from an upper bough. "To exemplify,—a beautiful glossy nut, which, blessed with original strength, has outlived all the storms of autumn. Not a puncture, not a weak spot any where.—This nut," he continued, with playful solemnity,—"while so many of its brethren have fallen and been trodden under foot, is still in possession of all the happiness that a hazel-nut can be supposed capable of." Then, returning to his former earnest tone: "My first wish for all, whom I am interested in, is that they should be firm. If Louisa Musgrove would be beautiful and happy in her November of life, she will cherish all her present powers of mind." (88)

Wentworth has returned to Somersetshire in search of a wife, and he has his formula ready: "a strong mind, with sweetness of manner" (62). It is a formula that is clearly derived from his previous abortive experience with Anne—her sweetness not being accompanied by sufficient strength to withstand Lady Russell's persuasion. By contrast, Louisa's claim of hypothetical constancy in love (85) and her selfish insistence that Henrietta complete the visit to Charles Hayter (thus ensuring that Wentworth will be left free for herself) seem to Wentworth to be evidence of fortitude: "Your sister is an amiable creature; but *yours* is the character of decision and firmness, I see" (88). And then he makes the nut analogy, quoted above.

One must be careful against too subtle a reading here, but I think we are to see Wentworth's misunderstanding of the nature of true fortitude in his words. A nut's destiny is not to remain whole and unharmed through autumn, but rather—like St. Paul's grain of wheat in I Corinthians xv: 36–38—to be trodden under so that it will flourish in the spring as a tree. If it is not too fanciful to see a pattern of resurrection here, the scene supports all those other references to seasonal death and rebirth that fill the novel. Anne's journey is through an autumn of depression to a spring of renewed hope. Lady Russell, meeting Anne "on a dark November day" (123), sees enough in her countenance to hope "that she was to be blessed with a second spring of youth and beauty" (124); and in the final reunion, Anne and Wentworth return "into the past, more exquisitely happy, perhaps, in their re-union, than when it had been first projected; more tender, more tried, more fixed in a knowledge of each other's character, truth, and attachment; more equal to act, more justified in acting" (240–41). Anne has moved through experience of suffering to a higher level of happiness.

There is perhaps more here. In insisting upon Anne's moral consistency through the novel I do not mean to impute to her a moral rigidity. Anne changes her outlook in *Persuasion*, not by repudiating her former position, but in a way that bears resemblance to the Victorian view of life and history as a continuum of deaths and rebirths. It has recently been suggested to me that the most illuminating analogues for *Persuasion* exist in the future, in Mill's autobiography, in Wordsworth's *Prelude*, and in Newman's *Apologia Pro Vita Sua*.[10] Certainly Newman's defense of the consistency and wholeness of his life, despite an obvious conversion of outlook, seems an appropriate comparison with Anne's final review of her past actions. How like Anne's words is the following passage from the *Apologia*, for example: "Certainly, I have always contended that obedience even to an erring conscience was the way to gain light, and that it mattered not where a man began, so that he began on what came to hand, and in faith; and that any thing might become a divine method of Truth . . . and have a self-correcting virtue and a power of germinating."[11] Anne will never reject Kellynch in the total way that Newman rejected the system of Anglican theory (though on revisiting Kellynch with Lady Russell [II, i], she will show how far she has moved from a nostalgia for her landed past),

[10] I owe the suggestion, and the argument of the following paragraph, to Douglas North, who plans to publish a full-length essay on this aspect of *Persuasion*. See also Jerome Buckley's chapter, "The Pattern of Conversion," in his *The Victorian Temper* (New York: Vintage Books, 1951).

[11] *Apologia Pro Vita Sua* (New York: Modern Library, 1950), p. 212. The whole of Newman's argument under the heading April 3, 1844, is of relevance to Anne's review of the past.

but her movement in the novel surely exhibits the same integrity, the same ability to "germinate" and to "correct" the self without repudiating a past identity, as that displayed by the great Victorian.

Of this Wentworth in the first volume has no notion. Instead he takes the spoiled wilfulness of Louisa for genuine fortitude, palpably misunderstanding her character which, to borrow a phrase that was once improbably used of Jane Austen herself, is that of "a husband-hunting butterfly." He must come to see that it is Anne who possesses true strength of mind. To this end, the "usefulness" that we have seen her to possess is stressed again and again, and the word (with its cognates) takes on something of the significance surrounding "business" in *Pride and Prejudice*. It is only her "usefulness to little Charles" that gives "some sweetness to the memory of her two months visit" at Uppercross (93), while at Lyme it is in the "hope of being of real use" to Captain Benwick that she converses with him about poetry (100). Finally, of course, it is Anne's usefulness and strength of mind that are stressed in the crucial central scene of the novel, Louisa's fall from the steps at Lyme. This, the second episode I wish to consider, is often considered a fictional storm in a teacup; in fact, it is the culmination in a concentrated setting of the whole sequence of Louisa's folly, Wentworth's misconceptions, and Anne's consistency. Louisa must again demonstrate her strength of mind:

"I am determined I will:" he put out his hands; she was too precipitate by half a second, she fell on the pavement on the Lower Cobb, and was taken up lifeless! (109)

The responses of those present perfectly fit their characters as these have been defined by their previous behavior. Mary screams and immobilizes her horrified husband. Henrietta faints into the arms of Benwick and Anne, and when Wentworth cries for help it is Anne only who has the presence of mind to answer:

"Go to him, go to him," cried Anne, "for heaven's sake go to him. I can support her myself. Leave me, and go to him. Rub her hands, rub her temples; here are salts,—take them, take them."

Captain Benwick obeyed . . . (110)

Some moments later:

Anne, attending with all the *strength* and zeal, and thought, which instinct supplied, to Henrietta, still tried, at intervals, to suggest comfort to the others, tried to quiet Mary, to animate Charles, to assuage the feelings of Captain Wentworth. Both seemed to look to her for directions. (111; my italics)

In the central chapter of the novel, Anne becomes a center of ethical reference and though her stock will fall again when she returns to her family in Bath, she is henceforth an ideal woman in Wentworth's eyes.

Several lessons are taught by the accident on the Cobb. Louisa's fall occurs when she tries to jump a *second* time. Her first jump ends safely, her second—"too precipitate by half a second"—disastrously. Surely we have here a dramatic comment on all "precipitate" actions. It is often possible, *once*, to act rashly without suffering ill consequences; but to persist in imprudent gestures may be to court disaster. Wentworth's precipitate proposal to Anne has been vindicated by his achievement of the fortune and rank which he then lacked, but is personal ambition always rewarded? Obviously not. In the lives of Harville and Benwick, which in a thematic sense "repeat" Wentworth's, no such successful completion of intention has occurred. Furthermore, when Louisa cries, "I am determined, I will," is she not revealing something of the same confidence in future success that the young Wentworth exhibited? And when she is taken up "lifeless" from the pavement, does not her imprudent and self-assertive action suggest the possible disaster that might have befallen an early marriage between Anne and Wentworth?

What the accident stresses is that the fortitude of Louisa, selfish, headstrong, and rash as it is shown to be, is morally inferior to the fortitude of Anne, which manifests itself in selfless and "useful" actions and which is characterized by self-control rather than by self-assertion. But this is not all. As Kenneth L. Moler has shown, the different versions of fortitude exhibited in *Persuasion* (and, indeed, the title term itself) exist in the context of a novelistic controversy over the degree of parental prerogative permissible in the matter of a daughter's choice of marriage partner. On the one hand, writers of the "romantic-revolutionary" school—Mary Wollstonecraft, Mary Hays, and other disciples of Rousseau and Godwin—

called upon individuals to assert their complete freedom from
parental authority in this matter; for them "persuasion" was the
forcing of a daughter to marry a man chosen by the parents. More
conservative writers, on the other hand, such as Hannah More and
Elizabeth Hamilton, repudiated the theories of the "modern
philosophers" and argued for a strong sense of filial duty, and, if need
be, obedience to the "negative voice" of a parent dissatisfied with a
daughter's choice of future husband, though it was also understood
that parents could not force on a daughter a man she did not like.
In this context, Anne's dutiful behavior is in accordance with conservative views on the subject (Lady Russell, she takes care to explain to Wentworth, was to her "in the place of a parent" [246]).
Wentworth's initial behavior, on the other hand, has some resemblance to the outlook of the "modern philosophers" and his journey
of education is from a mistaken approval of Louisa's false fortitude
to a recognition of Anne's true fortitude, from romantic individualism to a more, though never extreme, conservative position.[12]

Wentworth, effectively, has made this journey by the end of the
first volume, and the second volume will not so much question
whether Anne is the right wife for him as ask in what manner a
marriage may take place. Yet this early enlightenment of the hero
is neither thematically nor structurally a deficiency of the novel.
And the Bath scenes of the second volume, while providing the
setting for the rapprochement between Anne and Wentworth, will
also introduce ideas and moods new to Jane Austen's fiction. It must
be stressed that these departures do not mean that Jane Austen
rejects or abandons a social morality. Anne's consistent behavior in
accordance with social principles disproves this. What they suggest
is that, in a world lacking a public syntax, new means of communication may be required from individuals who retain an allegiance
to an older society and to a more traditional ethical vocabulary.

TWO OBSTACLES prevent an immediate reconciliation between
Anne and Wentworth. Wentworth's injudicious flirting with
Louisa has led to the general assumption that he will marry her;
and Anne, it seems to Wentworth at least, is also spoken for by

[12] See Kenneth L. Moler, *Jane Austen's Art of Allusion* (Lincoln: University
of Nebraska Press, 1968), pp. 187–223.

another. The first obstacle will be removed in time when Louisa and Benwick, mistaking mutual self-indulgence for love, become engaged. The second obstacle, Mr. Elliot, is a different matter. His interest in Anne is never really reciprocated and is, in any case, an expedient interest (as Sir Walter's son-in-law, he will be in a better position to prevent a second marriage, a possible future heir, and the consequent cutting off of the entail which is now to benefit him). But neither fact is known to Wentworth who—understandably in view of his knowledge of Lady Russell's powers of prudential persuasion over Anne—thinks a marriage of Anne to her cousin likely.

Wentworth's position in the second volume, it becomes clear, repeats that of Anne in the first. In the first volume, up to the trip to Lyme Anne was at a disadvantage, since she was constrained to watch her former lover flirting with Louisa before her eyes, as in the drawing rooms at Uppercross (I, viii). In the second volume, however, it is Wentworth who must suffer seeing Anne and Mr. Elliot in apparent league, as on the evening of the concert in the Bath rooms (II, viii). Then again, at Uppercross it was Anne who overheard the conversation of Wentworth and Louisa in the hedgerow, as (unaware of her presence) Wentworth made his open avowals of affection to Louisa (I, x). At Bath, however, it is Wentworth who overhears Anne's impassioned defense of woman's constancy to Captain Harville in the White Hart (II, xi).

What do these pivotal changes of triangular relationships tell us? They announce, of course, Anne's rise in moral importance, her superior constancy and more consistent behavior. Wentworth's wooing of Louisa is done quite frankly and with all thoughts of marriage, and he makes little or no attempt to shield Anne from hurt. Anne's relationship with Mr. Elliot, on the other hand, is unsought on her part, and as soon as she discovers that Wentworth is jealous she attempts to eradicate the cause of his jealousy. Furthermore, whereas Anne is able both to excuse Wentworth for his wish to marry Louisa and yet continue to love him for what he intrinsically is, Wentworth's jealousy, it is more than a little suggested, is the prompter of his regard for Anne: he is attracted not only to her for herself, but to her as she is valuable in another's eyes. At Lyme, when an unknown gentleman (who turns out to be Mr. Elliot) gives Anne a look of "earnest admiration" (104), Wentworth notices the fact. He too now looks at Anne with a look that seems to say, "That

man is struck with you,—and even I, at this moment, see something
like Anne Elliot again" (104). At the end, moreover, he will admit
that it was Mr. Elliot's "passing admiration" that had "roused"
him (242).

This partial mediation of desire on Wentworth's part announces
a major difference between the lovers. For Anne, value is intrinsic
in the object regarded; it does not depend in any degree upon the
approving gaze of another. The point need not be stressed—Jane
Austen is no Stendhal preoccupied with the mediated nature of all
values in a corrupt society—except to underscore the inferiority of
Wentworth's regard. Initially, his outlook had defined self as the
origin of order and value; Louisa's accident on the Cobb called this
into question, and Wentworth came to see Anne as his "model of
female excellence" (159). But in addition to Wentworth's growing
recognition of Anne's worth (which is subtly indicated at several
points), there remains just a taint of "rivalry" in Wentworth's attitude to adulterate the purity of his love.[13]

The suspicion that Jane Austen was moving in her last novel
toward a more "modern" examination of personal relationships increases when one comes to examine the nature of the novel's resolution. All of the previous resolutions not only bring about a marriage
of the central characters, but around this marriage they bring into
balance a set of themes in such a way as to reconstitute a sense of
social wholeness. To Darcy and Elizabeth in *Pride and Prejudice*,
for example, we need deny no psychological depth, but their marriage is not materially falsified if we reduce it to the reconciliation
of terms that is implied by the title—"pride" and "prejudice" being
complex omnibus terms which only receive full definition when
placed together. Anne and Wentworth, by contrast, do not really
resolve conflicting themes by their union; they exemplify rather a
deep and private relationship in a novel where the resolution of
public divisions has become of secondary concern. With the marriage
of Anne and Wentworth we are on the brink of the Victorian,
especially Dickensian, resolution in which the love of two people

[13] For a full discussion of the meaning of "rivalry" and mediated desire in the
works of, among others, Stendhal, Flaubert, and Proust, see René Girard, *Desire,
Deceit and the Novel,* trans. Yvonne Freccero (Baltimore: Johns Hopkins Press,
1965).

(or at most the affection of a small group) purifies an enclave within society, while society as a whole remains unredeemed.

In saying this, I am aware that there is in the Anne-Wentworth marriage an apparent union of landed and naval interests and that *Persuasion* seems to fulfill Jane Austen's perennial demand that social position be filled with individual worth. Many critics have noted the contrast between the effete characters of the landed order and the energetic naval officers. Joseph M. Duffy has argued that the contrast suggests the decline of the "aristocracy" and the rise of a "vigorous naval class," and whatever doubts we may have as to the historical credibility of such a cross-movement, there can be no doubt that Jane Austen intended a thematic contrast of some sort.[14] It is carried, for example, in the implied contrast between Sir Walter's love of Debrett, his "book of books," which gives him "occupation for an *idle* hour" (3, my italics) and Wentworth's appearance in the Navy List: the first book announces inherited but unearned status, the second marks advancement by virtue of performance. The contrast is implied, too, in Sir Walter's notorious dismissal of the navy: "First, as being the means of bringing persons of obscure birth into undue distinction, and raising men to honours which their fathers and grandfathers never dreamt of; and secondly, as it cuts up a man's youth and vigour most horribly; a sailor grows old sooner than any other man" (19). And it is ironically underscored in Mrs. Clay's obsequious support of his opinion (20–21), which says in effect that landed gentlemen retain their looks because they do nothing, while professional men grow old through hard work and the responsible observation of their duties.[15]

More can be said in support of the view that *Persuasion* describes the improvement of the landed order by the infusion of new naval

14 Duffy's argument was questioned by R. W. Chapman in his "A Reply to Mr. Duffy on *Persuasion*," *Nineteenth-Century Fiction*, 9 (Sept. 1954), 154. Chapman quite properly points out that Sir Walter is not, in any strict sense, a member of the aristocracy, and that naval officers were in no sense a distinct "class," for in general they came from landed families themselves. A thematic contrast between two quite different sets of men remains, however. Malcolm Bradbury has recently re-emphasized the point in his "*Persuasion* Again," *Essays in Criticism*, 18 (July 1969), 383–96.

15 David Spring has argued in "Aristocracy, Social Structure, and Religion in the Early Victorian Period," *Victorian Studies*, 6 (March 1963), 263–80, for the importance of the idea of the profession in Jane Austen's fiction, especially *Mansfield Park*; but *Persuasion* clearly has also much to say on the subject.

blood. Anne herself will admit that the Kellynch estate has passed into "better hands" (125) when she sees the Crofts in residence. The admiral has not made many improvements, but those he has made are of interest. He has rid his dressing room of "some of the large looking-glasses" (127) and replaced them "with [his] little shaving glass in one corner" (128). And it is perhaps from such evidence of his humility that Anne considers the parish "to be so sure of a good example, and the poor of the best attention and relief" (125).

From these and other examples it is clear that Jane Austen has utilized a temporary phenomenon—the return of a large number of naval officers from the wars—to illustrate professional dedication, without which, as she insisted in the earlier novels, the continuity of the land and of a publicly accredited system of manners and morals would be broken. Wentworth, who is always wanting to "be doing something" (65), is not only an instructive contrast to the indolent and vainglorious baronet; he follows in the line of such other dedicated characters as Darcy, Edmund Bertram, and Knightley in whom no trait is more prominent than commitment to profession. Yet, while the contrast between Sir Walter's betrayal of trust and the capability of the naval characters is well drawn, it does not function as one might expect from the example of the other novels. The Crofts have invigorated Kellynch, but they will move on, and the estate in more than one sense will descend to William Elliot, whose only idea of duty is "to do the best for himself" (202). As for Wentworth, though Mary fears he may be made a baronet, his future as far as we can see is to be professional, not landed. And Anne, in a phrase that bears repetition, has "no Uppercross-hall before her, no landed estate, no headship of a family" (250). As in previous novels, two contrasting styles of living have been set in opposition; but here there is no convincing reconciliation. No hope is held out that the frankness, resilience, and vigor of the Crofts and the Harvilles will modify the stupid pride of the Dalrymple set in Bath. As Malcolm Bradbury has perceived, in *Persuasion*, "the fascination of the movement toward social stewardship seems diminished."[16]

The dissociation of the heroine from her estate is, finally, the most significant of *Persuasion*'s departures from the norms of Jane

[16] Bradbury, "*Persuasion* Again," 386.

Austen's previous fiction. Two responses to this contingency are offered. The first, already examined, is the stoic and positive resilience in face of adversity and a reduced existence exhibited by Captain Harville and by Anne before her reunion with Wentworth. The second inheres in the developing relationship of Anne and Wentworth. The crucial question of the second volume—"How was the truth to reach him?" (191)— might be the question asked of other Austen protagonists, but, whereas with Elizabeth, Emma, or Edmund Bertram "truth" arrives rationally, either through retrospective analysis or sudden realization, here "truth" is conveyed by means outside of reason, or indeed of language, the prime rational system. Moreover, society, the arena of most previous *éclaircissements*, becomes in *Persuasion* a bar to the truth being conveyed as crowded drawing rooms and public streets frustrate rather than permit communication.

How does the truth reach Wentworth? Jane Austen has taken great care to emphasize the private, largely non-linguistic nature of the communication between the lovers. On several early occasions— when he relieves Anne from the boisterous attentions of the Musgrove boy (80), when he assists her into the Crofts's carriage (91)— Wentworth's actions speak louder than words, and in the second volume it will be "by manner, rather than words" (176) that he will offer his services to her. Anne, for her part, hoping that "our *hearts* must understand each other ere long," seems to have some doubts about her "argument of *rational* dependance" (221, my italics).

The new mode of communication discovered in *Persuasion* is most clearly evidenced in the White Hart chapter (II, xi) in which Wentworth finally comes to propose to Anne. Significantly, this chapter was revised from a previous version, still extant in manuscript, in which Anne's union with Wentworth is brought about in a totally different and rather contrived way, the Crofts serving as playful mediators of the proposal in their home, the proposal arising from Wentworth's somewhat clumsy discovery that Anne was not to marry William Elliot after all, and the whole scene resembling nothing more closely than the denouement of a romantic comedy.[17]

---

[17] For an excellent analysis of the repudiated manuscript and the significance of Jane Austen's revisions, see B. C. Southam, *Jane Austen's Literary Manuscripts: A Study of the Novelist's Development through the Surviving Papers* (London: Oxford University Press, 1964), pp. 86–99.

But it is not only the relatively maladroit handling of the manuscript version that led Jane Austen to reset her scene in the White Hart and to have Anne and Wentworth move toward an understanding without the comic aid of Admiral Croft. She had realized, I think, that this version did not properly answer the question posed, "how was the truth to reach him?" At the White Hart Wentworth learns of Anne's availability to his love not through any direct knowledge of her disinterest in Mr. Elliot, but through the unspoken discourse of the "look" and through overhearing her conversation with Captain Harville.

The sequence of the rapprochement is interesting. Anne and Wentworth are together in the same room but separated by mutual uncertainty. As Wentworth sits writing a letter to Benwick, Anne is at first somewhat isolated. Mrs. Musgrove and Mrs. Croft are discussing Henrietta's upcoming marriage to Charles Hayter, and they come to speak about the wisdom of short engagements. Both Anne and Wentworth find "unexpected interest" (231) in a topic of such relevance to their shared past:

She felt its application to herself, felt it in a nervous thrill all over her, and at the same moment that her eyes instinctively glanced towards the distant table, Captain Wentworth's pen ceased to move, his head was raised, pausing, listening, and he turned round the next instant to give a look—one quick, conscious look at her. (231)

The "quick, conscious look" becomes the first exchange in the "silent but . . . very powerful dialogue"[18] that follows. One may note, too, the force of "nervous thrill" and "instinctively."

The next exchange is similarly indirect. Responding to Harville's regrets over Benwick's inconstant memory of his sister, Anne discusses with Harville the relative merits of man's and woman's constancy. During the conversation Wentworth's pen falls down, and Anne is "half inclined to suspect that the pen had only fallen, because he had been . . . striving to catch sounds, which yet she did not think he could have caught" (233–34). Thus in the conclusion of her subsequent speech she is aware that she is speaking not only to Harville but to her lover too: "All the privilege I

18 The second quotation is actually from the rejected manuscript version, included in Chapman's edition of *Persuasion*, p. 258.

claim for my own sex (it is not a very enviable one, you need not covet it) is that of loving longest, when existence or when hope is gone" (235). Even here, however, it is not only what Anne says, but how she says it that conveys her love to Wentworth. The sound of her voice as much as the sense of her argument affects him. "You sink your voice," he writes in his secret note, "but I can distinguish the tones of that voice, when they would be lost on others" (237). And he ends his composition with a postscript that confirms the existence of a private language in *Persuasion*: "A word, a *look* will be enough to decide whether I enter your father's house this evening, or never" (238, my italics).

We have only to glance back to *Emma* to realize the distance Jane Austen has come. There Churchill's secret correspondence with Jane and the secret communication of the "look" that Knightley witnessed at the Eltons' and during the anagram game at Hartfield were highly suspect—dubious marks of a "closed" private world in a novel that called for openness in all personal dealings. Wentworth, of course, has none of Churchill's "intrigue" or "finesse," and Anne is a considerably more positive and resilient figure than Jane Fairfax. Nevertheless, even with these qualifications, it cannot be denied that a new validity is granted to private communications in *Persuasion*. The new direction culminates in the meeting of Anne and Wentworth after her receipt of the note. Though it is in a public place and Charles Musgrove is standing by, they are able silently to communicate. Wentworth "only looked. Anne could command herself enough to receive that look, and not repulsively" (239).

That a new sanction is given to personal relationships in *Persuasion*, therefore, is inescapable. The danger is that we may overestimate the degree of sanction permitted, especially when we consider how extreme Jane Austen has actually been in her descriptions of Anne's emotional responses. When, for example, Anne learns from Mary's letter that Benwick is engaged to Louisa, thus freeing Wentworth, she has "some feelings which she was ashamed to investigate. They were too much like joy, senseless joy!" (167–68). When Wentworth slips her the secret letter, Anne feels that "on the contents of that letter depended all which this world could do for her!" (237). And when she and Wentworth are finally together and alone, they retire to the gravel walk, "where the power of conversation would make the present hour a blessing indeed; and prepare for it all the immortality which the happiest recollections of their own future lives could bestow" (240).

Given Jane Austen's usual reticence, these are strong statements. The exclamation marks are unusual; "blessing" and "immortality" are not lightly used. Nevertheless, for a balanced reading of the entire novel it is necessary to set such statements not only against the emphasis that is elsewhere placed on "fortitude" and individual resilience but also against the more carefully considered remarks of Anne's review of her past actions at the end of the White Hart chapter. These remarks, which are not present in the manuscript version, are carefully weighed and represent not just Anne's final position but, I think, that of Jane Austen herself on the subject of the individual's duty to society.

"I have been thinking over the past, and trying impartially to judge of the right and wrong, I mean with regard to myself; and I must believe that I was right, much as I suffered from it, that I was perfectly right in being guided by the friend whom you will love better than you do now. To me, she was in the place of a parent." (246)

This does not mean, Anne adds, that Lady Russell was necessarily right in her decision, nor that she would ever herself give such advice. It does mean that she would have been wrong to go against the counsel of a figure who stood *in loco parentis*:

". . . I was right in submitting to her, . . . if I had done otherwise, I should have suffered more in continuing the engagement than I did even in giving it up, because I should have suffered in my conscience. I have now, as far as such a sentiment is allowable in human nature, nothing to re- proach myself with; and if I mistake not, a strong sense of duty is no bad part of a woman's portion." (246)

We recall that Anne was "glad to have any thing marked out as a duty" (33) as she left the Kellynch estate. Here, too, she affirms her belief in action in accordance with received principles, in "duty" (which is an inevitably social virtue), and in "conscience" (which acts internally on behalf of a social outlook). Despite Wentworth's wish, therefore, she refuses to admit that she had erred in acting in accordance with her surrogate mother's advice, for to do this would be to deny an external source of moral direction and to give to the self unlimited freedom. Such a burden, even when shared in a love relationship with another, is not to be sanctioned by either the character, Anne, or by her author.

Anne's constant love for Wentworth is comparable to her consistent observance of social principles. Her claim of "loving longest, when existence or when hope is gone" (235) resembles her subjective maintenance of her "estate," for as a love once chosen may be cherished even after all hope of renewal has passed (and cherished for itself, not for its mediated value), so the ideals of an inheritance may be continued even when this is abandoned or "rented." Both principles transcend the self's possession of them, and fidelity to the one must not contradict fidelity to the other.

Such, I think, is an explicit expression of Jane Austen's final view of the individual's role in society. Implicit in the novel, however, there is an incipient doubt as to the continuance of a socially based morality, and it is not fanciful to see *Persuasion* as the first in a line of English novels in which the felt inadequacy of secular values to embody ultimate truths leads to the end of a moral tradition based in Christian rationalism. Even the titles of such works as *Parade's End*, *Howards End*, and *Unconditional Surrender* are suggestive in this context of where *Persuasion*—on one of its tangents—leads. Mrs. Smith, we have seen, has negative value as an example of fortitude in the novel, but a remark of hers, almost Conradian in its cynicism, carries evocative resonance as a prophecy of what is to come. Explaining her initial refusal to expose William Elliot, she says, "Even the smooth surface of family-union seems worth preserving, though there may be nothing durable beneath" (198–99). This is not Jane Austen's view of society, but if Sir Walter Elliot is in any way typical of the landed order, the durability of the "estate" as a basis for human action is dubious. Whether Jane Austen would have gone on, had she lived, to explore new responses to a world where given certitudes are weakening, it is hardly possible to affirm. A glance at *Sanditon*, however, suggests that *Persuasion* was not her last word on the relation of the individual to society, of self to inherited estate.

POSTSCRIPT:

Sanditon

There—now the old House is quite left behind.

WRITTEN between 27 January and 18 March 1817, and abandoned a few months before her death, *Sanditon* goes further in the direction announced by *Persuasion*, convincingly suggesting that Jane Austen's art had not reached the end of its trajectory when her life came to its premature end. What is new in *Sanditon* is not so much its recognition of radical change (though this is pervasive) as the fictional response that such change elicits. Like *Mansfield Park*, *Sanditon* takes its title from a place endangered by "improvements," but unlike the former novel, Jane Austen's "last work," as far as we can conjecture from its fragmented state, gives little indication that the "improvements" proposed will be successfully resisted. In another important respect *Sanditon* follows the pattern of several previous novels, the heroine being separated from an initial security and made to encounter a world manifestly lacking in moral substance; but Charlotte Heywood's developing career, as far as we can see, is less likely than that of previous heroines to validate inherited "grounds," and there is little indication that her marriage to Sidney Parker, if this is indeed to come about, will bring together the sundered moral and social orders of her society.

In *Sanditon* Jane Austen describes for the first time a thoroughly Regency world, hectic, mobile, and in pursuit of novelty.[1] At the center of this world she places Mr. Parker, an "enthusiast" (*MW*, 371) and "projector" (412)—types long suspect to the Augustan mind. While it is probably true that his place in the total work would have been less prominent, Mr. Parker's importance in the fragment we have is considerable, for he is the last in a long line of false trustees in Jane Austen's fiction. "Succeeding as eldest son to the Property

[1] The most comprehensive and judicious account of *Sanditon* is B. C. Southam's, in *Jane Austen's Literary Manuscripts: A Study of the Novelist's Development through the Surviving Papers* (London: Oxford University Press, 1964), to which this postscript is much indebted. E. M. Forster's review of the Oxford edition of *Sanditon* (1925), collected in *Abinger Harvest* (1936; rpt. New York: Harcourt, Brace & World, 1964), has interesting suggestions about Jane Austen's new use of topography, but as most recent criticism has recognized, it is otherwise negative and misguided.

which 2 or 3 Generations had been holding & accumulating before
him" (371), Mr. Parker considers Sanditon to have the "highest
claims;—not only those of Birthplace, Property, and Home,—it was
his Mine, his Lottery, his Speculation & His Hobby Horse; his
Occupation his Hope & his Futurity" (372). Like Rushworth and
Crawford in *Mansfield Park*—without the gross stupidity of the one
or the pre-eminent intelligence of the other—Mr. Parker is an improver. Unlike these figures, however, his improvements are intended not merely to serve personal vanity, or to provide an outlet
for misguided creative energy, but to be a profitable "speculation":

[T]he success of Sanditon as a small, fashionable Bathing Place was the
object, for which he seemed to live. A very few years ago, & it had been a
quiet Village of no pretensions; but some natural advantages in its position & some accidental circumstances having suggested to himself, & the
other principal Land Holder, the probability of it's [sic] becoming a
profitable Speculation, they had engaged in it, & planned & built, & praised
& puffed, & raised it to a something of young Renown—and Mr Parker
could now think of very little besides. (371)

His principal "Colleague in Speculation" (375) is Lady Denham of
Sanditon House, who, we learn, "enters into the improvement of
Sanditon with a spirit truly admirable" (376). But they are not
alone in desiring improvement and pursuing commercial success.
The third landowner of Sanditon, Sir Edward Denham of Denham
Park, though "a poor Man for his rank in Society" (377), promises
to be a "noble Coadjutor"; he "is running up a tasteful little
Cottage Ornée, on a strip of Waste Ground Lady D. has granted
him" (377). In *Sanditon*, clearly, improvements are no longer a
fashionable innovation but a way of life. Even in the old part of the
town the "Spirit of the day" has been caught (383):

The Village contained little more than Cottages, but . . . two or three of
the best of them were smartened up with a white Curtain & "Lodgings to
let"—, and farther on, in the little Green Court of an old Farm House,
two Females in elegant white were actually to be seen with their books &
camp stools—and in turning the corner of the Baker's shop, the sound of
a Harp might be heard through the upper Casement.—Such sights &
sounds were highly Blissful to Mr P. (383)

Higher up the hill, the "Modern" begins, with a view of "a Prospect
House, a Bellevue Cottage, & a Denham Place" (384). On the Cliff

are further signs of Mr. Parker's project: "one short row of smart-looking Houses, called the Terrace, with a broad walk in front, aspiring to be the Mall of the Place" (384); while on the Beach, "the favourite spot for Beauty & Fashion," the Bathing Machines are visible.

Sanditon is a community in process of total transformation, "not simply the setting for a story, but a phenomenon . . . of contemporary life, the expression of a social ethos whose influence is pervasive, stimulating and dangerous."[2] As we shall see, Jane Austen's attitude toward Mr. Parker and his radical reinterpretation of his landed role is not as severe as one might expect from her treatment in *Persuasion* of Sir Walter Elliot, that "foolish spendthrift baronet," without "principle or sense enough to maintain himself in the situation in which Providence had placed him" (*P*, 248). If the folly of his "enthusiasm" is evident, his good qualities are also described: "Mr P. was evidently an aimable, family-man, fond of Wife, Child^n, Brothers & Sisters—& generally kind-hearted" (372). Nevertheless there is in *Sanditon* a concern over the changes which are overtaking society, a concern quietly conveyed through descriptions of houses and localities, which become, as in *Mansfield Park*, emblems of historically distinct social conditions.

As we travel with the heroine from her secluded home in Willingden to Sanditon and its various residences, we move through time as well as space, and experience, as it were, the very process of social change. Like Catherine Morland, Charlotte Heywood belongs to a "thoroughly respectable family" (370), whose worthy, if conservative, character is soon evidenced when Mr. Parker's ill-advised search for a surgeon for his health resort brings him precipitantly into the Heywoods' rural retreat. Mr. Heywood "happened to be among his Haymakers at the time" (365), a fact that marks his close relation with his work and workers. His hospitable reception of the Parkers and his belief that bathing places are "Bad things for a Country;—sure to raise the price of Provisions & make the Poor good for nothing" (368) also indicate his conservative social and economic values. But although Jane Austen underwrites Mr. Heywood's outlook to some degree, she is also, in the first two chapters,

2 Southam, *Literary Manuscripts*, p. 107.

revealing its anachronism. Like the Morland family at Fullerton, the Heywoods live in a kind of prelapsarian setting:

Marrying early & having a very numerous Family, their movements had been long limited to one small circle; & they were older in Habits than in Age.—Excepting two Journeys to London in the year, to receive his Dividends, Mr H. went no farther than his feet or his well-tried old Horse could carry him, and Mrs Heywood's Adventurings were only now & then to visit her Neighbours, in the old Coach which had been new when they married & fresh lined on their eldest son's coming of age 10 years ago. (373)

The limitations, as well as the virtues, of their old-fashioned ways are evident. The Heywoods are "stationary and healthy" (374), and if these adjectives set their existence against the "spirit of restless activity" (412) and the widespread hypochondria which Charlotte will later encounter in Sanditon, they also suggest the stasis of this way of life. Like Catherine Morland, Charlotte must "get out" if she is to develop. Her parents, indeed, are "glad to promote [her] getting out into the World" (374) when the Parkers invite her to Sanditon.

In Charlotte's experiences at Sanditon Jane Austen marks the progress of the moment, again by contrasting houses and settings. The transformation of the town is not immediately discovered, for the first house encountered is the old Parker residence: " a moderate-sized house, well fenced & planted, & rich in the Garden, Orchard & Meadows which are the best embellishments of such a Dwelling" (379). Charlotte's recognition that it "seems to have as many comforts about it as Willingden" (379) marks it as culturally coeval with the Heywood residence (in respect of its well cared for appearance it reminds us of Thornton Lacey in *Mansfield Park*). Mr. Parker sees that his old house, "the house of [his] Forefathers" (379), is an "honest old Place" (380), but like Rushworth at Sotherton Court he dislikes its low situation—"Our Ancestors, you know always built in a hole" (380)—and he has recently built a new home, with a view of the "noblest expanse of Ocean between the South foreland & the Land's end" (380). To this home he has given the name Trafalgar House, not so topical that he does not wish he had chosen Waterloo—but "Waterloo is in reserve—& if we have encouragement enough this year for a little Crescent to be ventured on . . . then, we shall be able to call it Waterloo Crescent" (380).

Almost forgotten in his exploitation of British victories for commercial ends is his old house: it has been given over to Hilliers, a tenant.

From the description of the two houses in chapter four, it is clear that Jane Austen has returned in part to the method of *Mansfield Park*. Rather than properly improve his house by giving it "modern dress," Mr. Parker has effectively abandoned it in the pursuit of novelty. Caught up in his projects and schemes, he has entirely lost sight of his traditional "grounds." The movement from one house to the other is a movement from one cultural orientation to another, and something of what is involved in the change is conveyed in the resonant conversation Mr. Parker has with his wife as they look at the old house. Mrs. Parker looks back "with something like the fondness of regret" on the old house with its excellent garden, but Mr. Parker points out that they can still get food from the garden "without the constant Eyesore of its formalities; or the yearly nuisance of its decaying vegetation" (380). Then Mrs. Parker remembers how shady in summer the old house was, but her husband counters by pointing with pride to the astonishing "Growth of [his] Plantations" (381), and by arguing that "you can get a Parasol at Whitby's for little Mary at any time" (381). Jane Austen perhaps intends us to recall Cowper's lines:

> Our fathers knew the value of a screen
> From sultry suns; and, in their shaded walks
> And long protracted bowers, enjoy'd at noon
> The gloom and coolness of declining day.
> We bear our shades about us; self-depriv'd
> Of other screen, the thin umbrella spread,
> And range an Indian waste without a tree.
> *(The Task*, I. ll. 255–61)

Certainly, when Mr. Parker himself refers to Cowper, his reference undercuts his intended meaning. Wishing to denigrate Brinshore, a rival bathing place, he says to Mr. Heywood: "Why, in truth Sir, I fancy we may apply to Brinshore, that line of the Poet Cowper in his description of the religious Cottager, as opposed to Voltaire— *'She*, never heard of half a mile from home' " (370). But the context of these lines from *Truth* shows, of course, that the Cottager is to be preferred to the "brilliant Frenchman":

> Oh, happy peasant! Oh, unhappy bard!
> His the mere tinsel, her's the rich reward;
> He praised, perhaps, for ages yet to come;
> She never heard of half a mile from home;
> He, lost in errors, his vain heart prefers:
> She, safe in the simplicity of her's. (ll. 331–36)

Mrs. Parker has another objection to raise:

"But you know . . . one loves to look at an old friend, at a place where one has been happy.—The Hilliers did not seem to feel the Storms last Winter at all.—I remember seeing Mrs Hillier after one of those dreadful Nights, when *we* had been literally rocked in our bed, and she did not seem at all aware of the Wind being anything more than common." (381)

To which Mr. Parker replies: "Yes, yes—that's likely enough. *We* have all the Grandeur of the Storm, with less real danger, because the Wind meeting with nothing to oppose or confine it around our House, simply rages & passes on" (381). Soon after this rebuttal from her husband, Mrs. Parker rests satisfied—glad, perhaps, to be relieved of the need for responsible thought: "There—now the old House is quite left behind" (382).

   In this exchange Jane Austen has provided another description of the transvaluation of social and moral attitudes in her society which she so deplored. Mr. Parker has left behind a life (as well as a garden) that was socially formal, yet in tune with the natural rhythms of the country. More important, he has left behind a society that provided protection and support from contingencies, whether natural, like the storm, or social. In flirting with his commercial ventures, he may be inviting "real danger." It seems probable that had *Sanditon* been completed the bubble of Mr. Parker's "speculation" would have burst.[3]

   The fragment, indeed, might well have been entitled *Speculation*.

---

[3] A suggestion also made by Southam. Jane Austen has surely foreshadowed the "crash" of Mr. Parker's schemes in the accident that befalls the Parkers' carriage in the first chapter (cf. Southam, *Literary Manuscripts*, p. 116). Another indication of his financial precipitance is evident in the conversation partly quoted here. Although plentifully supplied with vegetables from the gardens of his old house and Sanditon House, Mr. Parker has set up "old Stringer & his son" (381–82) as market gardeners, it being clear that there is insufficient demand for the extra produce.

The word appears at least seven times and always with its modern meaning of "an engagement in any business enterprise or transaction of a venturesome or risky nature, but offering the chance of great or unusual gain" (*O.E.D.*). In this sense, Adam Smith seems to have been among the first to use the word in *The Wealth of Nations* (1776), and the word had a like pejorative meaning for Burke and Cobbett. In a famous passage in the *Reflections*, Burke, referring to society, argues that "the municipal corporations of that universal kingdom are not morally at liberty at their pleasure, and *on their speculations of a contingent improvement*, wholly to separate and tear asunder the bands of their subordinate community" (*R*, 117–18; my italics), and Cobbett, whose views on social change were, as Raymond Williams has shown, often surprisingly close to Burke's, is continually critical of the new breed of landed gentry he encounters on his rural rides, particularly those who (like Mr. Parker) look "to the soil only for its rents, viewing it as a mere object of speculation."[4] "Speculation" appears on two other occasions in Jane Austen's work—in *The Watsons*, where Mrs. Robert Watson tells those assembled that "Speculation is the only round game now" (*MW*, 354), and in *Mansfield Park*, during the evening at the Grants' (II, vii) where Henry Crawford excels at this "round game of cards, the chief feature of which is the buying and selling of trump cards" (*O.E.D.*). On both occasions the word is associated with dubious characters and carries some of its modern, financial meaning. Significantly, in *Mansfield Park* Fanny Price has "never played the game nor seen it played in her life" (*MP*, 239). In *Sanditon*, by contrast, everyone plays the game (except the Heywoods). And this is the problem, since to no character in the fragment can we assign, as we could in previous novels, an outlook capable of opposing or resisting the prevailing "spirit of restless activity."

A COMPARISON of the heroine's role and development with those of previous heroines is helpful here. In former novels the heroines have, either consistently or ultimately, affirmed in-

---

[4] Quoted in David Thomson, *England in the Nineteenth Century* (1950; rpt. Baltimore: Penguin Books, 1966), p. 15. For Raymond Williams's discussion of Burke and Cobbett, see *Culture and Society: 1780–1950* (London: Chatto & Windus, 1958), chap. 1.

herited social principles and, in so doing, validated the proper moral grounds of their fictional societies. Elinor Dashwood and Fanny Price consistently adhere to ideal social behavior, and the novels in which they figure take final shapes that accord with their outlooks. Elizabeth Bennet and Emma Woodhouse, after initially rejecting the forms and restraints of their culture, come ultimately to accept and, in accepting, to vitalize, their worlds. Only in *Persuasion* is there a dissociation of the heroine and her inherited culture; even here, however, Anne Elliot does not so much reject her "estate" as discover its rejection of her. Set against these heroines, Charlotte Heywood appears as a new attitude and response in Jane Austen's fiction, with features that owe much to previous figures, it is true, but with an outlook that is finally unique to herself.

Unlike Catherine Morland, whom in respect of parental situation she resembles, Charlotte is not naive; unlike Marianne Dashwood, her sense is proof against sensibility ("She had not *Camilla's* Youth, & had no intention of having her Distress" [390]); unlike Elizabeth Bennet, she is not prone to wrong first impressions of character, or if she is, as with her initial assessments of Lady Denham (391) and Sir Edward Denham (394–95), she quickly redresses the balance and, at least in the latter instance, comes to an accurate appraisal of character. With Fanny Price, however much she differs in personality, she does have a functional similarity, often assuming Fanny's position of "quiet auditor of the whole" (*MP*, 136). But, unlike Fanny, there is no sign that she is fundamentally and irrevocably committed to a given form of society. Her relation to the mysterious Clara Brereton reminds us of Emma's to Jane Fairfax, but while Clara, like Jane, remains largely impenetrable to the heroine (and to the reader) throughout the fragment, Charlotte is not tempted, like Emma, to construct imaginative worlds around her secrecy. To put it in another way, the Quixotic conjectures she has are under the control of a self-conscious imagination, soon to be corrected by more rational views. In her first meeting with Clara, Charlotte "could see in her only the most perfect representation of whatever Heroine might be most beautiful & bewitching, in all the numerous vol:^{s} they had left behind them on Mrs Whitby's shelves," and she indulges in imagining fictional analogies: "She seemed placed with [Lady Denham] on purpose to be ill-used. Such Poverty & Dependance joined to such Beauty & Merit, seemed to leave no choice in the business" (391). But we are immediately to learn that "these feelings were not the result of any spirit of Romance in Charlotte herself":

No, she was a very sober-minded young Lady, sufficiently well-read in Novels to supply her Imagination with amusement, but not at all unreasonably influenced by them; & while she pleased herself the first 5 minutes with fancying the Persecutions which *ought* to be the Lot of the interesting Clara, especially in the form of the most barbarous conduct on Lady Denham's side, she found no reluctance to admit from subsequent observation, that they appeared to be on very comfortable Terms. (391–92)

Jane Austen seems no longer centrally concerned with the drama of a deluded imagination, the correction of which will bring the heroine to a recognition of her proper social role. Nor does she seem concerned to set Charlotte up as a figure of moral consistency and fundamental principle in accordance with whose outlook the novel will finally align itself. Charlotte's function in *Sanditon* is rather that of neutral observer and private commentator—both Lady Denham (393) and Diana Parker (410) catch her watching and judging them. She is the register not only of the quality and character of Regency England but of Jane Austen's own attitude in the year of her death.

What this attitude is may be further defined through a brief examination of the characters Charlotte encounters and responds to in the unstable and eccentric world of Sanditon. Of first importance in this world is Lady Denham, who has married one husband for his money, another for his title and, having outlived both, is now, at seventy years, fending off the overtures of three distinct sets of relations, while at the same time attempting to maintain through parsimony and increase through speculation her already large fortune. Among the seekers after this fortune is Sir Edward Denham, her nephew, a literary enthusiast who thinks he is "quite in the line of the Lovelaces" (405), and who plans to use his talents in the seduction of Clara Brereton, Lady Denham's favorite cousin. Sir Edward's sister Esther, too, is hopeful of currying favor with her aunt, aware that the latter expects her to marry for money. Other "originals" encountered by Charlotte are Diana Parker, a tirelessly active character with a "Zeal for being useful" (412) which is one misuse of energy in this society, and her hypochondriacal brother

Arthur, and even more fragile sisters, whose utter inactivity goes to the other, equally reprehensible, extreme. All of these characters are figures of affectation, in Fielding's sense, exhibiting various forms and degrees of vanity and hypocrisy. But while they often remind us of previous characters of affectation in Jane Austen's fiction (Diana Parker's "officiousness" bears some resemblance to Mrs. Norris's love of "direction," for example), cumulatively they have a prominence never before evident in Jane Austen's major works. True, the fragment leaves off at an early point, and Sidney has just arrived, "expecting to be joined there by a friend or two" (425). Even so, I do not think Jane Austen intended to have her eccentrics move into the background as, for example, the Palmers and the Middletons do in *Sense and Sensibility*. The Denhams and the Parkers define the world of *Sanditon* in a way that no other set of secondary characters does in Jane Austen, so that if we look for a model for this fragment, Smollett seems, finally, a more appropriate choice than Fielding. *Sanditon* often reminds us of *Humphry Clinker*—in its choice of a resort setting, in its concern with disease not only as a device of characterization but as a possible cultural symptom, in its distrust of luxury and of novelty, most of all in its grotesque characterization.

In face of this world of speculation, false literary enthusiasm, and hypochondria, Charlotte's response is, I have suggested, close to her author's. That it is a perceptive, moral, and "healthy" response is clear enough from a number of scenes. After her conversation with Lady Denham in chapter seven, for example, in which the latter makes it clear that she must not think of Sir Edward as a husband since, like his sister, he must "marry somebody of fortune" (401), Charlotte's response combines severe moral censure and a keen awareness of human motivation.

"She is thoroughly mean. I had not expected any thing so bad.—Mr P. spoke too mildly of her. His Judgement is evidently not to be trusted.— His own Goodnature misleads him. . . . He has persuaded her to engage in the same Speculation—& because their object in that Line is the same, he fancies she feels like him in others.—But she is very, very mean.—I can see no Good in her.—Poor Miss Brereton!—And she makes every body mean about her.—This poor Sir Edward & his Sister,—how far Nature meant them to be respectable I cannot tell,—but they are *obliged* to be Mean in their Servility to her.—And I am Mean too, in giving her my attention, with the appearance of coinciding with her.—Thus it is, when Rich People are Sordid." (402)

While it may be true that she is overreacting here—like Mrs. Jennings in *Sense and Sensibility*, Lady Denham may yet reveal unsuspected virtues—Charlotte's assessments of character and situation do not exceed "a sense of the probable."[5] With Sir Edward, moreover, whose attentions to her she soon recognizes to have an ulterior motive (the gaining of Clara's attention), her discrimination is complete and, in responding to his fantastic overtures, she can be moralistic or cutting, as the occasion demands. When he delivers his absurdly grandiloquent eulogy of Burns ("His Soul was the Altar in which lovely Woman sat enshrined, his Spirit truly breathed the immortal Incence which is her Due" [397]) she replies: "poor Burns's known Irregularities, greatly interrupt my enjoyment of his Lines" (398); and when Sir Edward responds to this with a polysyllabic defense of the poet and an "extraordinary stile of compliment" to herself, she changes the subject with splendid ease: "I really know nothing of the matter.—This is a charming day. The Wind I fancy must be Southerly" (398). Her response to the Parkers is less open, but no less perceptive. She immediately recognizes the "Unaccountable Officiousness" of Diana's desire to "be as extensively useful as possible" (410) and is aware of the egoistic impulse behind her frenzied attempts to organize the lives of other people and the business of Sanditon. And she is able, in the amusing scene in the drawing room of one of the Terrace houses, to observe the hypocrisy and indolent self-indulgence underlying Arthur Parker's hypochondria: "Certainly, Mr Arthur P.'s enjoyments in Invalidism were very different from his sisters—by no means so spiritualized—A good deal of Earthy Dross hung about him" (418). Earlier, all of the Parkers had come under her critical, if silent, scrutiny, and, in her reported thoughts at the beginning of chapter ten, her ability to define, as well as perceive, the neuroses of the family is made clear:

The Parkers, were no doubt a family of Imagination & quick feelings— and while the eldest Brother found vent for his superfluity of sensation

---

[5] Southam suggests that Jane Austen may have intended later to modify Charlotte's severe view of Lady Denham, "to give her a more temperate opinion" (*Literary Manuscripts*, p. 112).

as a Projector, the Sisters were perhaps driven to dissipate theirs in the invention of odd complaints.—The *whole* of their mental vivacity was evidently not so employed; Part was laid out in a Zeal for being useful.— It should seem that they must either be very busy for the Good of others, or else extremely ill themselves. (412)

In such instances Charlotte's right-minded and morally percep- tive responses are evident, but against these one must set other scenes in which she appears as a curiously detached figure, viewing her world with the "calmness of amused curiosity" (384) rather than revealing concern over the social and moral aberrations she witnesses. On her arrival in Sanditon, for example, Charlotte, rather than reflecting upon the great changes she has witnessed, "found amusement enough in standing at her ample Venetian window, & looking over the miscellaneous foreground of unfinished Buildings, waving Linen, & tops of Houses, to the Sea, dancing & sparkling in Sunshine & Freshness" (384). A little later, we learn that "Charlotte was glad to see as much, & as quickly as possible, where all was new" (389). And even as she observes the hypocrisy of Esther Denham, her response is curiously mixed:

The difference in Miss Denham's countenance, the change from Miss Denham sitting in cold Grandeur in Mrs Parker's Draw^g-room to be kept from silence by the efforts of others, to Miss D. at Lady D.'s Elbow, listen- ing & talking with smiling attention or solicitous eagerness, was very striking—and very amusing—or very melancholy, just as Satire or Morality might prevail. (396)

In this description, perhaps, we come closest to the special quality of Jane Austen's response in *Sanditon*. This is a world, it would seem, so far removed from traditional grounds of moral action that its retrieval through former fictional means is no longer possible, a world in which the heroine, though she remains a fundamentally moral figure, can no longer be an agent of social renewal. To adopt in this society an unswervingly moral stance would be to condemn oneself to a continually melancholic recognition of the disparity between moral ideal and social fact. Rather than this, "satire," or the ability to remain detached, even amused, in the face of ubiqui- tous vanity, becomes an acceptable response. In the earlier novels, the role of *spectator ab extra* had been criticized—when it appeared, for example, in the witty disengagement of Henry Tilney, or the private criticisms of Elizabeth Bennet. In *Sanditon*, by contrast, an attitude of detachment seems necessary; both heroine and author have to add to their moral perceptions a leaven of ironical disengagement if they are to retain their balance in a radically unstable society. As Charlotte is able to see in Esther's character both what is morally reprehensible and yet ironically amusing, so Jane Austen views Mr. Parker's projects both as a perversion of his true social role and yet as cause for humor. Such a position of ironic detachment is not, however, *pace* Professor Mudrick, the ultimate liberation of an irony always present but previously under the censorship of conventional pressures. Rather, it is a position into which Jane Austen has been driven by the untoward course her social world has taken.[6]

IF THE HEROINE of *Sanditon* differs from previous heroines in the degree of her detachment, Sidney Parker, the probable hero of the piece, is a strangely inconsistent figure whose character as it is adumbrated in the fragment gives little clue to the future progress of the work. His entrance, in the last chapter, has been carefully prepared by various accounts of him from Mr. and Mrs. Parker and, as with Frank Churchill in *Emma*, we have a good deal of information about him before he arrives on the scene. Much of this information suggests his special social and intellectual position. He is independently provided for "by collateral Inheritance" (371), which explains his "neat equipage & fashionable air" (382). Mr. Parker tells Charlotte that he is "a very clever Young Man," who is "privileged by superior abilities or spirits to say anything" (382). That he should laugh at his elder brother's "Improvements" (382) and his younger brother's hypochondria (385) suggest his discrimination. That he would find "something entertaining" in Diana Parker's letter (388) is—given the manifest self-revelation of her remarks— no more than we could expect from a rational person. Yet, even here, perhaps, his wit is not above suspicion. Certainly, as we know

[6] Marvin Mudrick, in *Jane Austen: Irony as Defense and Discovery* (Princeton: Princeton University Press, 1952), entitles his chapter on *Sanditon* "The Liberation of Irony."

from *Pride and Prejudice*, laughter need not be a normative attitude, and, if Sidney's wit bears any resemblance to the cynical variety embodied in Mr. Bennet (who also took great pleasure in reading stupid letters), his character is in some doubt. Other pieces of information, at any rate, reveal further grounds for suspicion. Like both his brothers and other dubious characters in Jane Austen's fiction, he has no profession; like Wickham and Crawford he is disturbingly mobile, "here & there & everywhere" (382), participating in, rather than opposing "the spirit of restless activity" that characterizes the new society. Another mark against him, at least if the themes of earlier novels still obtain, is that he is a poor letter-writer: "Not a line from Sidney," in response to Mr. Parker's letter announcing the accident (385). Finally, when he arrives at last in Sanditon, he comes, like Churchill to Highbury, unexpectedly and with no assurance of a long stay.

Such indications of his possible irresponsibility notwithstanding, it seems reasonable to predict that Sidney Parker is the hero of the piece, destined for marriage to Charlotte.[7] Perhaps, like Henry Tilney, also lively, discriminating, "with a decided air of Ease & Fashion," he would have had his attitude of witty disengagement modified in due course. Even if this were to happen, however, it is difficult to see what effect his developing character and marriage to Charlotte would have had on the total meaning of the finished novel. Certainly there seems little possibility of a marriage between this mobile and witty hero and this moral but detached heroine providing a fixed moral center around which—in the manner of earlier novels up to *Persuasion*—other less satisfactory marriages would fall into place.

A brief comparison with Jane Austen's other substantial fragment, *The Watsons* (1805?) will establish the uniquely uncertain status of *Sanditon*'s plot and thematic trajectory. Not only does *The Watsons* seem "almost to foreshadow its own fulfilment," in a way that *Sanditon* fails to do, but it also foreshadows a successful resolution in which, through the heroine's developing career and final marriage, its fictional society would have been properly reconstituted

---

[7] It is, however, possible that Sidney is the secret lover of Clara Brereton, his relation to her bearing resemblance to Frank Churchill's to Jane Fairfax in *Emma*. For interesting conjectures about Sidney's possible role, see Mudrick, *Irony as Defense*, pp. 251–52, and Southam, *Literary Manuscripts*, pp. 119–22.

on firm moral grounds.[8] *The Watsons*, I am convinced, was given up for other than artistic reasons, and the fragment we have, though admittedly somewhat "bleak" in its depiction of society, has within it the necessary thematic impulses to allow for the correction of its world.[9]

With a narrative economy that has been justly celebrated, Jane Austen in the early scenes of *The Watsons* describes a complex and tense social world. To the "winter assembly in the Town of D. in Surry" (*MW*, 314) come a number of families and figures subtly differentiated in social status: the rich and titled Osbornes from the Castle; the Edwardses, well established in town, with a solid house and a comfortable income, made in trade; their rivals, the Tomlinsons (the husband being the banker of the town); the handsome but irresponsible Tom Musgrave, with £800 to £900 a year; and Emma Watson herself, whose position and relation to her family are both uncertain. Brought up separately from her brothers and sisters with a rich uncle and aunt, Emma has been forced to return to her family by her uncle's death and her aunt's subsequent remarriage. The family to which she returns is itself a fragmented and neurotic structure, reflecting several aspects of the social condition as a whole. Rural, and poor for their station in life (the Watsons, unlike the Edwardses, have no carriage), they are reminiscent of several other families in Jane Austen's fiction. The father, like Mr. Woodhouse in *Emma*, is a senile valetudinarian, and Emma's three unmarried sisters have similar problems to those of the Bennet sisters in *Pride and Prejudice*. Emma's two brothers, however, give greater breadth to the social picture. Robert, the elder, has married "the only daughter of the Attorney to whom he had been Clerk, with a fortune of six thousand pounds" (349), and in the company of his wife from Croydon forms a partnership almost as despicable as that of the John Dashwoods in *Sense and Sensibility* or the Eltons in *Emma*. Sam, the younger brother, is a surgeon—not

---

[8] Quoted phrase from Mary Lascelles, *Jane Austen and Her Art* (Oxford: Oxford University Press, 1939), p. 39.

[9] Southam speaks of "the almost unrelieved bleakness of the social picture, and the asperity of the satire" (*Literary Manuscripts*, p. 63) in *The Watsons*; Miss Lascelles writes that Jane Austen seems here "to be struggling with a peculiar oppression, a stiffness and heaviness that threaten her style" (*Jane Austen and Her Art*, pp. 99–100). Both critics seem to me to read a very promising fragment too harshly.

yet a respectable profession—and he is in love with Mary Edwards. His suit is not prospering, however, since her parents, if they can cure her of her attraction to army officers, wish her to marry one of the Tomlinson sons.

Emma's role in this world bears some resemblance to Charlotte's in Sanditon; like Charlotte, Emma often appears as a neutral observer of the selfishness and hypocrisy of her society. Unlike Charlotte, however, Emma is a significantly moral agent both within her family and in the larger context of her society. Her generous suggestion to Elizabeth that she take her place at the assembly convinces Elizabeth of her good nature (320), and the "tranquil & affectionate intercourse of the two Sisters" (348) that ensues promises some improvement in a family hitherto divided by sisterly rancor and envy. Emma's most important function as a moral agent, however, occurs at the ball, in a setting which most vividly suggests a society divided, like the family groups and the dancers there, into "sets" and "circles." Between the Edwardses and the Tomlinsons, who, no doubt by virtue of their importance in the town, occupy the fireplace, a "very stiff meeting" ensues. Separate from these rivals are "three or four Officers . . . passing in & out from the adjoining card-room." Affable in the corridor of the Inn, "in a morning dress & Boots" (327) is Tom Musgrave, announcing in his lack of enthusiasm for the occasion a presumptive claim to a higher social status, to an acquaintance with the habits and outlook of the "Great People" (323) at the Castle. Last on the scene come the aristocratic Osbornes, stiffly aware of their superiority, enclosed like the other families within the boundary of their "set." In this tense atmosphere Emma's action in dancing with young Charles Blake, when he is abandoned by Miss Osborne for a more attractive partner, has an immense effect. It is, of course, an act of charity, stemming from an innate good nature: "Emma did not think, or reflect; she felt & acted" (330). But it is also an exemplary act (like Knightley's similar gesture when he dances with Harriet in *Emma*) which, in crossing the boundaries between groups, brings social fact and moral ideal together. The act is witnessed by the three important male characters of the novel, Tom Musgrave, Lord Osborne, and Mr. Howard, all of whom will thereafter make overtures to Emma. Tom Musgrave will discover that she is not, like her sisters, immediately susceptible to his charms (she refuses his offer to dance at the ball;

later, to his even greater discomfiture, she refuses his offer of con-
veyance home). Lord Osborne, after the failure of his intermediary,
will himself approach her and, like Darcy at Hunsford, discover
that his arrogant manners are not of much avail in face of the
heroine's natural good breeding and firm independence. Moreover,
though he is not, like Darcy, finally to win her hand, he is to be
educated in his outlook, a development already evident in the exchange he has with Emma at Stanton. The subject in question is
whether Emma has the inclination and the means to ride. Emma's
blunt response—"Female Economy will do a great deal my Lord,
but it cannot turn a small income into a large one" (346)—silences
Lord Osborne:

> Her manner had been neither sententious nor sarcastic, but there was a
> something in it's [*sic*] mild seriousness, as well as in the words themselves
> which made his Lordship think;—and when he addressed her again, it
> was with a degree of considerate propriety, totally unlike the half-awkward,
> half-fearless stile of his former remarks.—It was a new thing with him to
> wish to please a woman; it was the first time that he had ever felt what was
> due to a woman, in Emma's situation.—But as he wanted neither Sense
> nor a good disposition, he did not feel it without effect. (346)

That Mr. Howard's future courtship will be more successful than
the overtures of Musgrave and Lord Osborne, we do not really need
family tradition to tell us. Unlike Sidney Parker, he has no suspicious characteristics. All that can possibly be held against him is his
failure to modify the pride of Lord Osborne and his family, and by
refusing Miss Osborne, as we may assume he will, even this failure
will be removed. What we learn about him is uniformly favorable.
His modesty and good sense are revealed, for example, when he
dances with Emma at the Ball (335), and his reported excellence as a
preacher, a quality already discussed in chapter one of this study,
is another mark in his favor.

Admittedly, much remained for Jane Austen to do, before her
fictional society could be brought through the marriage of Emma
and Mr. Howard to a stable and morally reconstituted shape. Emma
is left in the fragment shattered by the unkind reflections of her
brother and discomposed by the sudden arrival and double enten-
dres of Tom Musgrave. She is relieved, in going to her father's
chamber, to be "as little among them as possible," to be "at peace

from the dreadful mortifications of unequal Society, & family Discord" (361). Furthermore, if family tradition is right, she has still to suffer the ordeal of her father's death and a subsequent stay with her brother and sister-in-law. That such a depressing prospect lies before her does not in itself, however, make the book "bleak" or explain its unfinished state. A period of social isolation is not uncommon for Austen heroines, and it is unlikely that Emma's stay at Croydon would have been any worse than Fanny's at Portsmouth. With the preparations already made, it would not have been difficult to have Emma return to Dorking, meet Mr. Howard again, and be asked for her hand in marriage.

With this marriage we would have a union of worthy outlooks, akin perhaps to the union of Elinor Dashwood and Edward Ferrars, or of Fanny Price and Edmund Bertram, a union, at any rate, which would have a morally centripetal effect on the fictional world of the completed work. It is possible that other marriages would have followed, between Sam Watson and Miss Edwards, between Musgrave and Margaret Watson (Wickham's marriage to Lydia does just allow for this unlikely event). Certainly there would have been a further chastening of Lord Osborne's pride following Emma's refusal; and, through Emma's ability to act as a continuing moral example, the world of *The Watsons* would, I think, have been reconstituted on firmer moral grounds, as new relations were opened between castle, town, and country, the Osbornes, Edwardses, and Watsons.

When we return to *Sanditon*, it is to recognize that no such sanguine predictions are possible for this fragment. Although the arrivals of Sidney, his friends, the West Indian heiress, Miss Lambe, and the two husband-hunting Misses Beaufort promise to complicate the inheritance plot, and perhaps add to the mystery of Clara Brereton, we cannot predict with any certainty the future development of the work. That Mr. Parker's speculation will result in financial disappointment, if not disaster, seems clear enough, but whether Lady Denham's fortune will suffer loss, too, we cannot say. That Arthur Parker will be roused from his lethargy to lay siege to one of the Miss Beauforts seems reasonably certain. That Clara will successfully resist Sir Edward is surely probable, but whether she will engage in further liaisons, and with whom, is not at all clear. The greatest enigma, however, in a story that has "a deliberate and meaningful enigma in almost every aspect," surrounds the fate of the heroine.[10]

The uncertainty which invests the future of *Sanditon* and its heroine is to be explained, I suggest, by its lack of an ultimate locality, or estate, for Charlotte to inhabit. After Emma Watson leaves her aunt's home and loses her expectations of being an heiress, Jane Austen is still able to reserve for her—as she is for all her heroines until Anne Elliot—the possibility of an ultimate and secure place in society. As the wife of Mr. Howard, clergyman to the Osborne estate, Emma, we may conjecture, would have taken her place, in the finished work, in a stable society properly improved by her own moral character and actions. But for Charlotte Heywood no such stable society beckons. After she leaves her enclosed, idyllic, but already slightly unreal home in Willingden, she enters an unstable world of shifting values, a world in which "every body must now 'move in a Circle',—to the prevalence of which rototory Motion, is perhaps to be attributed the Giddiness & false steps of many" (422). Old certainties are left behind as surely as Mr. Parker's old residence has been replaced by Trafalgar House. Sanditon is a society so totally transformed that inherited "grounds" can no longer support the individual, nor, conversely, can the individual any longer retrieve society from its errors, renew and invigorate time-tested and ultimately religious principles of being and action.

The fragment's last scene takes on interesting symbolic significance in this connection. It describes a visit to Sanditon House paid by Mrs. Parker and Charlotte. Sanditon House has previously been described as the "last Building of former Days in that line of the Parish"(384). Now its appearance, as the two women approach, seems to suggest it as a possible source of value and order—another Pemberley or Donwell Abbey: "The road to Sanditon H. was a broad, handsome, planted approach, between fields, & conducting at the end of a q^r of a mile through second Gates into the Grounds, which though not extensive had all the Beauty & Respectability which an abundance of very fine Timber could give" (426). But immediately following this description, replete with details which in former novels would have testified to the essential worth of the estate, Jane Austen provides a curiously insidious description of the gates and fence:

These Entrance Gates were so much in a corner of the Grounds or Paddock, so near one of its Boundaries, that an outside fence was at first almost pressing on the road—till an angle *here,* & a curve *there* threw them to a better distance. The Fence was a proper Park paling in excellent condition; with clusters of fine Elms, or rows of old Thorns following its line almost every where.—*Almost* must be stipulated—for there were vacant spaces. . . . (426)

Is it too much to see in this asymmetrical and disjointed scene a symbolic representation of a once worthy society twisted into a troubling new shape? Perhaps not, for it is through one of the "vacant spaces" in the estate's "enclosure" that Charlotte "caught a glimpse over the pales of something White & Womanish in the field on the other side;—it was something which immediately brought Miss B. into her head—& stepping to the pales, she saw indeed—& very decidedly, in spite of the Mist; Miss B—— seated . . . apparently very composedly—& Sir E. D. by her side" (426). As R. W. Chapman perceived, "all the items of *chiaroscuro*—the mist, the treacherous fence, the ill-defined flutter of ribbons—add up to an effect which is as clearly deliberate as it is certainly novel."[11] If the estate in Jane Austen's last fragment has not yet disintegrated into a handful of dust, its grounds have been partly obscured by mist. The new world is "very striking—and very amusing—or very melancholy, just as Satire or Morality might prevail." But in any case it is a world incapable of being redeemed through individual moral agency, or of being improved through fictional means.

---

[11] *Jane Austen: Facts and Problems* (Oxford: At the Clarendon Press, 1948), p. 209.

INDEX

Abrams, M. H., 24n
Addison, Joseph, 135n
Adler, Alfred, 75
Aldridge, A. O., 133n
Allen, Mrs. (*NA*), 84, 94
Amis, Kingsley, 6n, 61
Aquinas, Thomas, 24n
Arnold, Matthew, "Dover Beach," 25–26
Austen, Anna, 33
Austen, Cassandra, 54n
Austen, Edward, 88
Austen, Frank, 88
Austen, Mrs. George, 88
Austen, Henry, 8n, 45n, 88
Austen, James, 88
Austen, Jane: comparison with Fielding, 14, 27–28 (*see also* Fielding, Henry); comparison with Richardson, 14–20, 14n, 26, 76, 76n, 84; in the context of eighteenth century fiction, 10–20, 14n, 23, 25; in the context of nineteenth century fiction, 20–25; degradation, theme of, in fiction, 2–5; estate improvements as theme, 38–59 (*see also* Burke, Edmund; Cowper, William; *Mansfield Park*, estate improvements, theme of; Repton, Humphry); idea of profession in fiction, importance of, 61–70, 111–12, 131–32, 155–56, 202–3, 202n; intermediate nature of her novels, 24–26; letters, 33, 34, 54n, 93n, 194; limitation of individual choice, 31–32; money, attitude toward, 28–30, 83, 85–91; and moral individualism, 31–32, 119–21; moral standards, alleged class basis of, 30, 146, 146n, 153–55, 153nn; new directions in thought, 25–26, 180–83, 189, 210, 227–29; problem of perspectivism, awareness of, 121–25; relation of life to fiction, 4n, 5–6, 6n, 77n, 88; religion, allegiance to, 8, 26; and sentimental movement, 98–100, 106–9; society and traditional structures, allegiance to, 26–32, 73; spatial and temporal accuracy, 32–34; subject matter, 30–31; subjectivity, awareness of, 7–8, 20–23, 149–50, 156–62; "subversive" criticism of, 5–10, 6n, 9nn, 29–30; and sympathetic imagination, 98–100
Austen-Leigh, James Edward, *Memoir of Jane Austen*, 6n
Austen-Leigh, Mary Augusta, *Personal Aspects of Jane Austen*, 45n
Austen-Leigh, William and R. A., *Jane Austen: Her Life and Letters*, 45n, 88n

Babb, Howard S., 9n, 32, 62n, 130, 182n
Barish, Jonas, 59n
Barrett, Eaton Stannard, 148n
Bate, Walter Jackson, 24n, 98n, 106n
Bates, Miss (*E*), 8, 77n, 147, 155–56, 164, 168–71, 173, 176–77
Bates, Mrs. (*E*), 170
Battestin, Martin, 14n